Stage directors
in modern France

David Whitton

Stage directors in modern France

 Manchester University Press

Published by Manchester University Press
Oxford Road, Manchester M13 9PL, UK

British Library cataloguing in publication data
Whitton, David
   Stage directors in modern France.
   1. Theatre — Production and direction —
   History — 20th century. 2. Theatre —
   France — History — 20th century
   I. Title
   792'.0233'0944   PN2635

   ISBN 0-7190-2467-6 *hardback*

Set in Linotype Janson with Kabel display
by Koinonia Ltd, Bury

Printed and bound in Great Britain
by Billing & Sons Limited, Worcester.

Contents

Acknowledgements

Among the friends and colleagues who have helped with this work, I am particularly indebted to Claude Schumacher of Glasgow University Drama Department, Lindsay Newman of Lancaster University Library and Susan Taylor-Horrex of Lancaster University French Studies Department for their encouragement and perceptive critical advice. I should like to thank the British Academy for supporting this work, and my own University of Lancaster for granting a much appreciated period of research leave. In this connection, the good-humoured toleration by colleagues in the French Studies department of my prolonged absence from usual duties should also be recorded.

Preface

Directing as a profession is a recent phenomenon in the history of theatre. A product of the nineteenth-century obsession with naturalist illusion, the director quickly became one of the most powerful forces for renewal in the theatre. The first director's theatre, Antoine's Théâtre Libre, opened its doors in Paris just one hundred years ago in 1887. It seems a timely moment to take stock of a century of directorial achievement.

This book offers an introduction to seventeen key figures in French stagecraft. It is not a systematic study of *mise en scène*. Readers can consult the sections on individual directors who most interest them. But those who take the study as a whole will also, I hope, find a guide to the changing atttitudes and assumptions, the new ideas and controversies, that have shaped the French stage during the last hundred years.

The desire to tell the story of director's theatre in such a wide-ranging form inevitably imposes its own limitations. A book of this scope cannot pretend to deal comprehensively with each individual, many of whom in any case have been extensively studied by theatre historians. Faced with the competing demands of discussion and lengthy illustrative descriptions of productions, I have chosen to concentrate on defining the essence of each director's special contribution to his art. In each case my aim has been to bring into focus the distinctive balance of the director's approach to the resources of the stage.

The scheme adopted is generally, though not strictly, chronological. Each of the four chapters deals with a group of directors who might be said to share a common conception of the ultimate end of their art. Broadly speaking – very broadly speaking – these groups of directors may be said to have justified their art in terms, respectively, of:

- dramatic literature;
- art;
- life;
- society.

Two major strands in the complex pattern of development of *mise en scène* are reflected here. One is a movement away from directing seen as an interpretative art at the service of a text, towards directing as an autonomous creative art. A second strand is the shift of emphasis from theatre conceived primarily as an aesthetic manifestation towards a more socially-motivated conception of theatre's rôle.

The first directors such as Antoine and Lugné-Poe founded their theatres with two objectives: to provide stages for original new plays which were denied an outlet in the commercial theatre of the day; and, scenically, to rescue dramatic literature from a morass of empty spectacle and superabundant embellishment in an age when *mise en scène* had become virtually synonymous with decoration. Their article of faith was the centrality of the dramatic text. They hoped to bring about a renaissance of drama, but it was by encouraging new writers, rather than own scenic inventions *per se*, that they hoped to achieve this.

To a great extent the same was true also of the second generation of directors: Jacques Copeau, the father of the modern French stage, and his most brilliant followers Dullin, Jouvet, Pitoëff and Baty, the so-called Cartel des Quatre. These directors, while profiting from the scenic reforms advocated by theorists like Craig and Appia, and raising *mise en scène* to new standards of artistry, combined their mastery of the stage medium with a fundamentally conservative approach which held that theatrical creation began with the playwright.

Though there were, from the start, theorists and directors who wished to relegate the playwright and his text to an ancillary rôle and pass the primary creative rôle to the directors, *mise en scène* for a long time remained an essentially text-based art in France. The last forty years have seen the emergence of new directors for whom the text is more a pretext for the expression of their own aesthetic, metaphysical or ideological vision. Their belief is that the text is merely one component, and not necessarily the most significant one, in a complex medium. What counts, then, is not the transmission of a text but the *theatrical event* which is created when the director orchestrates all the means of expression specific to the art of theatre. This tendency, which has been called Total Theatre, includes Artaud, the most persuasive advocate of a theatre of "direct *mise en scène*"; his early disciple Jean-Louis Barrault; and three of the most original experimental directors who emerged in the 1960s, Garcia, Savary and Lavelli.

The idea of "*théâtre populaire*" around which the directors in my fourth chapter are grouped, has made several patchy advances during the present century and a few enormous strides in post-war years. *Théâtre populaire*, or "people's theatre", can be thought of as an attempt to bridge the gulf between elitist avant-garde theatre and low-brow popular entertainment by bringing worthwhile, relevant theatre into the lives of people who, for social, geographical or economic reasons, have formerly been denied its pleasures. This movement to democratise theatre by extending its class base beyond the narrow limits of the educated middle classes may yet prove to be one of the most far reaching developments in the modern theatre. Its practitioners discussed here include Firmin Gémier, the director of France's first Théâtre National Populaire in the 1920s; the T.N.P.'s two most successful directors in the post-war period, Jean Vilar and Roger Planchon; and the founder of one of the most vigorous and innovative companies working in French theatre today, Ariane Mnouchkine.

Inevitably I have had to be selective, and many notable directors such as André Barsacq, Roger Blin, Patrice Chéreau and Antoine Vitez receive barely a passing mention. Ideally, there should have been space too for Jean-Marie Serreau, Georges Vitaly, Jacques Mauclair, Reybaz, Maréchal, Vincent. . . Other people would no doubt have made different choices. I hope the artists I have chosen to write about will nevertheless serve as guides to the many and varied ways in which the modern French stage has been enriched by those who have responded to the creative challenge of *mise en scène*.

I have not intended this book to be of interest only to specialists in theatre history. It is an introduction to a rich and fascinating aspect of European culture and I should like it to be read by students and others who have an interest in the modern French stage. Titles of French plays are given in French, with an English equivalent where appropriate, and titles of other plays are in English. Quotations, which are my own except where stated otherwise, are in English.

Introduction

The advent of the director

Directors are such familiar and dominant figures in theatre today that one takes their presence for granted. Yet their emergence was one of the most recent and adventitious phases in the history of the art of theatre. Although the term *mise en scène* has a long history, the title of *metteur en scène* to describe a specialist charged with this rôle only came into use at the end of the last century, and well into the present century one occasionally finds it condemned as an inelegant neologism. For two and a half thousand years the theatre contrived to exist with only two terms (actor – spectator), or as a tripartite system of communication (author – actor – spectator), the essential intermediary between the writer and the audience being the performer. In the modern theatre a new intermediary exists in the shape of the director, whose functions are partly organisational but primarily creative. True, it is the actor who presents the play to the public, but the actor is no longer a free agent: his performance is guided or controlled by a super-ego. Curiously enough, the word *interprète* is still in common use as a synonym for *acteur* or *comédien*. But in practice it is the director who "interprets" the play.

Measured against the time span of world drama, the director was born only yesterday. Of course, some of his functions have always been present in drama down the ages because every group activity requires some form of organisation. These tasks have been discharged in a variety of ways at different times in history. Aeschylus, in the fifth century BC, is commonly said to have "directed" his own plays in the sense of instructing the performers in the proper manner of movement and speech. In the mediaeval theatre the *maître du jeu*, with a text in one hand and a baton in the other, acted as a kind of director-cum-stage manager, drilling the actors and arranging the special effects or *"secrets"*. Unlike the modern director, however, he would often conduct the performance from on stage and even on "the night" would not hesitate to make the actors repeat a sequence if it was not to his liking. Discipline rather than art seems to have been his chief objective. Later, in the eighteenth and nineteenth centuries, the actor-manager or leading actor such as Lekain and Talma, or Kemble and Macready in England, emerged as the most powerful organising influence in stage production.

Bernard Shaw, in a well-known essay on directing, stated that the ideal director is the playwright himself. Whether this is true today, given the high degree of specialisation that directing has acquired, is questionable. The only convincing modern example of writing and directing combined in a single person is Brecht. The seventeenth century, however, supplies a model for Shaw's ideal in the figure of Molière. Racine, too, spent many hours training his actors in the art of declamation which at that time constituted the essential component of production in classical tragedy. But it was Molière who most nearly approached the ideal of the universal man of the theatre. As writer, actor and company manager he had at his command all the resources which went to make up the dramatic event. Casting, for example, which nowadays is the responsibility of the stage director (sometimes the producer), was naturally his responsibility: not merely in the sense of allotting parts after the play had been written but in the process of conceiving and writing the plays for his troupe to perform. For Molière there was no divorce between writing and production: these were the twin phases of a single creative process. A member of his company, La Grange, has recorded how Molière as producer breathed life into his own writings on stage. It was Molière, he says, who infused the performances with their accuracy and truthfulness: "a glance, a step, a gesture, everything was observed with a degree of exactitude previously unknown in the Paris theatres".[1] Better still, in *L'Impromptu de Versailles* Molière gives us a fascinating glimpse of himself at work rehearsing a play with his company. We see him fixing entrances and exits, explaining to each actor his rôle and character, advising on diction and delivery, and generally coaching them with the calculated mixture of flattery and insult, cajolement and threat, which any modern director would instantly recognise.

And yet this is far from directing in the modern sense. For one thing, it did not involve the search for interpretation – interrogating the text to discover its meaning and relevance – which is what makes directing more than simply a matter of executing a performance. Nor did it require the command of scenic resources that a modern director has at his disposal. Molière's stage was a relatively simple instrument. Responsiblity for the stage was handed over to a separate member of the company. While the actor-manager coached the players, the *décorateur* worked as designer and stage manager and was also responsible for lighting the theatre. In the French classical theatre, as in the Elizabethan theatre, stage settings were simple and to a considerable extent standardised, often being made from stock items. Backcloths and legs painted in conventional perspective suggested the place. Nor was it deemed necessary for costumes to appear historically accurate. These were normally the property of the actors and their styles were dictated by contemporary fashion or, at the most, reflected some purely conventional notion of period dress. This did not entirely preclude costumes from being used as signifiers contributing to the play's meaning – notable examples from the inventory of Molière's personal wardrobe are the Miser's threadbare black velvet jacket or the Misanthrope's choice of an unfashionable juste-au-corps and green ribbons – but the principle does not seem to have been applied with any rigour. The overriding aim of most actors and actresses when stocking their wardrobes was simply to appear to best advantage. The science of stage lighting, one of the most important expressive media in today's theatre, was unknown. Plays were acted in natural light or with the aid of candles. These conventions obviously lack a certain form of realism but they reflect the relative unimportance of the plastic elements of staging and the fact that for seventeenth-century audiences it was the actor who created drama through speech and movement.

Given these conditions, it was natural that the task of producing the play should normally fall to one of the more experienced actors in the company. Conversely, as we shall see, the move towards realism and the greater importance attached to the plastic stage introduced a need for a more specialised approach to staging. These differences can be illustrated by Louis Jouvet's famous production in 1936 of Molière's *L'Ecole des femmes*. Written to conform to the seventeenth-century technical requirement of unity of place, the play presented Jouvet with a problem about where the different parts of the action take place. The problem, he said, arises because "the public today – which we have to admit is a cinema-going public – is used to *seeing* things much more than hearing them, which was not the case with a seventeenth-century audience who heard much more than it saw".[2] It was this thinking that led Jouvet to stage the action in not one but two settings, brilliantly achieved by a mechanised set with walls which pivot to disclose or conceal a garden in front of Arnolphe's house. This logical, visual separation of the play's "public" and "private" scenes was felt necessary if the action was to make sense to a modern audience. In the same way Jouvet was troubled by the speech in praise of Louis XIV by the King's officer in the closing scene of *Tartuffe*. Here was a long-ish speech of 45 lines which would have delighted Molière's audience but which has lost much of its point today. Jouvet's solution was to split the monologue into several parts, accompanied by a spectacular change of scenery. These are problems which have arisen since Molière's time because of changing theatrical conventions, and whose solutions are sought in the modern art of *mise en scène*. Given an audience for whom what was heard carried more weight than what was seen, neither of these "problems" would have been in the least problematic for Molière. They required, in fact, nothing more than competent acting.

Though the spoken word has continued until very recently to enjoy a uniquely privileged rôle in French drama, its supremacy was challenged by a process originating in a shift of emphasis from poetry to realism in the eighteenth century. (Or rather, a different concept of realism, for we should not forget that Molière, true to his stated aim of "painting according to nature", was praised for his life-like portraits drawn from contemporary society). The seventeenth-century notion of *vraisemblance* in the sense of credibility was gradually replaced by the more demanding requirement of literal verisimilitude. From this perspective classical tragedy seemed too remote and classical comedy too stylised and exaggerated, and the search began for a new type of drama to reproduce everyday life more faithfully. It was principally the playwrights themselves who initiated this trend by their approach to the writing of plays – playwrights like Sébastien Mercier, Diderot and Beaumarchais, and before them Landois who as early as 1741 in the prologue to *Sylvie* advocated greater realism in subject matter and treatment. In the middle of the century Diderot, the principal theorist of the new *drame bourgeois*, was arguing for a new dramatic genre in prose instead of the classical alexandrine, a prose which would mirror more faithfully the articulation of everyday speech with its hesitations and silences. This, like the more everyday characters and situations he prescribed, was in the name of greater realism or "truth". There were other influences at work, such as a taste for sentimentality and moralising, which ensured that the plays they wrote fell a long way short of the pure "slice of life" drama. That was not to be perfected until the following century. Nevertheless the slice of life was what Mercier was groping towards when he wrote that the playwright should "shape the play's action in such a way that it has the appearance of a vignette presented with the most exact verisimilitude".[3] According to Diderot in *Les Bijoux indiscrets*, the ultimate aim would be a total suspension of disbelief: "Perfection in the theatre means imitating an action so precisely that the spectator is continuously deceived into believing he is witnessing the action itself".

Once verisimilitude became the playwrights' obsession, stage settings and costumes were bound to acquire a new importance. As writers and audiences came to demand an ever-increasing approximation to real life, mere acting no longer sufficed to sustain the required illusion. The acting required a visual context which would not merely frame the action but would itself constitute an active component of the drama. Diderot pointed out that all the playwright's efforts to write true-to-life plays were futile as long as the stage conventions inherited from an earlier age prevailed. A hybrid of truth and obvious falseness was quite simply the worst possible form of drama, a "clumsy deception where certain details make it impossible to believe in the rest".[4] If this dichotomy was to be resolved, the stage painter had to be brought under the control of the playwright. He wrote: "Do you want your dramatic poets to show you the truth, both in their subject-matter and their dialogues? Do you want your actors to behave and speak as in real life? Then raise your voices, simply insist that the stage show you the setting represented as it should be".[5] Interestingly, though, Diderot already anticipated one of the dangers that later overtook the pictorial stage, the danger that the setting, instead of complementing the play's content, might swamp it. He issued firm strictures on this point: "There must be no distractions. . . Two artists cannot both display their talents to best advantage simultaneously. . . The stage painter must limit his efforts to sustaining the illusion".[6]

The theorists and playwrights like Diderot, Beaumarchais (in his *drames*) and Voltaire were seconded in their efforts to install the pictorial illusion by actors like Lekain, one of the great reformers of the eighteenth-century stage, and by designers like Jean-Nicholas Servandoni, a brilliant inventor who combined machines, dioramas and asymmetrical perspectives to create convincing illusions of nature. The middle decades of the century saw the stage which had evolved little since the time of Molière undergo striking visual changes. The conventional décor gave way to accomplished *trompe l'oeil* canvasses. Costumes became less fanciful and more realistic. For Voltaire's *L'Orphelin de la Chine* (1755) actresses appeared at the Comédie-Française wearing Chinese robes without the usual western hoops. Another landmark which caused quite a sensation was Talma's appearance in Voltaire's *Brutus* (1789) in an authentic roman toga with bare arms and legs. The practice of seating spectators on the stage (an impediment which had dealt a mortal blow to Voltaire's *Sémiramis* in 1748) was finally banned in 1759, causing one exultant writer to proclaim: "Theatrical illusion is now complete: we no longer behold Caesar knocking the powder off a fop sitting in the front row, Mithridate expiring on the laps of people of our acquaintance, or the ghost of Ninus colliding with a tax collector".[7]

In these ways the so-called pictorial stage came into being. It is clear that when Beaumarchais wrote detailed directions for the setting of each act of *Le Mariage de Figaro* (1784), the groupings of actors on stage and the cut of the costumes, he had in mind a radically different stage from that implied by Racine's perfunctory "the scene is in Trézène" or Molière's ubiquitous "the scene is in Paris". It is also clear that if truth is sought in the external paraphernalia of production rather than in characterisation and acting (which is where Molière found it), some specialised skills are needed to organise and control this paraphernalia. What for Molière was naturally a single creative process was starting to diverge into two discrete processes, and the conditions which would eventually lead to the emergence of directing as a separate profession were laid.

The director, then, or his forerunner, came into being in response to the need for some unifying agent to co-ordinate the increasingly elaborate scenic components of theatre. In his play *Intermezzo* Giraudoux imagines a benign spirit, L'Ensemblier, whose unseen hand controls the most disparate events to steer humanity on a safe course through a chaotic universe. The director's rôle in the theatre may be likened to that of L'Ensemblier. Set design and construction, stage painting, the provision of costumes, furniture and props, lighting effects and so on: each of these now indispensable elements had to be co-ordinated one with another and related artistically to the play.

Equally important, perhaps more so, was the need to supervise the individual performances of actors who, as creative artists, may easily find themselves pulling in opposing directions, or in altogether the wrong direction. In fact there had arisen an urgent need for some form of restraint and order to be imposed on the acting. The art of ensemble playing, which had flourished under Molière and with the Italian players, was extinct in France by the end of the eighteenth century. The cult of the star, begun when theatre lost its sacred character and the anonymous actor of the Mystery became the secular hero, had finally become exaggerated out of all proportion. With a few exceptions such as Lekain (1729-1778) and Talma (1763-1826) most actors and actresses came to regard the play as an opportunity to perform a rôle, in other words to display their talents in strongly marked individual performances, a tendency which can only have been encouraged by the lavishness of the sets against which they were forced to compete. Virtuoso performance attained its apogee in the late Romantic period when the exuberant liberality of the early Romantics degenerated into florid bombast. This was a splendid source of heightened dramatic and emotional effect in isolated moments but fatal to artistic unity. Overblown declamation and histrionics were pushed to the most impressive limits. The fact that leading actors might be distinguished by their scorched trouser legs suggests a practice – delivering tirades to the house from directly behind the gas footlights – not compatible with any attempt at consistent scenic illusion. A new word entered the language at the start of the nineteenth century to describe pejoratively these melodramatically amplified styles: *le cabotinage*.

That the best actors and actresses shunned these excesses is certain, though even their performances would appear strangely declamatory, even ridiculous, to modern spectators. At the same time, however, the very fact that the moderation of these few was singled out for praise reminds us how durable the fashion for *cabotinage* was. The tragedian Talma, recalling the late eighteenth century, wrote that, at a time when "all the arts of imitation had fallen into a false and mannered style", Lekain was distinguished by his belief that "tragedy must be spoken, not howled; that a continuous explosion fatigues without moving", and that "the spectator, shocked by the performer's continual ranting, ceases to pity the character portrayed and pities instead the actor".[8] This brief comment on Lekain's art speaks volumes about the prevailing taste for hyperbole against which he was reacting. But nearly half a century after Lekain's death we find the English actor Macready making much the same remarks about Talma's genius for treating virtuosity as a means to art rather than an end in itself. Talma, he wrote, "rose above all the conventionality of schools. . . His object was not to dazzle or surprise by isolated effects: the character was his aim".[9]

It may be no coincidence that one of the rare plays written

for the nineteenth-century French stage to achieve lasting popularity, Dumas fils' *La Dame aux camélias*, is one which capitalises on the appeal of virtuoso acting. The play is a superb vehicle for performance. The main reason for its perennial appeal is probably that in the heroine Marguerite Gautier, Dumas created a brilliantly effective starring rôle which few leading actresses, from Aimée Desclée and Sarah Bernhardt to Ludmilla Pitoëff, Marie Bell and Edwige Feuillère, have been able to resist.

Mostly, though, the growth of the star system was seen as an important factor in the disrepute into which the nineteenth-century stage fell. Taming the *monstre sacré*, for that is what it amounted to, converting his desire to please in isolation into a desire to serve a whole, was an abiding preoccupation for the early directors. Well into the present century directors like Antoine and Copeau were lamenting the anarchic state of acting regularly on show in the French theatres. To Copeau, nothing was more detrimental to the art of theatre than the stars and starlets who "condemn directors to ruinous expense, upset the balance of the performance, draw the public's attention to themselves at the expense of the play, and reduce the play-wright's talents to supplying opportunities for them to show off".[10] Nor should it be imagined that the commercial theatre, where stars like Bernhardt and Duse commanded huge fees, was Copeau's only target. At the Comédie-Française the rhetorical traditions led to plays being produced in conditions resembling artistic anarchy, if Jules Renard's description of a performance of *Hernani* by one of the great actors of the day is typical. The date is 1900: "Every few moments M. Sully beats his breast five or six times, then two or three more times for good measure. He barks like a seal, opens his mouth like an aperture on the entire digestive system, flares his nostrils right up to the eyes which are terrifying expanses of egg white. He is alternately inaudible and deafening; but along the way, some fifty lines are spoken like a god".[11]

It was, in fact, for his achievement in restoring ensemble playing that the man commonly regarded as the first specialist in production, Georg II of Saxe-Meiningen, was acclaimed. Soon after his accession in 1866 the Duke had taken charge of the court theatre and over the next two decades he raised it to a level where it was regarded as the most progressive theatre company in Europe. Inspired by the realism of the set-piece stage pictures which men like Kean had already achieved, his ambition was to apply the principle to the production as a whole, harmonising the actors and the stage picture within which they moved. To achieve a consistency of illusion at this level meant that a firm hand had to be taken with every aspect of theatrical production, beginning with the picture presented to the spectator's eye. It meant, for example, supervising the stage painter to ensure, as far as possible, that the painted flats blended almost imperceptibly with the solid three-dimensional objects in the set. It involved too a quasi-archaeological approach to accessories, to which the Duke himself devoted painstaking research. Genuine period furniture was used, costumes were reconstructed from original models using authentic materials, and genuine armour, weapons and other props were sought out with meticulous care. In all this Meiningen was helped by his wife Ellen Franz, a former actress, and especially by his stage manager Ludwig Chronegk on whom he relied heavily in practical matters of staging. But there was no doubt about who had the final say: the Duke assumed total control over the production, exercising it in an almost despotic manner to ensure that no stray detail could undermine the overall effect.

In Berlin where they first appeared in 1874 the Meininger troupe demonstrated what an outstanding impression of realism and unity could be achieved when scenery, costumes, acting and movement were rigorously co-ordinated. Meiningen's crowd scenes were particularly acclaimed for the new level of realism he injected into them. Rather than allowing a mob of actors to crowd on to the stage where, as often as not, they would vie with each other for attention, he divided his crowds into small groups, choreographing each group separately and even giving individual characteristics to each actor within the group. To us such procedures may seem an obvious way to go about things, but in the 1870s they were far from obvious because they depended on the actor, until then the undisputed lord of the stage, settling for a new, subordinate rôle. To achieve this Meiningen had to resort to heavy-handed disciplinary methods. There could be no stars for whom only the prominent rôles were reserved. All the members of the company were expected to take turns as supernumeraries, an indignity unheard of previously, and those who refused were dismissed. What was happening – and this, as much as the purely scenic innovations, was the true significance of the Meininger experiment – was that a director, not the actor, was becoming the dominant artist in the theatre.

It must not be imagined that the Duke succeeded in every respect in achieving wholly realistic performances. His actors were criticised for the unnaturalness of their diction which was too stagey and emphatic, at least for English and French tastes. What he did achieve, however, was the suppression of random virtuosity and the subordination of the actors to an overall sense of purpose. Evidently this new phenomenon was something which men of theatre in many European countries envied. In London where the Meininger company performed three of Shakespeare's plays in 1881 *The Athenaeum* reported that "the openly manifested desire to obtain an ascendancy over his fellows, which has been the disgrace of the English actor, is kept out of sight. . . The harmony and beauty which are the chief features of the performance are impossible under the conditions ordinarily prevailing in England, and can never be obtained while the vanity of the individual is allowed to override the requirements of art".[12] In Russia the director Stanislavsky drew inspiration from the Meininger players. So too, in Berlin, did Otto Brahm, the founder of the Freie Bühne and later director of the Deutsches Theater, and himself a crusading Naturalist.

In France Antoine was similarly inspired. He saw the Meininger troupe perform in Brussels in 1888, the year after the opening of his own theatre. Though critical of certain aspects of the production he too regarded their crowd scenes as models of their kind. "Their power is incomparable," he wrote to the critic Sarcey, "the groupings they achieve are remarkably life-like."[13] It reminded Antoine both what *could* be accomplished, and how much still remained to be done, for he added: "But just imagine applying that in our theatres and asking even a fifth-rate actor to play a supernumerary in the

Princesse de Bouillon's drawing room! And so we're obliged to use poor devils who hardly know what they're doing there or why they are there."

It can be said, then, that when the *metteur en scène* came of age in France in the person of Antoine this was not a truly revolutionary advance but an evolutionary step, a synthesis of various trends which had long been forming. The thorough-going Naturalist stage which Antoine set about creating at the Théâtre Libre was a modern refinement of the pictorial stage where realistic illusions had been sought with the aid of *trompe l'oeil* canvasses. The shift of focus from action and dialogue as the heart of drama towards stage pictures was the culmination of tendencies originating in the mid-eighteenth century. Even the unification of all the disparate elements of staging under the control of a single artist was the fulfillment of a need which had long been recognised, even if no-one in France before Antoine had achieved it.

These developments came about just as the new movement of Naturalism was at its peak in France, and it was in the application of Naturalist ideas that the director first proved his worth. The Naturalists saw heredity and environment as the chief factors determining human behaviour and they aimed to explore in art the operation of these forces in contemporary society. They advocated the application of scientific methods to literature so that the artist, in his search for truth, would observe, measure and record with as much objective detachment as a scientist conducting a laboratory experiment. The doctrine of Naturalism was not bred in the theatre. It rested partly on the theory of evolution given by Darwin in *Origin of the species* (1859); its methods were inspired by the positivist thinker Auguste Comte; and in art its chief exponents were novelists such as Zola and the Goncourt brothers. But Naturalism had obvious theatrical applications. It is only a small step from a stage considered as a facsimile of the real world to a stage considered as an environment where controlled experiments in behaviour can be conducted. Zola's *Le Naturalisme au théâtre* (1881) served as a manifesto for a new theatre which would be "in closer relationship with the great movement towards truth and experimental science which has, since the last century, been on the increase in every manifestation of the human intellect".

Dramatic literature, albeit lagging some way behind the novel, certainly seemed to be moving in that direction. The *drame bourgeois* of the eighteenth century had been succeeded, in the second half of the nineteenth century, by the bourgeois *pièce bien faite*, well-crafted plays which had in turn spawned a sub-group of well-observed plays and these often dealt honestly with social problems. In fact, however, Zola had in mind something different from the social thesis play. In Naturalist drama the accent would be less on overt discussion and more on the truthful portrayal of case studies. The Naturalist play would seek psychological truth above all. In this it was classical. But unlike classical drama it would feature individuals, not types, and would be soaked in their historical and social milieu. In this respect, an extreme application of the idea of local colour, it was Romantic.

Zola did not doubt that this "movement towards truth" which had already transformed the novel, painting, and the study of history and science, was about to conquer the theatre. The realist playwright Becque had started the process; conditions on the stage itself were ripe; all that was now needed was a playwright of the stature of Balzac to rise up and create a new dramatic genre worthy of Naturalism: "Which of us will stand up and be that man of genius? If the Naturalist movement is to become a reality, only a man of genius can bring it into being. Corneille and Racine created tragedy. Hugo created the Romantic drama. So where is the writer as yet unknown who will create the Naturalist drama?"[14] Zola automatically assumed the messiah to be a playwright. In the event, however, it was a director, Antoine, who did most to make the Naturalist theatre a reality.

As I have suggested, the emergence of the director was a by-product of the trend towards realism, of which Naturalism was the ultimate manifestation. It was therefore no mere coincidence that the early directors – Antoine in France, Stanislavsky in Russia, Otto Brahm in Germany, David Belasco in America – were specialists in Naturalist production. Without such directors to co-ordinate all the scenic components and integrate every significant detail, any implementation of the Naturalist doctrine in the theatre would have remained unthinkable. But out of this process the figure of the director emerged as a central, in fact indispensable power in the theatre and quickly outgrew the restrictions of any single narrow aesthetic. It might thus be said that the most enduring contribution of the Naturalist movement which enjoyed a brief heyday in the penultimate decade of the nineteenth century was to have ushered in a new age of theatre: the age of the director.

New theatres
1   for new playwrights

Problems facing new writers

By the 1870s, despite the enormous popularity of theatre-going
as a social pastime, the divorce between the French stage and
the serious writers who should have been serving it was greater
than at any time in history. The prosperous middle classes
whose interests it served looked to the theatre for safe and
undemanding entertainment: "an armchair between the dinner
table and bed", as one contemporary said. Those who would
have it otherwise had to contend with the laws of supply and
demand in a medium which had all but abandoned claims to
be anything more than a commercial commodity. So on the
one hand there were high-minded artists like Mallarmé who
displayed an almost despairing disdain for the contemporary
stage. For Mallarmé theatre-going was one of the perennial
disappointments of life, the hopeful anticipation of poetry and
magic always dashed by the same old tawdry display. A similar
mistrust born of experience could be seen in Maeterlinck, who
forbade performance of *La Princesse Maleine*, and among the
young symbolist admirers of Villiers de l'Isle-Adam. When his
mystical play *Axel* was performed in 1894 they protested that
the very idea of producing it at all on the prostituted French
stage was an insult to the late master.

On the other hand there were the aspiring playwrights
(among whom we should include the novelist Zola who passionately hoped to annexe the stage) struggling to breach the walls
of a fossilised theatre network. They too had good reason to
deplore its star system, the long runs accorded to commercially
successful plays and its endemic resistance to innovation. For
while the official Comédie-Française served mainly as a

museum for the classical repertoire, the commercial theatre was dominated by the handful of popular writers of the Second Empire – Scribe, Labiche, Sardou, Augier, Dumas fils – and a number of imitators who were content to follow the proven recipe of the well-made play. This is not to say that they were uniformly negligible. Although the *pièce bien faite*, epitomised by Scribe's inexhaustible stream of beautifully crafted comedies, was often coupled with trivial and platitudinous subject matter, some later writers like Augier and Dumas fils had made genuine, if somewhat earnest, attempts to steer plays towards realism and important social issues. But by the 1870s they were hardly *new*. The last event to send shock waves through the theatre world was Dumas fils' *La Dame aux camélias*, and that was in 1852. The vicious circle was completed by the restricted nature of the theatre-going public. Even when a manager willing to risk the investment could be found, conservative public taste generally ensured that original offerings were doomed to failure. Villiers de l'Isle-Adam's play *La Révolte* (1870) and Zola's first stage venture, an adaptation of *Thérèse Raquin* (1873), both closed after exactly five days.

The obstacles facing unknown playwrights or those who tried to write in an original vein were exemplified by Henry Becque. Becque was without question one of the most original voices in a generally undistinguished period of dramatic writing. His first play, a vaudeville comedy called *L'Enfant prodigue* (1868) was accepted readily enough, largely because it conformed to the familiar model. But when he aimed higher in *Michel Pauper* (1870), a realistic drama involving social questions set in a working class milieu, he found cautious managers closing ranks against him. To see it performed at all Becque had to hire the Porte St Martin theatre and stage it at his own expense. This bold venture aroused some interest but little support and it left the author facing heavy debts. But Becque's most notorious struggle with the established theatre involved his masterpiece *Les Corbeaux* (written c.1876). This bitter account of a widow and her children brought to ruin by her husband's friends and creditors must count as the most consistent and accomplished achievement of French dramatic realism. Becque tried to interest so many managers in it that it became the most widely rejected manuscript in Paris. Despairing of ever seeing it performed, he returned for his next two plays to the commercially acceptable formula of light comedy. These were readily performed. The lesson was obvious, and Becque was not slow to signal it: "Some twenty-five authors shared the theatres among themselves. The popularity of their plays, usually justified, sometimes excessive, was measured in terms of 200, 300 or even 500 performances. When they themselves were competing with each other and often having to wait their turn, how could outsiders have possibly hoped for a chance?"[1]

Les Corbeaux was admittedly several years in advance of public taste. By the time the Comédie-Française was persuaded to perform it in 1882 Zola's campaign for Naturalism in the theatre had already created a more receptive climate. It is nevertheless astonishing that the author should have struggled for more than five years to find an outlet for such a significant new masterpiece, and this at a time when the one thing everyone was agreed upon was the lamentable dearth of original drama. These experiences, repeated later with similar difficulties over *La Parisienne*, discouraged Becque from writing any further plays, and one of the most original talents of the period was stifled.

This state of affairs, I think, suggests why the malaise of French theatre went much deeper than any temporary or accidental paucity of original writing, and also why the remedy necessarily lay beyond the hands of the playwrights themselves. What was needed above all were small theatres where writers in advance of popular taste, and therefore financially risky, could be given a chance. To shatter the mould of the established commercial and official theatres, opening a door to new writers and cultivating a new public, was therefore one of the most important contributions that the so-called "free" theatres which sprang up in the 1880s could make towards the renewal of French drama. This indeed was the conscious aim of André Antoine at the Théâtre Libre and the other independent theatres that followed in his wake. Quantitatively, at least, they achieved this aim with singular success, though as we shall see their major contribution lay less in the dramatists they revealed than in establishing a new pattern of theatre with the emphasis on art rather than commerce. To escape the mercenary influence of investors Antoine organised his theatre on a subscription system. The thirteen hundred prospectuses he delivered by hand throughout Paris brought, initially, thirty seven subscriptions. But within a couple of years this had swelled to several thousand. It was to be a formula much imitated by his successors.

Antoine and the Théâtre Libre

Antoine's experiment lasted just seven brilliant years until 1894 when insurmountable debt forced him to close the Théâtre Libre. It began modestly in a rented wooden hall in the Passage de l'Elysée des Beaux-Arts where, in March and May 1887, he produced two separate programmes of short plays. The idea, a familiar ploy today, was to combine originality with public appeal by mixing new plays by well-known authors with those of completely unknown writers. Thus, on the first night Léon Hennique's adaptation of Zola's *Jacques Damour* lent substance to an otherwise light-weight programme, and on the second night a full-length verse comedy by the popular Bergerat (*La Nuit bergamasque*) shared the bill with a one-act Naturalist play by the then unknown Oscar Méténier. And when the Théâtre Libre, spurred on by its early successes, embarked on its first full season later in 1887, it presented a similar mixture of Naturalists (the Goncourt brothers, Tolstoy) and poets (Banville, the Parnassian Catulle Mendès). The success of this modest venture was immediate, demonstrating how pressing was the need for an independent art theatre. At the end of the first season Becque proclaimed: "Here is a young director of real culture and high sensitivity, a company of enthusiasts with two inestimable qualities: simplicity and naturalness. No sooner had this theatre opened than the educated public flocked to its door – and little wonder, since the only real dramatic life to be seen last winter was on its stage".[2]

As a director Antoine had a marked taste for realism and aimed at nothing less than the perfection of the facsimile stage.

The pictorial stage of the nineteenth century was essentially an elaboration of the stage inherited from the previous century, except that by now painted flats had replaced legs at the sides of the stage, thus forming a continuous box. A backcloth still masked the rear of the stage and windows and doors were not yet three-dimensional. Although the French stage painters had developed the art of *trompe l'oeil* to a level unsurpassed anywhere in the world, their efforts were still undermined by adherence to the old convention of the backcloth. The introduction of a solidly-constructed box set and the addition of a ceiling would at last open the way to a total scenic illusion. It was Antoine who first exploited this style. His first theatre offered neither the facilities nor the dimensions to permit the kind of productions for which Antoine later became famous. The naturalist illusion succeeds best when the stage is viewed from some distance, and must have been impossible to sustain in the intimate little theatre where Antoine began. But already most of the key innovations in staging were in evidence: training the actor to perform realistically – in fact, *living* his rôle rather than acting it, since Naturalism demands that the audience is supposed not to be there; dimming the auditorium lights (again, to inhibit the impression of a performance or display addressed to spectators); a modulated use of lighting changing in real time, instead of an overall glare; and, first implemented in the production of the Goncourts' *Soeur Philomène*, the concept of the stage designed as a real room with the fourth wall removed. When the company moved to the newly-built Théâtre de la Gaîté in Montparnasse, and thence to the Théâtre Libre on the Boulevard de Strasbourg, Antoine was able to use the larger and better equipped premises to achieve the total scenic illusion he was pursuing. His production of Tolstoy's *The power of darkness* (1888), which caused a sensation by the combined effect of authentic scenery, costumes, property and acting, marked the coming of age of Naturalism on the French stage.

Antoine's name is indissolubly linked with theatrical Naturalism. Indissolubly and, I think, inconsiderately since his practices were less doctrinaire than is sometimes supposed. It is true that he wholeheartedly endorsed the dramatic ideas Zola had been advocating since the early 1880s in *Le Naturalisme au théâtre* and *Nos auteurs dramatiques*. It is also true that for Antoine, the realist playwright Becque was "the real reformer of contemporary theatre" and "the greatest man at the present time".[3] Equally undeniable is Antoine's tenacious belief in stage realism which made him the leading exponent of the *tranche de vie* or "slice of life" style of drama. His quest for the perfect scenic illusion led to an obsession with authentic detail which nowadays may seem curiously irrelevant. Even at the time, the real lake complete with playing fountain (in Verga's *Chevalerie rustique*, 1888) struck uncommitted observers as excessive, while the notorious mutton impaled on hooks in a butcher's shop (in Icres's *Les Bouchers*, 1888) was seen by some as downright ridiculous.[4] Yet it is important to recognise that Antoine himself refused to acknowledge any doctrinaire attachment to Naturalism and the range of authors he staged bears this out. After only the second season at the Théâtre Libre he was at pains to redress the balance of his reputation. "We have not staged only the Naturalists. Remember *L'Evasion* and *La Femme de Tabarin*, *Le Baiser*, *Le Pain du péché*, *Matapan*, and *La Nuit bergamasque*. They were not Médan plays".[5]

In practice, then, Antoine's allegiance to Naturalism expressed itself more in his stage techniques than in his choice of writers. Paradoxically it is precisely because of this that Antoine, whose overriding aim was to create a theatre at the service of playwrights, was also the first to demonstrate how a director's ideas can conflict with those of the playwright. For his ambitions, as we have seen, were two-fold. Conceiving of his theatre as a *théâtre d'essai*, he regarded the discovery and promotion of talent which was excluded from the regular theatre as its primary function. So crucial was this rôle that he was able to say after the failure of Curel's *Les Fossiles*: "I am far happier to have discovered *Les Fossiles* in a pile of manuscripts and to have brought it to your attention than vexed at having played the piece badly. . . The essential thing is to continue assuring young writers of the certainty that their plays will be read and played, even very badly, for that is worth more to them than not to be played at all".[6] This led him to seek out non-commercial writers of the most varied tendencies, lyrical and comic as well as realistic. And when writers like Curel and Brieux, first discovered and promoted by Antoine, subsequently took their plays to the Comédie-Française or the Odéon this was seen not as a desertion but a vindication of the policy. At the same time, however, Antoine was greatly preoccupied with questions of staging, with carrying through the piecemeal innovations of his predecessors and with achieving the artistic unity of production that was the other function of the director. To Antoine these two functions went hand in hand; they were the necessary and mutually complementary requisites for the renewal of the theatre. Unless the ossified pattern of theatre organisation inherited from the Second Empire were broken, what original playwright could make his voice heard? Equally, unless artistic integrity were restored to the stage itself, what hope was there of encouraging the best artists to return to the theatre? Yet it was by meeting these two requisites that Antoine was led to the great heresy of modern stagecraft: the imposition of a particular style of staging on a varied repertoire of plays.

In his "Causerie sur la mise en scène" in 1903 Antoine described the process of staging a play. He observes, obviously enough, that it consists in two parts, the one tangible, involving the décor, the movements of the actors and so on, the other less tangible, concerning the interpretation of the play. What is interesting is the *order* in which these occur. In Antoine's account, staging appears as a process which works not from the essence of the play to its materialisation on stage but inversely, beginning with the material properties of the production. "First of all," he said, "I found it useful, in fact indispensable, carefully to create the setting and the environment, without worrying at all about the events which were to occur on the stage. *For it is the environment that determines the movements of the characters, not the movements of the characters that determine the environment.*"[7] Here we are at the heart of a Naturalist concept of staging, one in which drama is the reproduction of a pre-existing reality. And that reality is, in the prevailing scientific spirit, seen in the light of determinism. Human behaviour may be variable but it occurs in, and is conditioned by, a milieu which is concrete, observable, and capable of being reproduced in the minutest detail. Décor, as Antoine says, thus becomes the theatrical equivalent of description in the novels of Zola. Accordingly, the first step in the production process is to design a setting "in accordance with something seen", to determine the logical entrances and exits "with due regard for accuracy", to execute the design using the most authentic looking materials, to place the furniture in a natural manner ("still without any attention being paid to the audience"), and to fill the stage with that abundance of little objects and props which "make an interior look more lived in". Then, and only then, can the action of the play be considered: "we can now bring on the characters: their home is ready, full of life and brightness".[8]

Most of Antoine's successors would see this approach as the very opposite of the way a director should proceed, which is to start by assimilating the spirit of the play and then consider how best to express this using the plastic possibilities of the stage. The point about Antoine's method, however, is that it is a perfectly logical and consistent way of dealing with a particular type of play, namely that which "in the scientific and experimental spirit of the century" (Zola) investigates man and his milieu with the most objective detachment. Applied to plays by Zola, the Goncourt brothers, Alexis or Méténier, it could not have been more fitting. But its inherent limitations soon became obvious. It was Zola who said scornfully of Scribe, the master of the *pièce bien faite*, that "[his plays] do not need real milieux because his characters are made of cardboard".[9] But the same point – that they do not need a real milieu – may equally, but not pejoratively, be made of *all* playwrights who use the stage as an imaginative rather than facsimile medium.

How conscious was Antoine of this conflict? His pronouncements suggest that he saw the dangers clearly enough. He spoke of the need for renewed experimentation and stated, for example, that *"La Parisienne* must not be directed and played like *Le Misanthrope".*[10] But he remained too much a man of his generation to escape the world vision that led him to adopt the Naturalist stage in the first place, and all his productions from verse drama to the new realist plays, tended to be approached from the Naturalist angle. The first to accomplish with modern methods a thoroughly consistent *mise en scène*, Antoine was also the first to discover the potential antagonism between the intentions of the director and the intentions of the playwright.

It was a danger of which future directors would be acutely conscious. Baty, for example, wrote that "no formula is good for more than one play. Nothing is more vexing than directors who have a personal style and bend all manner of plays to it willy-nilly".[11] The lesson to be drawn from this was a kind of impossible ideal. The director, drawing his inspiration anew from the text, should acquire a different and unique style for each and every play he stages. No director yet has possessed such absolute versatility, though it became an ideal towards which many of Antoine's successors genuinely strove.

In spite of these limitations Antoine's production methods set new standards of artistic conscientiousness. They demonstrated an artistic unity which made it impossible henceforth to imagine theatre being created other than under the control of a professional director. Yet Cocteau was later able to summarise Antoine's contribution by quipping: "The Montgolfier brothers were geniuses too, but they set back the development of aviation by a hundred years". What Cocteau meant was that Antoine was both the initiator of the modern age in the theatre and also – in his association with Naturalism – the last exponent of a type of art whose death knell was already sounding in other quarters. Naturalism was the final flourish of a current of ideas stretching back to the emergence of scientific rationalism in the early years of the Enlightenment. But even as Antoine's experiment in the theatre began, a reaction against the whole rationalist-positivist tradition was gaining momentum. Ironically, the Théâtre Libre, demonstrating as it did the fatal *emptiness* of photographic realism, only served to hasten the reaction. It quickly extinguished the Naturalist theatre in France. Although a diluted form of stage naturalism spread through the commercial theatre where it remains the dominant mode to this day, experimental directors soon lost interest in Naturalism. In fact, an express hostility to Naturalist staging became the article of faith of the new avant-garde. In aesthetic terms it was the other independent theatres which poured through the breach Antoine had made in the established theatre network that pointed the way forward to the twentieth century.

The "Idealist Reaction"

It is a further sign of the impoverishment of dramatic writing weakened by half a century of neglect that the revolt against Naturalism in the theatre, no less than its advent, was the by-product of a movement begun in genres other than the theatre. The "Idealist reaction", as it has been called, embraced a grouping of artists, principally poets and painters, of diverse tendencies: Symbolists, Decadents, Naturists and others. What they shared was a rejection of bourgeois triviality, materialism and rationalism and the prosaic art it generated, and a determination to seek out essences and higher truths hidden beneath the surface of material reality. Realism, dismissed by Gordon Craig as "a vulgar means of expression bestowed upon the blind", seemed to condemn art to the trivial and mundane. Only the most determined rejection of realism could restore Truth and Beauty to art.

Perhaps no one person illustrates this changing tide more dramatically than the poet-playwright Paul Claudel who experienced it as a veritable conversion. Claudel was educated at the Lycée Louis-le-Grand, an important intellectual establishment of the day and one of the bastions of positivist thinking. In *Ma conversion* he describes the irresistible pressures to subscribe to the positivist climate of his youth in the 1880s and the oppressive sense of incompleteness it inspired. "When I was eighteen," he writes, "I believed what every so-called educated person believed then. I believed that everything was subject to 'laws' and that the world was a system of causes and effects which science was on the verge of deciphering. It all seemed to be dreadfully miserable and boring."[12] The key that unlocked this "intellectual prison", as he calls it, was contained in Rimbaud's *Illuminations* which were published in 1886. Reading these poems Claudel discovered a passionate call for the rediscovery of a lost purity, of the world of mysterious forces buried beneath the sordid façade of material reality. Thanks to this revelation, he says, "I finally saw a way out of the hideous world of Taine and Renan and the other nineteenth-century Molochs, out of that appalling mechanistic world governed by laws which were absolute, inflexible, and worst of all knowable and demonstrable. I received a revelation of the Supernatural."[13]

For Claudel this revelation was merely the first stage in a process which led to his conversion to Christianity and a career as France's leading Catholic playwright, and in this respect he is less typical of his generation. But when Claudel speaks of the need for the supernatural in art he enunciates a credo to which all the young Idealists in their different ways would subscribe: "that is where genius is revealed in its most sublime and pure state, springing from a truly unknowable source of inspiration."[14]

The Idealist reaction was not a specifically theatrical movement. But since the Symbolists hoped to transcend the rigid separation of genres to achieve a synthesis of all the arts, it was not long before a theatre dedicated to mysticism, magic and essences was being forged. Two men, Stéphane Mallarmé and Richard Wagner, exerted a particular influence on this emerging theatre.

Although a poet first and foremost, Mallarmé had long been interested in the theatre. Indeed his poem *L'Après-midi d'un faune* was originally intended to be performed dramatically and the first version in 1865 included stage directions. But he saw little in the theatre of his time to encourage him to put his ideas into practice. Like many of his contemporaries, he was torn between a low opinion of the current debased and trivialised stage and a lofty vision of what it might aspire to. His various pronouncements on the subject, esoteric and often very obscure, can hardly be regarded as a systematic programme to compare with Zola's, but they communicate a visionary sense of what might constitute a poetic drama. Drama should be the incarnation of the immaterial world, an expression of the hidden truths and mysteries of the universe. Passing beyond the frontiers of matter, it should reveal the spirituality of man's existence. It is, therefore, addressed not to the outward eye but to the inner eye of the soul. In contrast to the objectivity of Naturalism, its emphasis was subjective, but it should also aim to go beyond the individual to embrace the universal in the vast drama of the cosmos. To achieve such results required the invention of a dramatic language which, like the language of poetry, would be allusive rather than literal, impalpable rather than concrete. Form, colour, light, music and poetry would have to be harmonised, not to reproduce the specific and the contingent but to suggest the intangible and the universal.

Understandably, those Symbolists interested in the theatre looked towards Wagner for proof that their sometimes mystical intuitions were not only plausible but also capable of implementation. On the theoretical level Wagner had developed by far the most coherent concept of a transcendent art form: the *Gesamtkunstwerk* or "total art-work" in which music, spectacle and the human voice would blend in a combined appeal to the senses. Wagnerian opera, unlike Mozartian opera with its clear-cut division between recitative and aria, proposed to use music not decoratively, nor as an end in itself, but embedded in the drama and the characters. When *The Ring* was first performed at the Bayreuth Festspielhaus in 1876, musical drama seemed to become a living reality. In France the *Revue Wagnérienne* which first appeared in 1885 played a major rôle in disseminating Wagner's ideas. However, the chauvinism resulting from the Franco-Prussian War was still impeding a free exchange between the two nations. One result was that Wagner was known to some of his followers in France more by his writings and reputation than by any first-hand experience. Possibly this helped them to overlook the practical shortcomings of the Bayreuth productions – after all, Wagner's ideas were not matched by a grasp of the stage techniques needed to execute them. Be that as it may, the Wagnerian cult that was taking Europe by storm was a crucial factor in encouraging the young French poets to try out their own theatrical ideas.

Even as the Théâtre Libre was establishing itself as incontestably the most original stage in France, the reaction against all it represented was thus gathering force. (Claudel's conversion, as it happened, coincided exactly with Antoine's preparations for the opening of his theatre). Antoine's success naturally inspired a spate of similar ventures. The early 1890s saw the emergence of over twenty experimental theatre groups, mostly bearing names which proclaimed their partisan affinities: Théâtre Idéaliste, Théâtre Réaliste, Théâtre des Poètes,

Théâtre des Lettres, Théâtre de l'Avenir Dramatique etc. The majority of these proved to be short-lived. But two significant exceptions were the Théâtre d'Art which, thanks to its lively and ambitious director Paul Fort, exerted an influence in excess of its amateurish accomplishments, and its immediate successor, the Théâtre de l'Oeuvre.

Paul Fort's Théâtre d'Art

Paul Fort was a schoolboy aged seventeen when he launched himself into theatre in 1890. Like Antoine, he hoped to elicit original writing for the stage. But as a militant young Symbolist and self-styled Prince of Poets he declared his faith unequivocally in an exclusively poets' theatre. His intention was to prosecute the war against Naturalism using the stage as his battle-ground. Early in 1891, entering the fray in earnest, he announced: "The Théâtre d'Art will become totally Symbolist. It will henceforth be at the service of the masters of the new school – Stéphane Mallarmé, Paul Verlaine, Jean Moréas, Henri de Régnier, Charles Morice. At the end of March it will give the first Symbolist presentation, for the benefit of Verlaine and the admirable Symbolist painter Paul Gauguin".[15]

But finding Symbolist texts with real dramatic qualities proved difficult. Early productions varied from the wildly ambitious, such as Shelley's reputedly "unplayable" *The Cenci*, to the slight and mediocre offerings of the director's Parnassian poet friends. Fort did, however, give the first performances of *L'Intruse* (21 May 1891) and *Les Aveugles* (11 December 1891) by the Belgian writer Maurice Maeterlinck, the best representative of theatrical Symbolism in France and the one who most clearly anticipates the future in his obvious foreshadowing of the Theatre of the Unexpressed. Maeterlinck had developed a style of writing remarkable for its power to suggest doom-laden forces at work, buffeting the characters and filling them with inexpressible forebodings, without showing anything particularly concrete. With his gift for conveying an impression of the reality of immaterial sensation, the unknown and the unknowable, Maeterlinck makes what might be present in other plays as a hidden undercurrent into the very substance of his drama. Successful productions of his plays depend on a studied imprecision, and Fort's theatre, with the extraordinary vagueness of its settings and its anti-naturalist style of acting, was at this time the only one capable of revealing the playwright in anything like his true spirit. His productions of Maeterlinck were justly seen by many as a vindication of the movement against Naturalism. They showed that Symbolism *could* be a valid theatrical movement. Unfortunately, their promise was not borne out by other Symbolist writers who rarely managed to infuse their plays with real dramatic qualities.

Apart from this, Fort's major contribution was in demonstrating how the plastic elements of the stage could be turned to a completely different use from the descriptive function they had acquired over the previous one and a half centuries. His was the first modern theatre to put into practice the idea that theatre is above all a place to exercise the imagination. Visually, the most striking feature of his productions was their simplicity after all the realist bric-à-brac that had invaded the stage. At the Théâtre d'Art three-dimensional scenery – the "trivial and accidental details of actuality" which Fort said polluted the Théâtre Libre – was abolished. In its place one saw simple symbolic designs bordered by draped curtains. These settings responded to the principle that "every lyrical or dramatic work involves a pictorial accompaniment, *i.e.* a décor symbolising the sense of the poem of which it constitutes the frame".[16] This was a refreshing approach, even if at this stage it too often meant the mere juxtaposition of different art forms rather than their fusion.

The Naturalist theatre had ultimately come up against the old paradox of which seventeenth-century theorists had been aware, that the *introduction*, as opposed to the stylised *representation* of real objects from the natural world, is not *vraisemblable* and does not convey an impression of reality. Curiously, nothing can *be* and *seem* real simultaneously on the stage. But in the reaction against Naturalism, the early Idealist theatre placed too much faith in the painter. The initial efforts towards an abstract décor resulted in a natural antagonism between the flat, two-dimensional backcloth and the three-dimensional plasticity of the actor. This particular problem was not to be resolved until the theorist Adolphe Appia convinced the world that the introduction of colour and atmosphere in the theatre was the business of lighting and not of the painter. But it was a later generation of directors who profited from these advances. Fort, meanwhile, was understandably pinning his faith on the painter in the theatre to interpret the spirit of the production through the imaginative use of form and colour. Bonnard, Utrillo and Vuillard were among the artists who helped Fort to achieve the suggestive imprecision of his stage designs.

Harder to efface, though, was the flesh and blood reality of the actor with his particular physiognomy, voice, gait and all the other attributes that make up his individual presence. This was an abiding difficulty for the symbolist poet-playwrights. It brought many of them close to favouring the total banishment of the performer from the stage. In describing the actor as "features in solid flesh, leaning over the footlights into the well-spring of my being",[17] Mallarmé expressed the repugnance of those too-concrete presences intruding on the spectator's imaginative freedom. Maeterlinck was also preoccupied with the problem. He wrote: "Part of Hamlet died for us the day we saw him die on stage. The ghost of an actor defiled him and we can no longer extirpate the usurper from our dreams."[18] This was one reason why Maeterlinck preferred puppets to live actors, and even spoke about replacing them with shadows or reflections. Maeterlinck was not the only playwright who regarded the human presence as a hostile intruder in an art devoted to symbols. The chief spokesman for those who wished to push this minimalist approach to staging to the point where almost nothing was left to impinge on the resplendent solitary presence of the word was the playwright Pierre Quillard. He wrote in the preface to his play *La Fille aux mains coupées (The girl with severed hands)* that it was a lyrical poem written for the stage but "using only the precious instrument of the human voice and ignoring the imperfect trickery of scenery and other material devices. Such devices, useful for those who wish faith-fully to represent contemporary life, would be useless in works of the imagination, that is to say, works of real truth."[19]

Without going so far as to banish the actor from the stage, Fort aimed to effect a compromise between what are, after all, the conflicting demands of poetry and theatre. He developed a style of acting involving movements and gestures which were purely symbolic rather than mimicking natural behaviour. Animation was reduced to a low level, and so too was the lighting, which again helped to dissolve the material reality of the stage. For several productions a gauze curtain was hung in front of the stage, reducing still further the actor's specificity. This device first appeared in *La Fille aux mains coupées* (January 1891). The play was a lyrical poem about chastity and instinct and contained its own commentary in the form of a chorus. The setting, by the painter Sérusier, consisted of a golden backcloth with motifs of multi-coloured angels, and red drapes. The actors, who remained virtually static, intoned their dialogue behind the gauze curtain, in front of which a *récitant* clad in a long blue tunic made an explanatory liaison between the speeches, explaining in poetic prose the characters' emotions and their comings and goings.

In some cases, particularly with plays of dramatic merit such as Maeterlinck's, these experiments in indefiniteness achieved a genuinely mysterious, dream-like effect. But there were other times when the approach verged perilously on mere recitation. Only the most ardent of Fort's supporters affected not to notice how un-dramatic this was. But then, the Théâtre d'Art was always meant to be as much a militant arm in the crusade against Naturalism as a theatrical enterprise. For example, on one occasion Fort lampooned the Théâtre Libre by putting on a parody of a "scène naturaliste". The play was an exceedingly raw piece by a proponent of undiluted realism, Théodore de Chirac. It bore the archetypal title *Prostituée* and showed a starving mother driven to prostitution in order to feed her little children. The seamy subject, the hyper-naturalist detail of the staging, the vulgarity of the language, were all calculated as an act of provocation. In this limited sense, at least, the production was a success: it led to fighting in the auditorium accompanied by rival battle cries of "Vive Zola!" and "Vive Mallarmé!".

Naturally, such capers attracted plentiful abuse from the

critics but this was all to the good: the only really damaging response to such an enterprise would have been indifference, and of that there was not much sign. The influential critic of *Le Temps*, Sarcey, with his famous "Je ne comprends pas!", regularly recorded his bewilderment at Fort's antics. *Le Figaro*'s critic was not so much baffled as fearful of an imminent collapse of the national culture. "There are those who laugh at the vaporisers of the Théâtre d'Art," he wrote, "but can one be sure that the perfumes they exhale are not seriously turning our heads? I am inclined to think they are and I am starting to wonder if we are not losing the genius of our race: our reason."[20]

What prompted this sombre diagnosis was one of Fort's last and most audacious experiments, a production of *Le Cantique des cantiques*, presented as the climax of a blockbuster programme of five plays lasting most of the night at the Théâtre Moderne on 11 December 1891. The play was an adaptation by Paul-Napoléon Roinard of the biblical *Song of Songs*. Described as "a symphony of spiritual love in eight mystical tableaux and three paraphrases", it was an attempt to synthesise music, colour and perfume along the lines suggested by Baudelaire's *Correspondances*, Rimbaud's *Sonnet des voyelles* and René Ghil's *Traité du verbe*. Ghil had worked out a theory of correspondences for each vowel and consonant and its related colour and instrument. (A = black/organ; E = white/harp; I = blue/violins etc.). Roinard worked on similar lines for *Le Cantique des cantiques* but included also correspondences of perfumes. Thus, for example, for the sixth tableau ("Solitude") he prescribed:

> voice: *ui* highlighted by *o*
> music in *la*
> colour: light indigo
> perfume: lily of the valley

The subject, which had already been treated by Voltaire, Renan and others, had obvious dramatic potential, but it was on the staging that interest was chiefly focused. There was plaintive music by Mme de Labrély inspired by a native Egyptian song. Camille Mauclair said he wished that the orchestra had been not only out of sight in the pit but out of earshot too.[21] The set was heavy with symbolism, with a downstage screen on which were mounted a triangular cloud, a cypress and a cedar to left and right, symbolising the imperishable and the incorruptible, and a painted backcloth, probably by Roinard, featuring twenty-one lilies in seven triangular groups of three. The perfumes should have been produced by warming volatile liquids over a stove, but in the event Fort had to settle for an assortment of vaporiser sprays. The performance, which in any case was plagued by technical mishap, was given amidst a pandemonium unequalled since the uproar caused by *Hernani* sixty years previously. The novelty of seeing stage-hands solemnly drenching spectators with perfumes provoked help-less giggles which grew into facetious sneezing and ostentatious gasping for air.

The intentions behind this experiment in synaesthesia may have been laudable, or at least no less silly than the idea of bringing the contents of a slaughterhouse on to the stage to represent a butcher's shop, but they were hard to discern beneath the novelty and the chaos. *Le Cantique des cantiques* is generally cited as one of Fort's more outrageous fiascos. Perhaps it does lend weight to the opinion of Mauclair who, many years later, reflected that "if ever a literary movement has been incapable by its very essence of adapting itself to the stage, it was Symbolism".[22] But it was an instructive fiasco. It proved, as this extreme phase in the Symbolist theatre drew to a close, that the fusion of the arts in the theatre could not be achieved by merely technical means but only by inspiration. This in turn helped to define the qualities required of the director in the post-Naturalist theatre: rather than simply overseeing an admixture of the different contributory arts, combining poetry with painting and music in measured doses, he would have to become the master of a new independent art, the art of *mise en scène*.

The Théâtre d'Art enjoyed its animated hold on life for just seventeen months before Fort quit the stage to devote himself exclusively to poetry. The shortcomings which led to its demise were obvious. It lacked any permanent base and its finances, even by theatrical standards, were exceedingly precarious. Fort lacked the professionalism, even the sense of practicality, to match his artistry and ambitions. Chaotic last-minute improvisation somehow – though not always – managed to bring everything together before a performance started. (In *Mes mémoires* he recalls how on one occasion the backcloth for a reading of Rimbaud's *Le Bateau ivre* was placed upside down. Except for the irate artist Bonnard, no-one seemed to notice the mistake; indeed, the highly stylised submarine décor with fish swimming on their backs was greatly appreciated for its symbolism). Also, the vital distinction between what Cocteau later called "poetry *in* the theatre" and "poetry *of* the theatre" was never resolved, or even confronted. With rare exceptions the Théâtre d'Art remained a stage for poets rather than a home for poetic drama.

Fort's only concrete achievement was the introduction of Maeterlinck. Yet his theatre is rightly seen as a turning point for the French stage. Declaring Naturalism to be dead, its importance lay in the hopes vested in it by the many young poets and artists for whom it was a rallying point. Subscribers included Claudel and Gide, Jules Renard and Debussy. And it was deemed important enough to demand the attention of the leading critics, including Lemaître and Sarcey who appreciated that something living was in ferment, even if they had no idea what it was. Despite its amateurishness Fort's theatre, by the very fact of its existence, helped towards the long-term rehabilitation of the stage in the eyes of artists and intellectuals.

Lugné-Poe and the Théâtre de l'Oeuvre

On these foundations a more substantial enterprise was built when Lugné-Poe founded the Théâtre de l'Oeuvre in October 1893. Aurélien Lugné, or Lugné-Poe as he chose to be known in homage to the poet Edgar Allan Poe, had created an amateur group, the Cercle des Escholiers, in 1886. He also worked under Antoine as an actor and stage manager at the Théâtre Libre and had appeared briefly at the Odéon. When Paul Fort opened his theatre in 1890 Lugné-Poe recognised a kindred spirit and transferred his allegiance to the Théâtre d'Art where he acted in the two plays by Maeterlinck. When this theatre broke up he joined with Camille Mauclair, a young poet and critic, to create the Théâtre de l'Oeuvre which then became the focus of Symbolist activity in the theatre. For five years after the Théâtre Libre closed, it stood alone as the most serious champion of dramatic art in France until it too closed in 1899.

To begin with, at least, the general aesthetic principles were in direct continuation of those of the Théâtre d'Art. Unlike Fort, however, Lugné-Poe was able to distinguish between poetic recitals and theatre proper and did not mix the two in a single programme. But his stage productions began by resembling Fort's in their extreme vagueness. They gave an impression of shadowy indistinct forms barely moving and barely distinguishable in dim light from the soft pastel and grey backgrounds. The gauze curtain became a familiar device for dissolving the action into an insubstantial vision. In Maeterlinck's *Intérieur* (1895) and Quillard's *L'Errante* (1896) the text was recited by two performers standing downstage while behind them the action they described was dimly visible behind the gauze screen. Whether this was really speech lending a poetic dimension to drama, or mime contributing a visual dimension to poetry, is hard to say.

As for the acting, Lugné-Poe subscribed to the Symbolist preference for maximum self-effacement of the performer's individuality. Ideally the actor should be no more than a "shadowy projection of symbolic forms", to use Maeterlinck's formula. In its initial extreme phase this attracted widespread derision. It was said that under Lugné-Poe's direction the actors "assume a perpetually ecstatic and visionary air. As if hallucinated, they stare before them, gazing afar, very far, vaguely, very vaguely. Their voices are cavernous, their diction chopped. They endeavour to give the impression that they are deranged. This is in order to awaken us to a sense of the Beyond. They would have us dream of the Beyond when they say 'Bring me my boots, Nicholas'."[23] Lugné-Poe's own remote presence on stage, where he invariably appeared in a black frock coat and intoned in a uniformly slow monotone, earned him a memorable nickname: *le clergyman somnambule*. A further peculiarity of his productions was the diversity of acting styles they contained. In a single performance there might be realistic or illusionist acting alongside varying degrees of visionary vagueness. This bizarre hotch-potch was partly a result of Lugné-Poe's negligent approach to the actors, and partly because the Théâtre de l'Oeuvre never built up a permanent troupe but depended on a mixture of amateurs, regular professionals and other professionals hired for specific rôles.

Lugné-Poe's artistic policy, like Antoine's, was to shun commercialism, but like the Théâtre d'Art's, his repertoire was intended to foster original playwrights with Idealist tendencies. In this context mention should be made of Maurice Beaubourg (*L'Image*, 1893), Henry Bataille (*La Belle au bois dormant*, 1894) and Henri Régnier (*La Gardienne*, 1894). Maeterlinck, whose reputation was now well established, provided *Intérieur* in 1895, as well as *Pelléas et Mélisande*, the major work whose production in 1893 had led to the creation of the Théâtre de l'Oeuvre. But Lugné-Poe would certainly not have been able to sustain a worthwhile programme without casting his net wider. From the first season the repertoire was more wide-ranging than the prospectus had led subscribers to believe, and it continued to become progressively more catholic. It included classical sanskrit drama (Kalidasa's *Shakuntala*), Chinese theatre (*La Fleur Palan enlevée*) and Jacobean revenge tragedy (Ford's *'Tis pity she's a whore*). Principally, though, it was to the best of contemporary foreign theatre, especially in Scandanavia, that Lugné-Poe turned for his major revelations. In 1893-4 Strindberg (*The creditors*), Bjornson (*Beyond human power*) and Hauptmann (*Lonely lives*) were all premiered in France at the Théâtre de l'Oeuvre. Later Oscar Wilde and Gogol entered the repertoire with *Salomé* and *Revizor*.

The tempestuous event that immortalised the Théâtre de l'Oeuvre was the creation in 1896 of Alfred Jarry's *Ubu roi*. Lugné-Poe seems hardly to have realised what he was getting involved in. This was understandable, since *Ubu roi* was totally unlike any play previously written – though its author's reputation for eccentric and extravagant behaviour should have given some indication of what was to come. Jarry, a precocious, diminutive firebrand, was a familiar figure in Symbolist circles and a friend of Alfred Vallette, the director of the symbolist review *Mercure de France*, but the play he wrote belonged to no school. It is true that in common with other Symbolists he asserted the futility of representational staging and the suggestive power of the stage symbol. For all that, however, his *Ubu roi* was a timely counterblast not only to pedestrian realism but also to the cult of other-worldly latencies practised by his more mystically-inclined friends. Jarry exchanged the rarified atmosphere of Parnassus for a thoroughly earthy and scatological parade of the most abject and despicable aspects of human nature. He invented a craven anti-hero of bourgeois tastes and aspirations and followed him on a rampage of greed, ignorance, stupidity and bullying. In his grotesque mock-epic Jarry unleashed a figure the like of which had never been seen on the stage, and in the process created a modern myth. In form the play was equally original, going way beyond anything the Symbolists had imagined. The latter were seeking inspiration in the incantatory power of verse and music, an approach which in its extreme form was bound to lead down an anti-theatrical impasse. The avenue Jarry explored was, in contrast, anti-literary and anti-poetic but, discovering as it did a new theatrical language rooted in performance, it proved eventually to be the main thoroughfare of the theatrical avant-garde.[24]

The relationship between director and author was a curious one, without parallel. Although ostensibly sponsored by Lugné-Poe, the whole Ubu phenomenon was actually mastermined from the start by Jarry. Early in 1896 he was engaged as assistant to the unsuspecting Lugné-Poe, giving him to understand that he was writing a new play for the Oeuvre. "I was far from imagining the kind of play he was preparing" wrote Lugné-Poe.[25] In fact, the play Jarry was getting ready to launch had started life as a schoolboy farce eight years earlier, when Jarry was fifteen, and had been given several private performances in front of friends, the most recent for Vallette and his wife Madame Rachilde. The final version appeared in print in the summer of 1896, whereupon Lugné-Poe discovered what he was now committed to. "It all fills me with apprehension" he confided to Rachilde.[26] Jarry, on the other hand, knew exactly what he wanted and campaigned assiduously to make Lugné-

Poe go along with his ideas about the play's staging and to prepare the public by a steady stream of publicity, culminating in the publication in the *Mercure* (September 1896) of a potent little article entitled "De l'inutilité du théâtre au théâtre". While the letters he was simultaneously sending to Lugné-Poe were placatory and reassuring, the article was obviously intended to prime a bomb. His argument was that the public is stupid and can appreciate nothing except characters it identifies with and situations it recognises as being everyday. It is futile for the artist to take account of public taste, since the public has no taste, being incapable of understanding anything except what it is told. The time had come for artists to stop descending to the spectators' pitiful level, and in particular to deprive them of the comforting conventions that have brought dishonour on the theatre – *i.e.* "certain notoriously horrid and incomprehensible objects which uselessly clutter up the stage, beginning with the *scenery* and the *actors*". So far there was nothing particularly new except the provocative, attention-seeking tone of the argument. Jarry then went on to outline the reforms that were needed: a simple abstract décor (he suggested a "heraldic" décor consisting of fields of symbolic colour); the replacement of actors representing characters by de-personalised masked performers moving like puppets; the use of special unnatural voices to give the impression that the masks themselves are speaking; actors whose physical attributes match the rôles they are playing, and none of this nonsense about having young actresses to play the parts of boys. In all of this there was not a word about Jarry's own play, the article being presented as a purely theoretical programme of reform. In reality, however, it anticipated point for point the *mise en scène* of *Ubu roi*, even down to the previously unheard-of device of using a teenage boy to play the young Prince Bougrelas.

Notwithstanding Lugné-Poe's qualms, the play was performed in December 1896. Jarry had stated that scenery must be abolished. What he meant was that there was no place in theatre for scenery which duplicates reality, since this is both redundant and inimicable to the spectator's imagination. Far from abolishing décor, whatever that might mean, the production of *Ubu roi* was given in a brilliantly illogical and, in modern terms, utterly theatrical décor. Designed by Sérusier and painted with the help of Bonnard, Vuillard and Toulouse-Lautrec, it was a synthetic set showing simultaneously interior and exterior scenes, Russia and the tropics, landscape and sea-scape, night and day. On one side was a painted bed with a tree and snow at its foot. Opposite was a group a palm trees. Upstage, against the sky, stood a window and a large fireplace through which characters trooped in and out. It was this anti-illusionist staging, as much as the play's obscenity, that scandalised the audience. Tastefully painted abstract pictures and drapes were one thing, but a deliberately childlike and contradictory jumble was an outrage of quite another order. The accessories, such as Ubu's sceptre (a lavatory brush) and the hobby-horse which Gémier insisted on having for his mount, were also provocatively unrealistic. To complete the anti-illusionist effect, the location of each scene was announced with a scrawled sign brought on to the stage by a bearded octogenarian in evening dress – a device which roused the Symbolists to applaud his every appearance but was particularly resented by others. Jarry also had his way with the actors. Lugné-Poe had initially intended to play Père Ubu himself but could find no way into the rôle. According to Jarry he thought it should be played as tragedy. Jarry, who saw far better what was needed, asked for it to be played "en guignol" – like a puppet show. Firmin Gémier, the leading actor at the Odéon, was brought in to play Ubu. He too found the style elusive until it was suggested that he imitate Jarry's own bizarrely clipped and expressionless manner of speaking. Other characters adopted whatever regional or foreign accents they fancied, exaggerated to varying degrees of grotesqueness. Some wore masks, though Gémier declined to use the mask with elephant's trunk designed for the part by Jarry, and they adopted the jerky puppet-like movements Jarry had stipulated. Since the satire was intended to be both modern and timeless they were dressed in a tatty assemblage of contemporary clothes.

To mount such a crude spectacle was a flagrant provocation, a blatant assault on the public's idea of what constitutes theatre, and without even the redeeming virtue of good taste. The public's reaction suggests that Jarry's attack found its target. The riotous performances on 9th and 10th December 1896 have been described many times over – by Gémier, whose professionalism alone enabled the performance to continue in spite of the interruptions, by bemused onlookers such as W. B. Yeats and Arthur Symons, and by Lugné-Poe who was left to pick up the pieces and pay the debts.[27] Jarry, feeling let down by Lugné-Poe's lack of support, promptly decamped, to the great relief of Lugné-Poe who regarded the production as a nuisance and a failure. Thirty-five years later he was to muse: "If, on that first night, *Ubu* had been recognised as the key work, the revolutionary play it was later taken to be, many things in the theatre would have turned out differently. Where might we have been now?"[28] By then Jarry had been acclaimed by the surrealists as a great precursor of irrational art and the modernity of his theatrical language was better understood. In 1896 it was not clear what had been accomplished, beyond an indisputably well-aimed assault on theatrical proprieties. Not only well-aimed but timely too. After the hyper-refined delicacy of perception offered by artists who, as Symons put it, had "perfected the fine shades to their vanishing point", a return to the primitive and elemental must have seemed invigorating, to those able to stomach it. This, however, was no immediate consolation to Lugné-Poe who regarded *Ubu roi* as a near-disaster which he was lucky to survive. He was in the business of promoting serious drama and could ill afford the distraction of a dubious *succès de scandale*, not to mention the loss of subscribers who withdrew their support as a result. That Lugné-Poe had neither understood nor sympathised with the *Ubu* venture seems very probable, but it says much for his generous eclecticism that he gave Jarry his head in a project which seemed all too likely to deal a blow to his theatre's reputation.

Of the many foreign dramatists staged at the Oeuvre, the most important by far was Ibsen. Lugné-Poe developed a close rapport with Ibsen and returned repeatedly to his plays. Three were included in the opening season (*Rosmersholm, An enemy of the people* and *The master builder*) and a further six, mostly premières, followed in the next five years. The figure of Ibsen looms large in the history of the early French avant-garde. Naturalists and Symbolists alike claimed him as their own. The first productions of Ibsen in France were given by the Théâtre Libre which staged *Ghosts* in 1889 and *The wild duck* in 1890. As productions both were judged to be failures and Antoine himself later agreed that he had misunderstood the plays. Yet the performances left the impression that an original playwright who merited further interest had been uncovered. It was left to Lugné-Poe to reveal the true nature of Ibsen's originality.

Neither Naturalist nor Symbolist, Ibsen's plays take over the conventions of the realistic stage, which detractors accused of giving only an empty reproduction of objective reality, and inject into them an irresistible impression of hidden forces at work. In furnished interiors that look real enough, and dialogue that sounds like natural conversation, they weave a complex and deceptively precise web of symbols. Their power to suggest that objects and dialogues function on two levels, with a literal meaning and a hidden significance, caused Maeterlinck, in an article inspired by the première of *The master builder*, to question: "What is it that Ibsen has added to ordinary life to make it appear so strange, so profound and so disquieting beneath its puerile exterior?"[29] The answer is symbolism, but a symbolism achieved by totally different means from those being pursued by the French Symbolists.

Ibsen's plays presented a challenge to the French directors, imprisoned as they were within their aesthetic schools. The Théâtre Libre with its style of factual realism failed to capture their allusiveness. Lugné-Poe, in contrast, began by approaching them from quite the opposite extreme, in much the same way as he approached Maeterlinck. But through Ibsen he learned to attenuate the excesses of symbolist staging. After a few productions in the familiar style of dimly-lit imprecision he gradually developed a style mid-way between the symbolist and the realist. This did not mean the invasion of the stage by all the material trappings of the Naturalist theatre; rather, it meant treating the characters as individuals, not as mere cyphers, and allowing the undertones to surface through a style of acting which was neither totally abstract nor excessively fussy. Ibsen himself, who saw *Rosmersholm* and *The master builder* when the company toured Scandanavia in 1894, and with whom Lugné-Poe corresponded regularly, encouraged him in this direction. By the time he came to stage *Peer Gynt* in 1896, *John-Gabriel Borkman* in 1897 and the second productions of *An enemy of the people* and *Rosmersholm* in 1898, the murky stage, the static silhouetted actors, the plaintive intoning and the long silences had totally vanished and had been replaced by a simpler, unaffected and altogether more natural style of presentation.

Unfortunately these changes came too late to correct the false impression of Ibsen that had grown up in France. Ibsen had acquired a clinging reputation as an obscure playwright, so that nearly forty years later Copeau wrote that "in France the adjective Ibsenesque has long been, and still is, synonymous with incoherence, hermeticism and moroseness".[30] Ibsen really had to wait for Pitoëff's productions in the 1930s to release him finally from what Robichez called his "five years of captivity among the Symbolists".[31]

Ibsen, who was unquestionably the most important new playwright produced by Lugné-Poe, was the master which both the Naturalists and the Symbolists longed to see emerge but which neither school succeeded in generating. Lugné-Poe's association with him was especially significant because it corresponded to a shift in his ideas as a whole away from Symbolism towards the middle ground that was now beginning to form between the two aesthetic camps. Behind this shift lay Lugné-Poe's growing impatience with the French Symbolists for their immaturity and their failure to provide him with a single worthwhile playwright other than Maeterlinck. Citing this as his reason, he broke publicly with them at the end of the 1896-7 season. The outstanding artistic success of 1896 had been Ibsen's *Peer Gynt*. Of the French plays presented in the third season only one, *Ubu roi* – which Lugné-Poe pointedly failed to mention – was of any significance. Even as the controversy over *Ubu* rumbled on around him, he wrote "And still not a single symbolist writer to get our teeth into".[32] Wisely concluding that the best policy was independence, he wrote in the manifesto for the forthcoming season: "The Théâtre de l'Oeuvre does not belong to any school. If some people have been misled by the welcome we gave to mystical tendencies it is time to put an end to it since, apart from the admirable plays of Maurice Maeterlinck, they have contributed nothing to dramatic art." Henceforth, he continued, "we shall take no account of the provenance of the works we stage, looking only for plays about humanity and life; and if such plays only come from abroad then we shall perform only foreign plays."[33]

In the event Lugné-Poe did not close the door to French playwrights, far from it, but pursued his search for new talent on a wider front. The newly formed Naturist school, rejoicing over what they saw as Lugné-Poe's public disavowal of the decadent excesses of Symbolism, were quick to woo him. They were eager to carry their Rousseau-esque programme of simpler, more natural values into the theatre. Their leader Saint-Georges de Bouhélier, whose Naturist Manifesto had been published in *Le Figaro* earlier that year, offered him his play *La Victoire*. This lyrical drama, neo-classical in form but supposedly modern in spirit, was heralded as the first of a cycle of works through which a great new national drama would rise from the ashes of the dying century. Lugné-Poe must have been less confident about its qualities because the preparations for *La Victoire* were marked by much delay and prevarication, as was habitual when his enthusiasm was not fully engaged. The two performances which were eventually given were judged universally to be failures. The Symbolist cabbale was there in force to manifest its hostility and to make the performances as tumultuous as those of *Ubu roi*. Actually, its efforts were superfluous because even Lugné-Poe's supporters were forced to concede the play's weakness. By this venture the Naturist experiment was nipped in the bud and the Théâtre de l'Oeuvre emerged with its reputation somewhat bruised.

The final years of the century did, however, witness a more fruitful collaboration between Lugné-Poe and one of the most significant writers of the period, Romain Rolland. Rolland, chiefly remembered today for his later political and pacifist writings, had composed a series of historical dramas inspired by the ideals of the Revolution. They displayed an affinity with the movement towards moral renewal and common sense that was emerging in reaction against the decadent tendencies of the period. As Robichez observes in *Le Symbolisme au théâtre*, Rolland's partnership with L'Oeuvre, which until then had seemed to epitomise all the dilettantism, refined sensibility and

parisianisme that he detested, could not have been more improbable. But Rolland had spent years trying to interest managers
and publishers in his work and was still looking for a public;
and Lugné-Poe, now freed from his Symbolist links, was still
seeking original writers. Moreover, at a time of social and political ferment when many, including Lugné-Poe, were becoming
increasingly conscious of the divorce between theatre and life,
Rolland's plays had the merit of dealing with subjects closely
related to contemporary affairs. In *Les Loups* dealing with the
Dreyfus Affair and other plays inspired by the 1789 Revolution
but presenting parallels with the situation in France after the
Franco-Prussian War, Rolland tapped a hitherto unexplored
vein of interest among the Oeuvre's public. The three plays by
Rolland *(Aert* in 1897, *Les Loups* in 1898 and *Le Triomphe de la
raison* in 1899) provided some of Lugné-Poe's most interesting
discoveries.

Apart from these, the last two seasons at the Théâtre de
l'Oeuvre were sustained mostly by foreign plays, especially
Ibsen, and revivals of earlier successes. A special event of 1898
was the revival of *An enemy of the people*, a production which
became notorious not for any intrinsic reasons but because of
the Dreyfus Affair. The play's hero, Dr Stockman, threatens
the prosperity of his spa town and wins himself the enmity of
his fellow townsfolk by warning them that their water supply
is polluted by industrial waste. Audiences were quick to identify
Stockman with Zola in his solitary campaign for justice on
behalf of the discredited Captain Dreyfus: a somewhat far-
fetched parallel, but typical of the way the Affair had taken a
grip on French life. The play was thus given in rowdy performances attended by intellectuals and liberals brought to the
theatre not out of interest in the play but more with a desire
to manifest their sympathy.

Such exceptions apart, a scent of debility was now hanging
over the company and the press was showing clear signs of
indifference to its fortunes. No longer propelled by the crusading spirit of the early years, Lugné-Poe was succumbing to the
struggle to keep a company, a repertoire and and a public united
in a common enterprise. Material and financial contraints
which earlier had been overcome by sheer force of enthusiasm

weighed more pressingly as the itinerant company moved from one temporary base to another. Several long foreign tours had been undertaken to maintain the company's momentum, though these too took a heavy toll. Lugné-Poe was, however, determined to end this phase of his career on a high note. Summoning all his personal resources, and calling on his subscribers to do likewise, he staged Rolland's *Le Triomphe de la raison* with an unusually meticulous attention to detail and then, in June 1899, closed the Théâtre de l'Oeuvre.

As with Antoine, these first crusading years marked the high point of Lugné-Poe's career, the time when battle was joined and when, for a few years, his theatre was the focus of all that was original and promising in the avant-garde. The Théâtre de l'Oeuvre did, however, reopen in 1900, though no longer on a subscription basis, and continued to operate irregularly under Lugné-Poe until 1929. Many more new writers were revealed there. The list which had begun with Tristan Bernard, Edmond Sée, Coolus, Bouhélier, Maurice de Faramond, Régnier and Rolland was continued with Alfred Savoir, Jammes, Nozière, Sarment, Achard, Passeur, Salacrou and Claudel, whose standing as a major playwright was established by Lugné-Poe's production of *L'Annonce faite à Marie* in 1912. Edmond Sée was speaking for all these when he declared Lugné-Poe to be "the most militant, the most eclectic, the most generous dramatic 'prospector' to whom two or three generations of writers remain indebted".[34] In his own memoirs Lugné-Poe, describing himself as a "ferryman" (*"passeur"*), reminds us what he considered to be the principal asset of a *metteur en scène*: a disinterested capacity to nurture the talent of others, to become a creator vicariously by serving their creative genius.

*****

How far did these early directors fulfill the promise of a renewal of dramatic art in France? If we take as a yardstick their aim of stimulating an immediate resurgence of dramatic writing, the answer must be that they met with qualified success. Quantitatively the floodgates were certainly opened. In his seven years at the Théâtre Libre Antoine is credited with the introduction of over one hundred new plays by seventy new writers, by no means all of them belonging to the Naturalist school. Lugné-Poe pursued his quest for new manuscripts with even greater eclecticism. Viewed qualitatively, however, the record is more mixed. It is true that several writers who first appeared at the Théâtre Libre went on to pursue successful careers, among them Jules Renard, Courteline, Brieux, Curel and Porto-Riche. Thanks to Lugné-Poe, Maeterlinck found the audience he merited, as, later, did Claudel. But it has to be said that in the short term their harvest was disappointing, as both Antoine and Lugné-Poe recognised. The reliance on adaptations of novels at the Théâtre Libre, rather than works conceived in the dramatic mould, and on poetry at the Théâtre d'Art and to some extent at the Théâtre de l'Oeuvre, must be taken as symptomatic.

In the short term, therefore, both Antoine and Lugné-Poe tended to rely on foreign imports. This policy, pursued partly from inclination but mainly from necessity, is sometimes seen as an admission of defeat. In fact, its consequences in the long term were wholly positive. It achieved far more than temporarily plugging a gap. For too long the French theatre had been insular almost to the point of xenophobia. Antoine and Lugné-Poe began the transformation of the Parisian stage into a cosmopolitan centre. And just as the infusion of German ideas earlier in the century had helped to formulate French Romanticism, so too the introduction of Hauptmann and Tolstoy, Strindberg and Ibsen, and the re-appraisal of Shakespeare, long overdue in France, proved important elements in the brew of fresh ideas from which the modern drama emerged.

But beyond the particular merits and limitations of the new writers they staged, their outstanding contribution, as I suggested earlier, was in instituting an alternative pattern of theatrical activity. Under their influence a theatrical system which had hardly changed since 1830 was completely transformed in the last fifteen years of the century. In this respect what unites Antoine and Lugné-Poe is more important than the aesthetic choices which separate them. For they were both more than simply artistic directors: they took control of the totality of the means of theatrical production. Without this their efforts were doomed to fail. Unlike their counterparts of today, who can be invited as visiting directors into thriving, fully-equipped theatres to direct productions, they were obliged to create from scratch the enterprises needed to house the contemporary drama which neither the commercial or state theatre of the day would consider. This meant bringing together a company of actors, a repertoire, finding a theatre to house them, and creating a public to share in the adventure. If, as was the case, this produced few real masterpieces, it did at least ensure that worthwhile plays were no longer being stifled at birth.[35]

At the start of this chapter I referred to the divorce that existed between the French stage and the would-be writers struggling to gain a foot-hold in an ossified theatre system. The unquestionable merit of Antoine and Lugné-Poe, aided by the other independent theatres, was to have bridged this gap by creating theatres dedicated to artistic values. In doing so they created a new polarity: between the *boulevard* (safe, undemanding, commercial theatre) and the *avant-garde* or experimental theatre. That process continued apace in the early years of the twentieth century. Many new studio theatres sprang up and disappeared like mushrooms, but some, like the highly experimental Art et Action group of Edouard Autant and Louise Lara, were serious and durable affairs. There was also Jacques Rouché's Théâtre des Arts (1910-13) which, although relatively short-lived, provided a model for other arts theatres and led directly to the creation of Jacques Copeau's Vieux-Colombier theatre. The latter in turn inspired the Cartel theatres of the inter-war years. It is theatres such as these that have housed the progressive drama of the last hundred years. Though the boundaries between experimental and commercial theatre have become blurred subsequently (Jouvet, for example, courted popular success, and the boulevard theatre is not entirely resistant to avant-garde tendencies) the system introduced by the Théâtre Libre and the Théâtre de l'Oeuvre has persisted in a recognisable form to the present day. In this sense the last fifteen years of the nineteenth century were truly the cradle of the modern theatre.

Finally, what view emerges from the period of what was

quickly to become the most controversial aspect of the director's work in the theatre: the respective importance of the *metteur en scène* and the playwright as originators of drama? Antoine and Lugné-Poe were both conscious of the potential of their art to distort or even supplant the texts from which they believed drama should originate. Essentially, they both saw themselves as interpreters, servants of playwrights. If, unlike later directors, they did not discuss the issue at great length, it is because for them the question did not arise in those terms. The answer was implicit in every aspect of their work. Their entire programme of activities rested on an unquestioned assumption that the art of the theatre is organised around dramatic literature. If a theatrical renewal was to come about, it was not the directors themselves who would invent the new theatre; their contribution was to usher it in by creating the conditions in which it could occur. Why else should they place such emphasis on stimulating new plays?

Nevertheless, the fact that a director makes it his aim to serve the playwright does not in itself make it impossible for there to be some conflict of interest between *mise en scène* and dramatic writing. Already, in this early phase of director's theatre, there were signs of such a clash. Certain Symbolists, as we have seen, had difficulty accommodating themselves to the conditions of performance; but this reflects not so much a rejection of the function of the director as a denial of the stage itself. Of wider significance than this special case is the tendency for a particular production style, conceived for a particular form of play, to be extended to a more eclectic repertoire. The example of Ibsen illustrates how this was the case with Antoine and Lugné-Poe, the former stifling the plays' symbolism in an excess of factual detail, the latter, at first, approaching them as full-blown Symbolist dramas at the expense of their realism. This particular problem would not be overcome until directors ceased to see their art as the theatrical extension of a literary school and came to understand *mise en scène* in terms of a specifically stage-orientated language of performance.

Paradoxical as it may seem, Lugné-Poe saw his essential task as *metteur en scène* as being to rid the stage of *mise en scène*. "No décor!" he prescribed in 1896, "and may the words 'mise en scène' be erased for ever from the list of credits".[36] This is fully consistent with the Symbolist stage aesthetic and it suggests that the natural complement to unobtrusive décor and self-effacing performers must be a self-effacing director. But the notion of the self-effacing director remains anchored in Lugné-Poe's concept of theatre long after the Symbolist period. In 1927 we find him fulminating against the spectacular and enormously costly productions of Edward Gordon Craig, the designer-director whose advent, claimed Lugné-Poe, had signalled the demise of true theatre. Each of Craig's productions, he said, was a "resplendent interment" – a burial, that is, of the author and his play within a grandiose mausoleum erected to immortalise its architect, the director.[37]

Of course, the idea that there can be a self-effacing director is an illusion. The fact of opting for this choice implies a particular (minimalist) view of the plastic elements of staging, and so has an impact on the way plays are presented every bit as profound as when a director sets out intentionally to mould a play into his own vision. Nevertheless the notion of the director functioning as a kind of unseen midwife, breathing life into the author's play without making it his own creation, remained the ideal shared by the second generation of French directors who followed Antoine and Lugné-Poe.

2 The scenic revolution

Theorists of the scenic revolution

"Directing", stated Antoine in 1903, "is an art that has just been born. Nothing – absolutely nothing – prior to the last century prefigured its emergence".[1] Antoine could have added that, as he spoke, theatre throughout Europe was entering a period of intensive reform triggered off by this new phenomenon and by the anti-naturalist reaction in particular. By now, thanks to Antoine's own example, the need for a director to control theatre production and give it coherence was an accepted fact. But what of the stage itself? The great contribution of the Symbolist movement to theatre had been to focus attention on questions concerning the specificity of the stage. Previously, the one goal towards which two centuries of theatrical endeavour had tended was the suppression of overt theatricality, disguising the artifice of the stage in conventions which tried to pretend they were not conventions but life itself. The culmination of this tendency, the Naturalist theatre, was in a sense an attempt to negate the very essence of theatre. The Symbolists, although their approach was sometimes naive and they placed too much emphasis on painting, initiated the return to a creative, imaginative use of the stage. The aim of the second wave of reformers was then to define a new art of staging not derived from a literary aesthetic but based on the specific properties of the stage itself: form, movement, colour and lighting. Not surprisingly, then, the scenic revolution which transformed European theatre in the first decades of the twentieth century was the work of designers and directors rather than playwrights. Its principal theorists were a Swiss stage designer named Adolphe Appia and an eccentric Englishman, Edward Gordon Craig.

Among its leading practitioners were the directors Reinhardt and Piscator in Germany, and Stanislavsky, Meyerhold and Taïrov in Russia, and in France Jacques Copeau.

The importance of Appia's work is that it was the first thorough-going programme for scenic reform which examined every component of the stage and assumed them all to come under the unifying control of a single artistic consciousness, that of the director. His main interest was in musical theatre, especially the music-drama of Wagner whom he venerated, though his most original and lasting contribution proved to be in the field of stage lighting. It was the discrepancy between Wagner's concept of musical drama, which Appia believed to be the art form of the future, and the limitations of actual productions, that convinced him of the need for a total scenic reform. He believed that Wagner's Bayreuth productions were being hopelessly undermined by the stage conventions of the time with their painted flats illuminated by fixed lights. Wagner had formulated an exciting, original artistic concept but had failed to see that his musical drama implied a radically new approach to the stage, believing instead that ever-more sumptuous settings would eventually carry the day. In reality, Appia said, this was simply accentuating the internal contradictions of performances where the lavish spectacle offered to the eye was competing with the music offered to the ear.

Less a visionary than a clear-sighted practical thinker, Appia subjected all the ideas about staging currently being advanced to a probing scrutiny and tracked down their weaknesses. The talk was about fusing poetry, music and painting. Appia replied that the idea of a *fusion* of these arts, however beguiling, was based on a false premise, and he pointed to the Symbolists' ambivalence about the place of the actor as a symptom of a basic flaw in their theories. Painting and theatre were fundamentally incompatible because they were different in essence. How could dramatic art, which is created in time and space, and is therefore by definition an ephemeral art of movement, accommodate art forms like painting and sculpture whose essence lies in the creation of fixed, static artefacts? It could not: "either painting must relinquish its fictive character in favour of the living body, which amounts to its self-suppression;

or else the body must renounce its plastic and mobile life and hand the stage over to painting, which is the negation of dramatic art. So there is in reality no choice".[2] The stage, to begin with, is an empty, latent space, waiting to be filled. But with what? Appia's answer was that, if it is to remain consistent with its own essence, drama can only use the arts of time and space, *i.e.* music, speech and the human body. The implications of such thinking were enormous: above all, it showed how the actor could once more be restored to his central place in dramatic art.

In *Music and the art of the theatre* (1899), one of the key sources of modern stage theory, Appia showed how the components of the stage, instead of contradicting each other, could be blended into an aesthetic whole. A central problem that demanded a comprehensive solution was the disparity between a three-dimensional, mobile actor and a two-dimensional painted set, and between the vertical plane of that set and the horizontal plane of the stage floor. Appia reasoned that, in the first place, it is the music and the musicality of the text that must determine the movement of the actor in time and space. This in turn suggests the vital link between actor and set: the rôle of the set is not to give a redundant pictorial background but to furnish a three-dimensional space which the actor inhabits. Appia referred to this functional, non-representational stage as a "rhythmic space". He illustrated these ideas in his own designs which were conceived entirely in terms of volume and space, and consisted of steps, platforms and ramps, Finally, since Appia realised that even a three-dimensional structure can look flat under flat lighting, the whole picture must be given depth and light and shade and colour by a non-realistic play of light. Appia was the first to explore in a coherent way the immense creative possibilities opened up by the introduction of electric lighting. He showed that the lighting artist not only disposed of the full range of the painter's palette but could also clothe the actor's plasticity, modelling him into the stage in a way which footlights and border lights used with a backcloth could never achieve.

At first these ideas were slow to win acceptance, especially at Bayreuth. Wagner's widow Cosima considered them ludicrous and said his grey chiaroscuro sketches for stage settings resembled nothing so much as Fridtjof Nansen's pictures of the North Pole expedition. Indeed, it was not until Wieland Wagner's productions in the 1950s that Appia's vision eventually penetrated Bayreuth. In spoken theatre, however, where realism was already on the wane, his ideas were more readily received. Their first partial implementation came in 1903 when Appia was invited to work in the Comtesse de Béarn's private theatre in Paris. It was here, in a production of part of Schumann's setting of Byron's *Manfred*, that a constructivist multiple-level stage made its first appearance in France.

Between 1906 and 1914 Appia worked with Emile Jaques-Dalcroze. Appia had always considered rhythm to hold the key to the staging of drama and had sensed the need for a new approach to the training of the actor. Jaques-Dalcroze, meanwhile, as a teacher of music in Geneva, had evolved a system of musical kinetic exercises which he called eurythmics. In partnership with Appia he went on to expand his method to express not only pure tempo and rhythm but also human emotions. (Later, when Copeau and Dullin set up their acting schools in France it was on Jaques-Dalcroze that they based their method). The question of movement and rhythm came to preoccupy Appia increasingly, and in his last major work, *The work of living art* (1921) he stated: "The future of our whole artistic culture – and, obviously, the very existence of *living* art – depends on a correct bodily pedagogy. Its importance is incalculable."[3] Hence, stage design, lighting, theatre architecture itself, came more and more to be seen as a means of exploiting the plasticity of the actor's body. An opportunity to try out these ideas arose in 1911 when the German patrons Wolf and Harald Dorn invited Jaques-Dalcroze to work at Hellerau near Dresden. The theatre he had built at Hellerau, the most avant-garde in Europe at that time, was designed by Appia. The stage and auditorium formed a single continuous space, with no proscenium arch, thus creating the first open stage to be built in Europe in modern times. This theatre was the venue for two highly influential festivals in the summers of 1912 and 1913. The second of these, featuring a production of Gluck's *Orpheus and Euridice*, was particularly successful. A showcase for Appia's ideas about stage design and lighting, it was acclaimed by an audience of international figures including Stanislavsky and Reinhardt, Claudel and Pitoëff, Granville-Barker and Shaw.

At about the same time as Appia, but in a blaze of publicity and controversy, Edward Gordon Craig was hammering out his own vision of a reformed theatre. After an early career as an actor and a brief period of directing between 1900 and 1902, he achieved celebrity with a series of theoretical writings: *The art of the theatre* (1905), *On the art of the theatre* (1911) and *Towards a new theatre* (1913).

Craig abhorred Naturalism with its slavish and redundant imitation of material reality. His theatre was dedicated to the expression of an ideal beauty. He was the first and most persuasive advocate of stagecraft conceived as a totally autonomous art – not a union of all the arts as Wagner and the Symbolists had proposed, but a separate art created out of a multiplicty of raw materials. "The Art of the Theatre," he wrote, "is neither acting nor the play, it is not scene nor dance, but it consists of all the elements of which these things are composed: action, which is the very spirit of acting; words, which are the body of the play; line and colour, which are the very heart of the scene; rhythm, which is the very essence of dance".[4] As to which of these was the most central to the theatre, he refuted any notional hierarchy. None was more important than another, "no more than one colour is more important to the painter than another, or one note more important than another to the musician."

In reality, though, Craig subordinated everything to the visual. He believed the theatre had allowed itself to become enslaved by words and wanted to bring it closer to its origins which lay in dance and mime. In *Towards a new theatre* he cites this dictionary definition: "THEATRE: derived from the Greek *Teatron*, a place for seeing shows, derived from the Greek *Teasthai*, to see". To which he adds: "NOTE: Not a word about its being a place for *hearing 30,000 words babbled out* in two hours."[5] What really interested him most were stage settings, which he regarded as a form of architecture. Like Appia he considered the reduction of the stage to a two-dimensional picture to be absurd. He wanted to re-introduce the sense of light and space that had characterised stage settings in ancient

Greece when productions took place in the open air. His designs were powerful and spectacular, though often impractical. Like Appia's they were non-representational and conceived in terms of volume and space, but they contained soaring vertical lines in grandiose proportions that no known theatre building could contain. Some of his plans, it is thought, would translate into structures five or six storeys high. He also experimented with mobile sets. One of his most fertile ideas, though unfortunately he himself never succeeded in making it work properly, was the use of sliding screens which could be moved by invisible machinery, thus permitting rapid transformations of the stage in full view of the audience.

Craig's most provocative ideas concerned the creative rôles of the playwright, the actor and the director. Craig was one of the first to argue that the theatre must first break free from the centuries-old tyranny of the written text. In *The art of the theatre* he envisaged the theatrical renaissance that would occur when stagecraft ceased to be a mere technique and became instead an autonomous creative art. This could only happen when theatre was taken away from the playwrights, who were merely wordsmiths, and put in the hands of directors. Then, he claimed, "the Art of the Theatre would have won back its rights, and its work would stand self-reliant as a creative art, and no longer as an interpretive craft."[6] In his ideal theatre there would be no play in the usual sense of the word. Instead there would be Drama organised around an idea or vision emanating from the mind of the master creator, the director.

Once the playwright had been deposed there remained one further obstacle to the director's supremacy: the actor. Of all the raw materials manipulated by the director, the animate material is the hardest to dominate and hence the one most likely to ruin the whole enterprise. Here Craig was completely at odds with Appia who regarded the actor's living presence as the key resource of dramatic art, and the only one capable of binding the otherwise "dead" or inert matter of the stage into a living whole. Craig, however, mistrusted the actor's ego and prescribed the most rigorous discipline to keep it in check. He likened the theatre to a ship and warned that any disobedience from the actors would be as disastrous for the enterprise as mutiny would be for the navy. He wanted ideally to reduce the actor to an *Uebermarionette*, an impersonal super-puppet whose every move and gesture would be controlled by the master-creator. This was Craig at his most cranky. Unlike Appia, he had personal experience of acting, yet he would willingly have sacrificed, in the interest of some abstract notion of purity, the theatre's oldest and most precious resource. Fortunately it was Appia's concept of the actor as a living presence, rather than Craig's, that took root in the modern theatre.

Throughout this time he continued to draw up grandiose plans for productions to illustrate these ideas but only five were ever implemented, and they would have been unthinkable without the help of more practical men of the theatre. Stanislavsky struggled for two years to translate Craig's vision of *Hamlet* into a workable reality at the Moscow Art Theatre (1911). Craig regularly declined offers to work in the theatre, or else imposed exorbitant conditions. For example, when Jacques Rouché invited him to work at the Théâtre des Arts he accepted on condition that the theatre remained closed for ten years while he prepared his opening production. Such preposterous behaviour in his dealings with real men of the theatre has led some people to conclude that he was simply a *poseur*, which may well be true. In a sense, though, that did not matter. Craig's chosen rôle was that of guru and prophet of the New Theatre. As such, from his villa in Florence, he projected a bold and vivid vision that had an immense influence on the work of progressive directors everywhere.

In 1922 the International Theatre Exhibition in Amsterdam was devoted to the work of Craig and Appia, and by now their ideas were being widely implemented. The need to subjugate all the elements of production to the overall control of the director, the use of light and colour on stage, rather than re-presentational scenery, to create mood and atmosphere, the extension of the actor's expressive powers to include mime and dance, these were becoming the new orthodoxy. In addition, Craig's more radical notion of the director as a master-artist replacing the playwright no longer seemed such an extravagant ambition. Craig's reluctance to serve a written text, and his more general hostility to speech in favour of the visual, were echoed in the practices of Reinhardt and Piscator, Meyerhold and Taïrov, the constructivists, expressionists and futurists, all of whom in their various ways were intent on exploring new forms of theatricality. Reinhardt's motto "The theatre belongs to the theatre" stood for all those who believed there was far more to the art of theatre than the production of a dramatic text.

*****

Against this background the prevailing values of French directors in the first third of the century may appear timid and conservative. Of course they knew of and were influenced by the reforms taking place elsewhere and they saw themselves as working with, not against, people like Craig as partners in the scenic revolution. But they were more mistrustful of theory, and more cautious in applying it, than their foreign counterparts. This was most evident in the value they attached to the dramatic text. Inverting Henry Irving's famous pronouncement that "the theatre is bigger than the playwright, plays are made for the theatre and not the theatre for plays", they based their approach on the conviction that the theatre exists to serve the playwright and that good theatre depends on good writing.

In France the second wave of theatrical renewal began when Jacques Rouché published *L'Art théâtral moderne* in 1910. This contained an enthusiastic account of the theories of Appia and Craig and the work of Reinhardt, Stanislavsky, Meyerhold and Komissarjevskaya, making plain just how far the French theatre lagged behind the rest of Europe in the matter of scenic reform. Although stage naturalism had been discredited, France could offer no example of a contemporary *mise en scène* based on architecture, painting, music and the decorative arts to rival that of Russia and Germany. At the Théâtre des Arts which he took over in 1910 Rouché staged a modern repertory in highly simplified stylised settings, inspired partly by the exciting new visual style of the Ballets Russes. Rouché remained at the Théâtre des Arts for only three years, not long enough to accomplish a substantial programme of reform but long enough to give the lead to men like Copeau, whom Rouché first introduced to the stage, Jouvet and Baty.

Jacques Copeau and the Vieux-Colombier

The influence of Jacques Copeau on the course of French theatre was decisive. Although his theatre, the Vieux-Colombier, mounted only six seasons (1913-14 and 1919-24) Copeau left an indelible stamp on the French stage throughout the inter-war period and well beyond. Significantly, this director who was so to shape the French stage came to the theatre at the age of twenty four as a critic and man of letters. In 1909 it was Copeau who, with André Gide and Jean Schlumberger, founded the influential *Nouvelle Revue Française* which he directed until 1913. The NRF group were keenly interested in theatre and they lent the Vieux-Colombier moral, financial and even practical support. The novelist Roger Martin du Gard once acted on its stage and Georges Duhamel occasionally prompted. Most of the group, however, were devoted to the novel and saw the theatre as a secondary pursuit. For Copeau it was the only art form that really counted.

Copeau's only practical involvement in theatre prior to the founding of the Vieux-Colombier had been his adaptation of *Frères Karamazov* for Rouché's Théâtre des Arts in 1911. He was neither an outstanding actor nor a technician and depended heavily on other members of the company in practical matters. But he was a man of vision whose dedication to the art was total. As a man of letters he brought to the theatre a passion and respect for dramatic literature, both classical and modern. As an individual he brought to it a love of simplicity and sincerity – some saw it as a calvinist austerity – which gave his approach to art an ethical as well as aesthetic foundation.

Copeau signalled his intentions in an article entitled "Un essai de rénovation dramatique" *(Nouvelle Revue Française* of September 1913) whose publication was intended to alert the informed public to the imminent opening of the Théâtre du Vieux-Colombier. There is no better introduction to Copeau's ideas than this passionate yet modest call for a purified art theatre. It is a manifesto without dogma. "We do not stand for any school," he wrote, "nor do we pretend to offer any formula in the certainty that from this embryo the theatre of the future will emerge."[7] The implied contrast with the Théâtre Libre and the Théâtre de l'Oeuvre is obvious. Starting from no pre-conceived positivist or idealist position, his aim was neither to create a new school of drama nor systematically to champion the avant-garde, but simply and honestly to create *good* theatre. Action, not theorising, was what was needed. The Vieux-Colombier never pretended to be other than a practical attempt to set up a secure base where actors and authors could confidently practise and develop their art.

A conviction that beauty is born of honesty and simplicity permeated Copeau's theatrical endeavours. Surveying the con-temporary stage he perceives a temple filled with dishonest traders: "a commercialisation, becoming more cynical by the day, degrading our theatre. . . the seizing of most of our theatres by a handful of shameless wholesale purveyors of cheap enter-tainment; everywhere the same fairground spirit of vulgar speculation; everywhere the same bluff and overstatement and exhibitionism sapping the last strength of a dying art."[8] And more. These remarks are directed against the commercial theatre. As for the national theatres, Copeau objected to the stifling weight of conservative traditions accumulated over the centuries, deforming the classical repertoire. His hope, then, was to restore some integrity to a once great but now prosti-tuted art form. In Copeau's mind this involved a return to the sources of theatre in order to rediscover its original purity, and as such, therefore, it was less a revolutionary programme than a reforming mission.

What did this mean in practice? Copeau's manifesto outlined a programme bearing on five main areas: the practical task of establishing the Vieux-Colombier; its public; its repertoire; the formation of a company of actors; and its stage aesthetics.

If it was to fulfill its reforming mission as Copeau intended, his theatre had to be free from the commercial pressures of investors yet at the same time sufficiently stable financially to endure. Small capital funding, low overheads and economical operations were combined with a subscription system. In return for a guaranteed regular income, this offered subscribers a wide variety of plays (three a week alternating in repertory) at excep-tionally low prices. The Vieux-Colombier boasted the cheapest seats in Paris. The building itself had two peculiarities. It was long and narrow, rather like a hall, with a platform at one end, no wings and no proscenium arch separating the stage from the small (500 seat) auditorium. Although impractical in some respects, it had a certain intimacy and lack of opulence entirely suited to Copeau's general view of theatre. Secondly, it was located unfashionably in the 6th arrondissement on the edge of the Latin Quarter. This had a symbolic value, signifying how far removed it was both from the commercial theatres on the large boulevards in the north of Paris and from the Comédie-Française on the right bank of the Seine. For Copeau intended to liberate France's great comic genius from the fossilised traditions of the so-called Maison de Molière and create in his modest left-bank theatre a new home where the national playwright's freshness and spontaneity would come to life again.

The Vieux-Colombier's location was also significant in relation to Copeau's aspirations for his public. The theatre, he believed, was not a place of entertainment but a point of convergence for society and humanity. A public was not an arbitrary assemblage of individuals but a corporate body of people "drawn together in the same place, at the same time, by the same need to live together, to experience together the force of human passions".[9] Participating in drama meant experiencing "a heightened sense of, and love for, one's own humanity."[10] Although the ultimate ideal was to bring this common heritage within the reach of all men, Copeau set his sights first on recruiting a faithful nucleus of supporters among the artists, students and intellectuals of the Latin Quarter. Copeau was accused of fostering a cultural elite. Indeed he did exactly that, and openly declared his intention of doing so in his manifesto, but always in the belief that from this practical base the virtues of dramatic art would be disseminated progressively to reach a truly popular public. This never happened during Copeau's career. But others whom Copeau inspired, from Charles Dullin and Michel Saint-Denis to Jean Vilar, went some way towards furthering his hopes for a popular theatre.

Only genuine dramatic works worthy of such a high enterprise would feature in the Vieux-Colombier's repertoire. This meant according an especially privileged place to the classics so that, as Copeau put it, "the writers of today, inspired anew with a filial respect for an art they have seen sullied, will aspire to take their place upon the stage."[11] Here again it can be seen how Copeau's approach was essentially reformist, since it involved returning to the principles on which the great dramatic works of the past were based. Molière, described by Copeau as "the poet in the theatre and the theatre incarnate, the living poet and, through him, the written work brought to life on stage",[12] was to be the Vieux-Colombier's patron, mentor and inspiration. Of particular interest to Copeau were the *commedia dell'arte* and the farces of Molière related to this tradition. The *commedia dell'arte*, a popular art form based on mask, mime and improvisation, and possessing a wholesome naivety, offered a medium in which the actor could rediscover the basic resources of his art in their purest form.

Unlike Gordon Craig, whom he knew well and respected, Copeau saw the actor as the key to interpretation. The artistry and asceticism of Craig's stylised stage designs held great appeal for Copeau but his concept of the actor as a marionnette who must be sacrificed to the overall stage design – and hence ultimately to the director – was totally at odds with Copeau's idea of theatre. Here Copeau was closer to Appia and Dalcroze, believing that it was through characterisation, speech, gesture and movement (*i.e.* the art of the actor) that a playwright's intentions are best expressed. Since the actor was the author's interpreter the director's aim should not be to dominate him and dictate his every move, as Craig was arguing, but rather to submit him to a programme of rigorous training designed to enable him to realise his own expressive potential.

So from the outset Copeau attached the highest priority to the formation of his troupe. The Ecole du Vieux-Colombier was central to the life of the company and eventually the school came to be Copeau's over-riding preoccupation. He wanted to build up a homogeneous troupe capable of unaffected ensemble playing. The star performer and the cult of personalities could have no place in such a company; it was to be "a troupe of young, unselfish, enthusiastic actors whose aim is to *serve* the art to which they are dedicated".[13] In addition to cultivating their sense of vocation Copeau taught his actors one cardinal

principle: submission to the play. "Originality" was to be shunned like the plague: only the text should inspire their performance. The disciplined training was deliberately conducted away
from Paris in a country retreat. Moral and intellectual self-discovery went hand in hand with the acquisition of technical
skills. The training involved improvisation upon a *canevas* or
scenario, as in the *commedia dell'arte*, coupled with exercises to
develop corporal and vocal flexibility and to co-ordinate speech
with movement, taught by Suzanne Bing along lines suggested
by Jaques-Dalcroze. Overall, the aesthetic was dominated by a
quest for movement which was both beautiful and eloquent,
fusing idea and expression in the human body.

The results in performance were most impressive. They
amply justified Copeau's policy of recruiting novices rather
than established actors corrupted by the old rhetorical traditions of the Conservatoire and the Comédie-Française.
Simplicity, verve, spontaneity, freshness were the qualities most
often evoked by the critics – the same qualities, in fact, that
Molière's admirers had hailed in his performances in the 1660s.
Gone was the fussy detailed business of the Théâtre Libre and
the eccentric somnambulism of the Théâtre de l'Oeuvre.
Instead, Copeau instilled a striking economy of movement so
that each sparing gesture the actors made appeared all the more
significant. Contemporaries like Kenneth Macgowan and
Robert Jones found the gymnastic approach to acting irresistible. They wrote: "Their bodies can be seen from all sides, and
still keep their expressiveness and beauty. They have learned
to master their bodies, as well as their voices, and they are able
to make the lines of arms and torsos and knees speak directly
to the audience. When Jouvet sharply underlines and caricatures the salient shape of old Karamazov he is able to escape
from ordinary representation and is able to push his conception
of the wicked, vital old man into almost direct physical contact
with the audience."[14] Overall the productions had a balletic
quality. In *The producer and the play*, a book nourished by half
a century of first-hand experience of European theatre, Norman Marshall vividly recalls their extraordinary spontaneity:
"What I chiefly remember about these productions was their
lightness, their grace and their gaiety. Pictorially they were

exquisite because of the skill with which Copeau composed his grouping and movement on the various levels of the stage. But one was never conscious of a producer composing effective groupings for their own sake; they seemed the natural result of the action of the play, just as the movement about the stage had an ease and fluidity which gave the impression that it had been spontaneously created by the actors themselves instead of being the work of the producer."[15]

This emphasis on the art of the actor determined Copeau's view of the director's function. The actor was always the one who communicated the play to the public and nothing permitted the director to substitute himself in this capacity. The latter's rôle was that of Giraudoux's Ensemblier, which was to ensure a harmonious synthesis of all the scenic elements. *Mise en scène*, in Copeau's terms, meant "the arrangement of movements, gestures and poses, the blending of faces, voices and silences, the totality of the scenic spectacle springing from a single mind which conceives it, regulates it and harmonises it".[16] In one sense, then, the director was indispensable and fundamental to the whole enterprise; but it remained a discreet, self-effacing rôle whose success was measurable by the extent to which it remained invisible.

As for the more material, external components of the production – décor, props, machinery – these were to occupy the place due to them, *i.e.* strictly subservient to the interpretation, and in the event strictly minimal. Copeau's suspicion of visual effects which do not depend on the text and the actor extended equally to the discredited naturalist staging and to the majority of anti-naturalist reforms now sweeping across Europe. While acknowledging his general sympathy for the latter, he nevertheless added: "But, it must be said, the ideas of the afore-mentioned masters [Meyerhold, Stanislavsky, Reinhardt, Craig etc.] are not always without a degree of clumsy pedantry. We detect in them certain simplistic leanings which are sometimes at odds with real simplicity, and, above all, a tendency, incompatible with the delicacy and moderation of French taste, to underline the playwright's intentions and to overstate them by naive material effects."[17]

In sum, Copeau's staging process can be described as reductive. Instead of adorning a play with a style, effects etc., it aimed to subtract all the polluting accretions until one arrived at the residual essence of drama: a text, some actors and a *tréteau nu*, that is, bare boards. On this bare stage the actor, the only true artifice of the theatre, deprived of artificial refuge, is forced to "condense all truth into the characters' feelings and actions".[18]

The principle of the bare stage presided over Copeau's productions from the beginning, but was refined over the years. The first productions featured only a few bits of scenery or furniture – a tree, a couple of chairs – to suggest a place. The idea was taken a step further in 1919 when the stage of the Vieux-Colombier was completely re-built to designs drawn up by Louis Jouvet. Copeau had sensed instinctively that scenic action resides in the living presence of the actor, an actor with a three-dimensional body whose setting must be three-dimensional. What he learned from Appia and Jaques-Dalcroze, whom he visited in 1915, was that the body in motion requires obstacles to meet for its self-expression and that the beauty of bodily movement depends on the variety of points of contact with the floor and objects set on it. The *dispositif scénique fixe*, or permanent stage setting, which Jouvet designed for him, was intended to provide exactly that: a three-dimensional acting area based on blocks, platforms and steps. It was a permanent concrete structure with a wide bay upstage, flights of steps at either side leading to a balcony, and a number of practicable openings down the wings. The concrete soon took on a drab and tatty appearance but that did not trouble Copeau. Functionally, it supplied a neutral but dynamic non-representational space sufficiently versatile to serve, with a minimum of props, for each and every production. In this way, unlike Craig for whom stage architecture was the principal means of dramatic expression, Copeau allowed the actor to animate the stage instead of being overwhelmed by it. Paul Léautaud, admittedly not an impartial observer, assessed the results thus: "There has never been a better demonstration of how self-sufficient a really worthwhile play can be, without any of the experiments, not to say excesses, in staging and scenery which all too often only detract from the play by distracting the audience's attention."[19]

It should be added, however, that the stripping away of

superfluous elements and presenting the play in its unadorned integrity is a relative rather than absolute condition. Like the notion of a self-effacing director, the idea of a "neutral" stage is in absolute terms a myth. Even a bare stage, by its very novelty, has the inconvenience of drawing attention to itself. The English producer Granville-Barker said as much when, in a friendly letter to Copeau, he gently rebuked him for what he saw as mannerism in Copeau's early abstractions. "I fancy," he wrote, "that you were at first a little too intrigued by all those clever devices of staging and decoration that were then in their heyday. That was natural. Some of them were very good and others quite amusing. But the game of dressing up your stage in odd shapes is an easy one to play and it contributes just as much to the art of the theatre as the costume of the actor does to the playing of Hamlet or Tartuffe."[20]

Copeau's text-centred approach to directing obviously sprang from a conviction that the playwright is the *fons et origo* of theatre. What importance, then, did he attach to the discovery of new writers? He was certainly not a systematic champion of the avant-garde and his repertoire showed a marked predominance of classical revivals. But this did not mean he regarded the promotion of modern dramatic literature as unimportant; it meant, instead, that he had a more gradualist view of how it would come into being. In the minds of his predecessors, Antoine and Lugné-Poe, the immediate priority was to provide an outlet for the new writers excluded from the regular theatres. In Copeau's mind the first prerequisite was a return to original values and sources as the foundation upon which, given time, a worthwhile dramatic renewal could be built. Thus he could justifiably say of a theatre where works from the past were given pride of place that "by founding the Vieux-Colombier we are building a secure home for future talent".[21]

The growth of a contemporary dramatic literature could be fostered in two complementary ways. Firstly, and indirectly, by restoring the theatre's prestige, creating a theatrical environment which would stimulate writers to choose to express themselves in the theatre. Among the many authors who testified to Copeau's influence in this respect was André Gide who wrote:

"It needed the Vieux-Colombier with Copeau's artistry and dedication and his good-humoured troupe to entice me back to the stage."[22] It was for the Vieux-Colombier that Gide, ending twenty years of self-imposed exile from the stage, wrote *Saul* in 1921. Similarly Régis and de Vienne, who dedicated their *Bastos le hardi* to Copeau with these words: "If it were not for his work, this play would never have been written." Secondly, and more directly, the new theatre could be fostered by commissioning and staging new plays. In this respect Copeau's eclecticism, which was real enough, was circumscribed by his uncompromising regard for high standards. In *Un essai de rénovation dramatique* he announced: "we reserve the right to exercise strict selection, believing that in the pursuit of an ideal no good is achieved by encouraging false vocations." Thus his idealism tended to de-throne eclecticism, formerly regarded as the director's most valuable quality, in favour of discrimination, and the idea arose, as the playwright Salacrou later put it, that "a director's greatness is shown not only by the plays he accepts but also by those he rejects".[23]

At least, that was the theory. In practice a further influence on Copeau's choice of new plays was his involvement with the *Nouvelle Revue Française*. The dominant rôle played by novelists in the NRF is mirrored in Copeau's repertoire. Jules Romains, René Benjamin, Georges Duhamel, Ghéon, Bost, Gide, Schlumberger, Martin du Gard – all of them novelists trying their hands at plays – supplied more than half of all the new works staged at the Vieux-Colombier. The result was plays which were competent in varying degrees but which would hardly merit revival today. It is true that masterpieces are rare by definition and that what a healthy theatre needs is a regular supply of worthwhile texts. Copeau certainly contributed to this, even if time has not sanctioned his choices, by recruiting a number of writers who would not have written for the stage without his encouragement. All the same, there remained this weakness in Copeau's discernment. The plays he chose – and even more so, those he rejected, like Pirandello's *Six characters in search of an author* and Jules Romains's *Monsieur le Trouhadec* – reveal a director who was more responsive to a text's literary virtues than to its theatricality.

The main successes among his modern repertoire were Vildrac's *Pacquebot Tenacity*, Romains's *Cromedeyre-le-vieil* and an unusual modern farce, *Le Testament du Père Leleu*, by Roger Martin du Gard. The latter was so popular that Copeau included it in every season mounted by the Vieux-Colombier. Apart from these plays the theatre's reputation was founded on outstanding productions of traditional farces, classics such as *L'Avare* and *Twelfth night* and some more unusual works from the past like Prosper Mérimée's Romantic comedy *La Carrosse du Saint-Sacrement*. As one might expect, established works outnumbered new plays in a proportion of two to one. But the most striking aspect of the repertoire is the sheer number and variety of plays presented. The total for the six Parisian seasons and the two seasons in New York (1917-19) is a staggering eighty-five plays by sixty-three authors, in many cases with the number of performances for a play in single figures. The combination of such frequency with high standards is an achievement which only Jean-Louis Barrault among French directors can match.

In 1924, after five hugely successful post-war seasons, Copeau abruptly closed the Vieux-Colombier and retired with some of the company to the village of Pernand-Vergelesses in Burgundy. Explaining this remarkable step he cites, in *Souvenirs du Vieux-Colombier*, an awareness of the shortcomings in his work so far and a sense of mission, as yet undefined, which he felt could only be pursued away from the contaminating influences of the capital. It is also probable that the recent defection of key figures like Dullin and especially Jouvet on whom he relied heavily, was keenly felt.

In the provinces Copeau and his troupe, Les Copiaus as they were dubbed, studied mime and improvisation and gave performances in the villages of Burgundy. Local themes such as the life of the *vignerons* furnished the material for their performances. Later Copeau did return to Paris to direct occasional productions and even assumed the management of the Comédie-Française for a few months in 1940 until the German occupation put an end to it.[24]

Despite its short life, the Vieux-Colombier had a great influence: first, because Copeau was a pragmatist who asked to be judged on his results and not his theories. Secondly, because his theatre looked beyond the limits of the immediate present; instead of seeking instant gratification it aimed to retrace the steps that had led to the former greatness of theatre. And finally because of the idea of the school where young artists acquired not only skills but the sense of a vocation. Copeau's ideals were perpetuated most directly by the Compagnie des Quinze, a group which emerged from the Copiaus in 1931 under the leadership of Copeau's nephew Michel Saint-Denis. With them, Copeau's *tréteau nu* became, literally, a bare trestle stage erected in barns or the open air. Combined with the consummate mime artistry of the performers, it created what was probably the nearest approximation in modern times to the pre-literary popular culture in which Molière's art had its roots. But because the Ecole du Vieux-Colombier was a veritable seed-bed of talent, Copeau's heritage was disseminated in many other ways: through Louis Jouvet who wrote in 1949 "Everyone who works in the theatre today is to some degree indebted to him. Even those who seem furthest from his work have their roots there"[25], and no less through Charles Dullin who in turn trained Artaud, Barrault and Vilar. Even today his influence is felt among some leading European directors such as Giorgio Strehler of the Piccolo Teatro in Milan who cites Copeau along with Jouvet and Brecht as one of his masters.

What did this heritage comprise? It resided not so much in the study of acting techniques (though Dullin, Michel Saint-Denis and Barrault perpetuated the mime tradition), nor in his stage aesthetics (his followers soon went beyond Copeau's "degree zero" and started filling up the empty stage), nor indeed in any of the specific practices he introduced. It lay rather in the underlying principles that inspired him. These can be summarised as: the moral sense he vested in the director's vocation, the centrality of the text, and, flowing from this, the accent on the living presence of the actor in preference to scenic inventiveness.

Copeau thus established a notional hierarchy (in descending order: author-actor-director) which, with the questionable exception of Gaston Baty, remained immutable beneath the obviously different production styles of his successors between the wars. This emphasis on the centrality of the text expressed through actors, it should be recalled, appears restrained and conservative when compared with developments taking place elsewhere in Europe. The advance of directing as an art form was tending towards a situation where more and more directors were "creating" theatre themselves using the text, the actors and the stage as their raw materials. Thus, a variety of alternative hierarchies were being tested: director-actor-text, director-décor-actor and so on. Indeed the only real echo we find of Copeau's views at this time come from Granville-Barker, the director closest in spirit to Copeau, to whom he once wrote: "The art of the theatre is the art of acting, first, last and all the time." But these were conservative voices. Gordon Craig, as I have noted, saw the actor as only a figurative element within stage designs whose soaring lines reduced the human being to dwarf-like proportions, and anticipated the eventual extinction of the playwright as a species. Max Reinhardt, though he claimed this was never his intention, had a manifest tendency to dominate his actors, dictating their every word and gesture in order to mould them into his personal vision of theatre. Stanislavsky was at this time moving towards a re-evaluation of the actor, whom he had previously subordinated to his overall staging arrangements. But as a director with strong personal ideas he found it impossible not to impose these on his productions. Some writers felt they were being sacrificed to Stanislavsky's ideas. Chekhov went so far as to claim that his production of *The cherry orchard* was a massacre of the play. Stanislavsky himself maintained that he had tried to interpret the play faithfully – perhaps with justification, since Chekhov's insistence that *The cherry orchard* should be played in the style of a farce does seem strange. Still, the fact that Stanislavsky could make this claim, even if the author disputed it, does show the value he attached to the text as a starting point. Other directors had no such compunctions. In Meyerhold's propagandist productions, and even more in Piscator's revolutionary agit-prop spectacles, plays were seized and freely adapted as components of a theatre dedicated to political ideology. It was not until much later that Piscator's emphasis on the rôle of theatre in the political life of a society eventually penetrated France through the intermediary of Bertolt Brecht. In the 1920s French directors looking eastwards were inclined to disparage the excesses of German experimental theatre and to congratulate themselves on their own Gallic moderation. It would be pointless to speculate what course French stagecraft might have taken if Copeau had not appeared on the scene or if some other master with different ideas of the director's rôle had dominated the theatre as he did. What can be said, however, is that in making the French stage worthy of its playwrights, he also made it safe for them.

Interestingly, Copeau, like Lugné-Poe before him, eventually became impatient with the meagre harvest he reaped in terms of original plays. In 1930 he wrote somewhat testily: "Our 'movement' had just one aim: to provide playwrights with an instrument that was worthy of them, minds capable of understanding them, and enthusiasts willing to serve them. Well, I say the writers have not repaid us in kind. They are still abstaining. Most of those who followed us have shown neither the disinterestedness we expected from them nor the genuine love of theatre we tried to inspire in them."[26] The failure of writers to respond was doubly dangerous. For, along with the lacuna it created, it was responsible for the art of the director being elevated to a status which the directors themselves were the last people to wish for it. The most brilliant *metteur en scène*, Copeau continued, knows full well that he will never be anything other than a playwright *manqué*. But: "what do you expect him to do, this poor conjurer left alone to play with his tricks? He mistrusts his own judgement, but he is forced to expose himself, to answer for everyone, to be all-powerful, to become the creator and master."

Copeau's jibes at the absent writer-figure were not the grumblings of an embittered individual. They echoed an anxiety that has troubled many like-minded French directors. In Dullin's eyes the director only came into existence because writers had abdicated their responsibilities in the theatre. He declared bluntly that "the abuses which come from the excessive importance assumed by the director are really the result of writers neglecting their art".[27] Vilar, too, would willingly have restored the central creative rôle to the playwright. Given the obvious and theoretically unlimited power wielded by the director, the marked resistance of French *metteurs en scène* to their promotion from Caliban to Prospero is a singular phenomenon. Again, Copeau's influence in this area was paramount.

The Cartel des Quatre

In Burgundy, Copeau and his troupe devoted themselves to exploring new types of community theatre with provincial audiences, anticipating some of the approaches adopted by theatre workers involved in decentralisation and *théâtre populaire* after the Second World War. In Paris, meanwhile, the avant-garde theatre movement he launched was now in the hands of four directors who dominated the French stage between the wars. Two of these, Dullin and Jouvet, had worked at the Vieux-Colombier until 1918 and 1922 respectively. In 1927 they were joined by Georges Pitoëff and Gaston Baty in a professional association calling itself the Cartel des Quatre.

The Cartel was a loose association based on the recognition that the four companies were working towards a common goal. On a practical level it allowed for joint publicity of each other's programmes and, to a limited extent, a pooling of resources. It aimed, among other things, to provide a shelter from commercial pressures and to break the power of critics in the press as arbiters of a production's success or failure. Insofar as there was a shared artistic policy, it was modelled on Copeau's ideal of a theatre functioning as a school for writers, actors and public alike. Aesthetically there was tacit agreement along the lines of Copeau's theatrical reforms: judicious scenic reform at the service of a classical and contemporary repertoire; a rejection of realism in favour of poetic values; but also a rejection of art for art's sake in favour of work rooted in contemporary life.

Within these broad lines each theatre preserved its distinctive style and to some extent its own public, so that it was not uncommon for regulars to go to the Athénée or the Théâtre Montparnasse expressly to see Jouvet's or Baty's latest production rather than such a play by such an author. Jouvet's brilliantly polished stylised realism, Baty's sumptuous spectacles, Pitoëff's poetic *mises en scène* and Dullin's colourful, animated productions, each offered a unique dramatic experience to Paris theatre-goers between the wars. The Cartel organisation did, however, give the new public that was growing up the idea of a "family" of independent theatres united in pursuit of a common ideal, rather than four rival enterprises.

Charles Dullin

Of Copeau's immediate successors, Charles Dullin in some ways remained closest to his principles. Like Copeau he had a moral sense of the theatre, seeing it as "a source of spiritual enrichment for the people"[28] and drew his inspiration from farce and the classics. This was not in the vain hope of reviving extinct traditions like the *commedia dell'arte* but rather in order to build a modern theatre on proven foundations. This was made clear in the artistic formula he proposed for the Théâtre de l'Atelier which he opened in 1921: "To return to the great traditions of dramatic art, and from this solid base set forth in search of new forms in keeping with the spirit of our times."[29]

Without Copeau's jansenism, Dullin had nevertheless the same disinterested dedication and total identification with his vocation. The highly developed art of mime and gesture he had perfected under Copeau remained a central feature of his style. However, he was no mere imitator of Copeau. Unlike the latter, his first passion was for acting. He was an actor of outstanding expressive talent and already had a rich fund of experience as a reciter and improviser in the Paris cabarets and bars, as well as melodrama and straight acting, when he joined the Ecole du Vieux-Colombier. Possibly this is why his own productions tended to communicate not so much a reverential respect for the text as the sheer exhilaration of its re-creation.

Along with Jouvet, Dullin had been Copeau's closest partner until the two men fell out in 1918. Both were strong, intransigent personalities, tending towards authoritarianism in

Copeau's case and mulishness in Dullin's. Working with Copeau had broadened his cultural horizons and inspired a sense of mission which he now intended to pursue independently. Unable to put a company together immediately, he first went to Firmin Gémier's Comédie Montaigne to set up an acting school modelled on the Ecole du Vieux-Colombier. By 1921 he had recruited a little company of six enthusiasts, including the young Artaud. After two successful productions, *L'Avare*, which had provided Dullin's most popular rôle at the Vieux-Colombier, and Calderón's *Life is a dream*, he was able to secure the lease on the Théâtre Montmartre. Re-named the Atelier, it was Dullin's stage until 1939.

In his seventeen years at the Atelier Dullin staged an eclectic programme of some sixty-nine plays. The major successes included Pirandello's *Each in his own way* (1924), Ben Jonson's *Epicoene, or the silent woman* (1925) and *Volpone* (1928), Evreinov's *Comedy of happiness* (1926), Aristophanes' *The Birds* (1928) and the première of Salacrou's *La Terre est ronde* (1937). But Dullin did not regard these popular successes, welcome though they were, as the most important part of his work. The Atelier was not a factory for producing commercial successes but an exploratory workshop where what really counted was the sustained programme of research. In public and commercial terms many of its productions were failures but for a number of young artists, including Barrault, it was a complete way of life.

Dullin was an exacting director, but the special appeal of his productions lay not in a high-minded artistry but in their warmth and generosity of spirit. As with all directors his personality permeated his productions. In Dullin's case, a sharp sense of humour and a taste for carnival and rumbustuous popular entertainments like the *foire* steered him away from Copeau's asceticism. His tendency to approach theatre in the light of his own temperament sometimes gave rise to criticisms that he deliberately twisted plays to suit his own ends. This was said, for example, of his colourful production of *Volpone* where Jonson's black-edged satire took on a lighter, more cheerful hue. But to accuse him of infidelity is really to underrate Dullin's scrupulous honesty. The truth lies more in Norman Marshall's assessment that "although his view of life was too personal, too individual to make him a good interpreter of the works of those who saw life from a different viewpoint, he produced plays as he saw them, with complete sincerity, and was often genuinely puzzled when other people saw them differently".[30] The playwrights he worked with certainly never complained of being betrayed. Armand Salacrou, a writer with a well-publicised aversion to self-indulgent directors, often paid tribute to Dullin's respect for his texts. Even when Dullin lightened the tone of *L'Archipel Lenoir*, characteristically playing it as a black comedy rather than a tragedy, Salacrou declared the interpretation totally justified.

In fact, once one makes allowances for his tastes and temperament, Dullin was the least doctrinaire of directors. "I have always tried to seek out the *mise en scène* in the substance of the play itself, establishing the most direct contact possible between the author and the public," he wrote.[31] Having first accepted the basic principle that the director is a specialist whose job is to translate the playwright's world as faithfully as possible in the theatrical medium, it followed from this that no immutable theory could be valid for any two plays. Putting aside prejudices and preconceptions, the director approaches each play in a state of "virginity" with the aim of immersing himself in the world of the play. When its essential and unique truth has been disengaged the appropriate means of expression will begin to suggest themselves. It was significant that only once did Dullin come to rehearsals armed with a written *mise en scène* prepared in advance. After struggling for some time to implement it he threw it away and returned to his usual method of creative improvisation.

Thus Dullin looked on his art as a process of constant research and his life as a series of provisional attainments. More than any other art, the art of theatre is one of ephemeral and perpetual re-creation, a process of creating then destroying in order to create something different. The important thing is never to delude oneself into believing one has created a definitive truth: when it seems this has been achieved, that is the time to start again. Eventually this meant that searching and experimenting, rather than making, were the most important parts of artistic activity. No doubt this is what Dullin was signalling when he chose to call his theatre the Atelier, or Workshop.

It was in this spirit of research that, for example, whenever the Atelier revived a former success from its repertoire, it was never a straight repeat but a substantially new production. *L'Avare*, one of Dullin's popular successes, was given three times at the Atelier but each time in a quite different setting. The original production in 1922 simply used plain black curtains, the first revival was played in a more elaborate arrangement of multi-coloured drapes, whilst for the third production Dullin designed a tripartite set representing a street, a garden and an interior. Dullin himself played the part of the miser. One particularly difficult scene is where Harpagon, searching for the thief who has stolen his treasure, takes himself for the robber. Conventionally this is done by the actor catching hold of his own arm. In his first production Dullin relied on traditional mime for comic effects in this scene. Subsequently he invented an ingenious yet logical approach by arranging for a spotlight to cast a gigantic shadow of himself on the curtains upstage, permitting an original comic interplay between the distraught miser and his own shadow.

The same questing spirit prompted Dullin to call a halt to the phenomenally successful run of Jonson's *Volpone* in 1929. The first real box-office success of the Atelier, which had teetered on the brink of insolvency for seven years, this production showed signs of being able to run indefinitely and transforming the economy of his theatre. Yet after the 400th performance Dullin declared that *Volpone* was "mucking my theatre up" and withdrew it. He was suspicious of success, both for the sense of complacency it was apt to induce and because the long runs given to popular plays undermined the theatre's rôle as a foyer for research and creation. This attitude was not uncommon among directors of the time but few of them practised it so selflessly.

The eclecticism of the early avant-garde theatres was also a feature of the Atelier. Its repertoire included a high proportion of foreign playwrights: Shakespeare and Jonson, the Spanish Golden Age classics (Lope de Vega, Calderón and Cervantes) whose broad and colourful canvas of life appealed to Dullin, and Pirandello, a name usually associated with Pitoëff though in fact it was Dullin who introduced him in France with *The pleasure of honesty-* in 1922, followed by *Each in his own way* (1924) and *All for the best* (1926). Some accused him of neglecting the native drama – unjustly, since in addition to the classics he promoted some two dozen new playwrights. Among them were Jean Cocteau, Max Jacob, Marcel Achard, Bernard Zimmer, Stève Passeur, Armand Salacrou and, towards the end of his career, Jean-Paul Sartre. His close association with Salacrou was particularly fruitful. Salacrou's tricky style with its overtones of Pirandello and surrealism and taste for incongruity and parody has fallen out of fashion today but in Dullin's hands plays like *Atlas-Hôtel* (1931) and *La Terre est ronde* (1938) enjoyed a well deserved popularity.

What was the secret of Dullin's productions? To appreciate this, and to see incidentally how Dullin understood the idea of "serving the playwright", it is necessary to go back to the moment when the director makes his initial encounter with the text. Here again I think Dullin's background as an actor was crucial. There are directors, such as Jouvet, who are above all responsive to the value and nuance of words, the harmonies and rhythms of speech. There are other directors whose reading of a play is strongly shaped by a visual imagination, whose mind's eye sees movements, patterns and gestures. Dullin belonged to a third type who lives with the characters. He described the initial reading as "a charming flirtation with the characters". His description of this flirtation is worth quoting at some length because it reveals both the intensity of the encounter and the way it helped to shape the eventual production:

The more one sees these characters, the more one grows to like them. They can come and wake you in the night, interrupt your reading, prevent you from writing urgent letters. In the morning you are in such a hurry to meet them you forget to shave or do your exercises. . . So many intrusions into one's private life, and all this because one is grooming them, with a face, a build, a hair-style, ready for them to meet the public. There are costumes to be found to dress them with the necessary splendour or simplicity, an architect to draw up the plans for the house they will live in. . . You must trace each of the steps they will take, organise their movements which must be adapted to the needs of art whilst all the time remaining true to life.[32]

On another occasion Dullin described a visit which Smerdiakov, the character he was to play in *Frères Karamazov*, paid to him in his room one night and their conversation which lasted throughout the night.

A faithful interpretation of a play thus meant *listening* to the characters and bringing them to life in all their plenitude on stage. For the actor it required a triumph of instinct over the intellect, of sincerity over artifice. It also required the actor to exploit the fullest possible range of expression, without excessive reliance on speech alone. Dullin believed that on stage actions speak, if not louder, at least as loud as words, and that a servile respect for the text at the expense of *le jeu* is fundamentally anti-dramatic.

Dullin's attitude to the plastic components of theatre often seemed ambivalent. He was deeply mistrustful of machinery and elaborately staged productions, believing that unrestrained decoration meant certain death for the text,[33] yet he had a marked taste for colour and spectacle. Some of his stage designs were outstandingly spectacular, like the set for Pirandello's *Each in his own way* where a huge corridor receding away from the public allowed the actors to surge dramatically into sight when making an upstage entrance. He abhorred the ingenious mechanical tricks being invented to permit rapid multiple scene changes, remarking witheringly: "to hear the advocates of these systems, one would think that playing Shakespeare at 25 sets an hour would finally make his plays accessible to everyone"[34] yet he used the revolving stage himself when it suited him.

These practices may seem to contradict his assertion that "the most beautiful theatre in the world is a masterpiece on bare boards".[35] In reality, although he replaced Copeau's asceticism with a richer sense of spectacle, the underlying principle of stage effects at the complete service of the text, and never in competition with it, remained constant. It was all, as he saw it, a question of moderation and tact. Basically – and this is where as a practitioner he differed from the theorists – he believed that what was needed was mastery over the existing technology and a judicious application of it where appropriate to highlight the text. From Appia he learned that, of the technical resources available to the director, lighting was the most valuable. He said lighting was a proper medium for the imagination because it was fluid, living matter, as opposed to scenery which was inert. Applied with subtlety it could achieve an effect comparable almost to music in its power to stir the spectators' emotions. And in combination with music it generated a cumulative poetic effect beyond the sum of the parts. Dullin made much use of music, not merely by way of overtures and interludes but integrating it into the dramatic action. One of his devices was to give each character his own musical "atmosphere" so that a distinctive air accompanied his entrances or exits – a technique later adopted to superb effect by Darius Milhaud and Anouilh for *Le Bal des voleurs*.

It might seem odd, given his emphasis on characterisation, that his productions of what one might call psychological plays – those of Stève Passeur for example – were among his least successful. But this was because Dullin was at his best as a director and an actor in plays which lent themselves to expressive stylised playing rather than individual composition rôles. He was never at home within the confines of realism. He scored a particular success with Balzac's *Mercadet ou le faiseur* (1935), a black play depicting the world of financial speculators which most directors would treat as a realist drama. Dullin characteristically played it in a cheerful pink and yellow candy-striped set with musical accompaniments almost in the style of a comedy by Beaumarchais. He loved to include spectacular elements of ballet or mimed dance and did so in nearly all of his productions. To critics who objected that he dragged them in willy-nilly he argued that these were not gratuitous *divertissements* but served either to highlight the play's theme (like the apothacaries' dance in *George Dandin* or the creditors' ballet in *Mercadet)* or (as with the mimed entr'actes for Salacrou's *Le Soldat et la sorcière)*) to bridge the gap between acts, thus giving the theatre something of the fluid continuity of cinema.

It was at the Atelier in the Place Dancourt (now Place Dancourt-Charles-Dullin) that Dullin enjoyed his greatest successes. The Atelier was a small, under-equipped theatre with a cramped, almost circular stage but it had a uniquely cosy and intimate character. (After the war the Atelier enjoyed a second distinguished phase of life under André Barsacq's management). In spite of its constantly precarious finances it survived for seventeen years – far longer than any previous avant-garde theatre – thanks largely to Dullin's ability to make a positive virtue out of poverty. It was typical of him that when Philippe de Rothschild offered the Cartel directors his ultra-modern Théâtre Pigalle Dullin declined, though Jouvet and Baty felt no compunction about using its magnificent equipment. When men like Piscator and Gordon Craig were spending vast sums to realise grandiose projects, Dullin showed how the most effective sets could be contrived from the slenderest means: a forest built from packing crates picked up from the local grocer's shop *(Huon de Bordeaux)* or a garden made of newspaper mounted on wires *(Le Camelot)*.

The devotees who followed Dullin's work were a faithful, supportive public but relatively few in numbers. As the 'thirties wore on Dullin, in common with the other members of the Cartel, became increasingly concerned with the need for a popular theatre catering for a wider public. In 1937 he submitted a report to the minister Jean Zay arguing the need for theatrical decentralisation, and he was one of the first directors, well before Jean Vilar, to organise tours of the provinces with his productions. These initiatives bore fruit later in the *théâtre populaire* movement which gathered strength after the Second World War. Meanwhile, it seemed a natural step for Dullin to move to the larger, more modern Théâtre Sarah-Bernhardt (re-named Théâtre de la Cité during the Occupation) in 1941. This final venture was a failure both artistically and financially, in spite of an audacious programme which included Sartre's anti-collaborationist play *Les Mouches* in 1943. The theatre's wide stage and cavernous auditorium imposed its own restrictions on the repertoire, being quite unsuited to the intimate style of production Dullin had evolved at the Atelier, and no popular public came to swell the ranks of the faithful who had followed him from Montmartre. By 1947 an accumulated deficit of four million francs forced him to relinquish the post. The popular theatre he helped to plan needed an organiser of the calibre of Jean Vilar to make it succeed. The natural milieu for Dullin's special genius was a studio theatre. In 1947 he abandoned the struggle with the Théâtre de la Cité and went to Geneva where he directed theatre operations at the Maison des Arts until his death in 1949.

Louis Jouvet

If Dullin was the most Shakespearean of Copeau's successors, Jouvet must be considered the most classical. This is curious, because apart from three of Molière's comedies and Corneille's *L'Illusion comique* it was not with the classics but with contemporary playwrights that he made his mark. Yet his tastes were urbane and sophisticated – like the classical writers he saw society as man's natural milieu – and he brought the most rigorously Cartesian scrutiny to bear on his working methods. Above all, his productions had the clarity and economy of expression that for French people are the hallmarks of classicism. They perhaps lacked the poetic suggestiveness of Dullin's or Pitoëff's. Instead of depth they had lucidity and polish. As it happened, there was a vein of contemporary writing that suited his talents to perfection: not the avant-garde experiments of iconoclasts like Apollinaire, Vitrac and Tzara but the stylish literary and sociable plays of Jules Romains, Marcel Achard and, above all, Jean Giraudoux.

Jouvet's career followed a similar pattern to Dullin's. Like the latter he came under Copeau's formative influence before setting up his own company, and like him he also survived long enough to be involved with the radically different existentialist and so-called "absurdist" theatre of the post-war and to take an active interest in the process of decentralisation. But he remains pre-eminently a figure of the elegant and conservative theatre world of the 1920s and 1930s, a scene swept away by the Second World War. Perfectionist rather than radically innovative, he brought theatre of the highest calibre to a relatively select public.

Jouvet the director is inseparable from Jouvet the actor. In fact, it is as an actor that many people remember him, partly because of his celebrated stage performances in *Knock*, *Don Juan* and *L'Ecole des femmes*, and also in his frequent film rôles. His influence was also extended through his teaching at the Conservatoire d'Art Dramatique. He showed little interest in the traditions of *commedia dell'arte* and Noh, being primarily concerned with diction. And whereas the acting styles of the Vieux-Colombier and the Atelier, partly based on these pre-classical and oriental traditions, tended towards stylisation and the presentation of types, Jouvet's acting strength lay in his creation of individuals. But at the same time he had little sympathy for the fashionable methods of Stanislavsky which aimed at total identification with the rôle. His own approach was based on a lucid and critical analysis of character which, coupled with total mastery of voice and gesture, enabled the actor to give a precisely controlled performance.

In a similar way, his approach as a director combined the qualities of intelligence and technique. He studied all the tools of his craft in infinite detail. It is doubtful, for instance, whether anyone knew more about the behaviour of reflected light. Jean-Louis Barrault in his memoirs characterises the directors of his youth by imagining the rôles they might have had in other walks of life: Copeau as a cardinal, for example, and Baty as the initiate of some arcane society. He pictures Jouvet as a space technician at NASA. The image is partly true but a trifle misleading because Jouvet was not devoid of intuition and artistic flair, far from it, though he did mistrust their subjective promptings as a basis for creation. I would say Jouvet was more akin to an alchemist pursuing a double-pronged programme of theoretical study and laboratory experiment in order to understand the properties of the elements and other substances, and then operating with and upon these substances in his quest for the Philosopher's Stone. Jouvet's Philosopher's Stone, the consummation of all theatrical activity, was what he termed the "dramatic moment": the elusive "precipitation of feeling" that can occur when an auditorium filled with complete strangers haphazardly assembled, suddenly coalesces into "a single unique being, responsive and warm, which we call a *public*".[36]

A letter he wrote to Copeau during the First World War gives an early insight into the way Jouvet conceived his task. He wrote that if the real problems of lighting, scenery etc. had not yet been answered it was because "up to now, only theoretical technicians or else 'artists' have tackled them. The former have done a lot of talking, and the latter haven't wanted to listen. All this because there has not been some little fellow who didn't think too much, or too well, but who loved canvas and thread and wood and metal and electric lights – who took one of these materials and tried to make it yield up its secrets. I would dearly love to be that little fellow." And he adds: "I try to reason my art, consciously, in order to possess it. . . I think all the time so, sometimes, I hit on something that's right."[37] As these words reveal, Jouvet nourished no immodest ambition to revolutionise theatre, but simply a painstaking pursuit of perfection.

Jouvet first became stage-struck while a pharmaceutical student in Paris before the war, though he failed three times to win a place at the Conservatoire. He was avid for acting experience and seized it almost indiscriminately: at the experimental Théâtre d'Action d'Art (an offshoot of the militant Groupe d'Action d'Art) which he also managed, at the Théâtre des Arts where Jacques Rouché cast him with Dullin in *Frères Karamazov*, at the Théâtre du Château d'Eau (of which he was manager briefly in 1912) and at the popular Châtelet theatre. It was at the Théâtre des Arts, playing in Ghéon's *Le Pain*, that he caught the eye of Copeau who was prospecting for his new company. Copeau recruited him, officially as stage manager, though Jouvet also acted at the Vieux-Colombier, with particular success in comic rôles like the doctor in *La Jalousie du barbouillé* and Andrew Aguecheek in *A midsummer night's dream*. Soon Jouvet was designing and building sets, arranging the lighting, assisting with directing, and he quickly became Copeau's most versatile and indispensable factotum.

In 1921 the energetic entrepreneur Jacques Hébertot replaced Firmin Gémier as manager of the Théâtre des Champs-Elysées, a move which was to have repercussions not only for Jouvet's career but for all the members of the future

Cartel. Hébertot planned a number of changes in the theatre. The Théâtre des Champs-Elysées (misleadingly situated on Avenue Montaigne) was an imposing modern complex boasting two auditoria of 2,100 seats and 750 seats, as well as rehearsal rooms, a gallery and bars. The so-called Grand Théâtre was the scene of some of the most exciting productions given by the Ballets Russes and Rolf de Maré's Swedish Ballet. In recent years it had seen the première of *The rite of spring* given by Diaghilev, Stravinsky and Nijinsky, and the first performances of Cocteau's surrealist farces *Le Boeuf sur le toit* and *Les Mariés de la Tour Eiffel*. A dazzling variety of celebrities also appeared there, from Isadora Duncan, Taïrov's Kamerny Theatre and Stanislavsky with the Moscow Art Theatre, to Mistinguett and Josephine Baker! The smaller theatre, known as the Comédie des Champs-Elysées, meanwhile, had already been let to Pitoëff. In 1922 Hébertot made Jouvet what must have been an irresistible offer to share the Comédie with Pitoëff, while also giving him a free hand to design and install an experimental studio theatre in place of the picture gallery above the Comédie. The tiny Studio des Champs-Elysées, inaugurated in 1923, became the home of Gaston Baty between 1924 and 1928. Pitoëff left in 1924, perhaps having been squeezed out by an over-demanding Jouvet, leaving the latter in sole possession of the Comédie. Eventually, in 1934, Jouvet too was driven out of the Comédie by its high running costs. During the second half of his career he occupied a boulevard theatre, the Athénée-Louis Jouvet, though he also mounted productions at Philippe de Rothschild's Théâtre Pigalle and the Comédie-Française.

Copeau looked upon Jouvet as his spiritual heir in the theatre. When he closed the Vieux-Colombier it was to Jouvet that he bequeathed its repertoire, subscriptions and those members of the company who chose not to follow him to Burgundy. If the Vieux-Colombier's mission was to stage good works of the past with the ultimate aim of "preparing a home for future talent", the disciple might be said to have realised the second part of the programme more effectively than the master. Apart from Mérimée's *La Carrosse du Saint-Sacrement*, acquired from the Vieux-Colombier's repertoire, the occasional foreign play such as Sutton Vane's *Outward bound* (translated as *Au grand large*) and Gogol's *Revizor*, and (later in his career) Molière, Jouvet produced nothing but contemporary French playwrights. Three important names predominate: Achard, Romains and Giraudoux, but there were also premières of plays by Bernard Zimmer *(Bava l'Africain*, 1926, *Le Coup du deux décembre*, 1928), Cocteau *(La Machine infernale*, 1934), Genet *(Les Bonnes*, 1947) as well as Bost, Crommelynck, Gignoux, Sarment, Savoir, Passeur, Supervielle, Vildrac. . . Quite simply, no other director has worked so consistently at building up a repertoire of contemporary writing.

Curiously, though, he rarely risked staging the first play of an untested writer. Romains had already acquired a reputation with *Cromedeyre-le-vieil*, Cocteau with *Orphée*, produced by Pitoëff. The only major exception was Giraudoux. This measure of caution was probably induced by his craving for popular success – not merely to finance his next production, nor to assuage the self-doubt that beset him permanently, but for the quite legitimate reason that success was incontrovertible proof that what he was doing was valid and worthwhile. He fully appreciated the importance of playing to full houses. Giraudoux, in *L'Impromptu de Paris*, has him say: "When a theatre is full it's a smiling angel. Empty, it's a monster. In the daytime a theatre only radiates that engaging aspect, that good humour, that picturesque charm which like a little hypocrite it's polishing up for you, if it knows it will be packed in the evening. When you have to live with a monster you prefer to see it smiling." This was one of the major differences he had with the resolutely anti-utilitarian Copeau. Of the phenomenal success of *Knock* he claimed: "It's not a literary judgement but an evidence – irrefutable and certain evidence – which pulverises all the opinions, verdicts or points of view that can be voiced about the play. Success is an argument."[38] The sentiment, if not the style, is precisely that of Molière in *La Critique de l'Ecole des femmes*.

Jouvet's opening production at the Comédie in 1924 was Romains's second play, *Monsieur le Trouhadec saisi par la débauche*, a lively if light satire strangely turned down by Copeau who claimed the cast had fallen asleep at the first reading. Jouvet directed, designed the set and acted. The set design retains the simplicity of the Vieux-Colombier period. But it also foreshadows a return to decoration, albeit stylised, after the Appia-like abstractions he had explored at that time. It suggests too the impeccable and effortless stylishness that was one of his hallmarks. It features a simple backcloth representing Monte Carlo and a pair of palm trees which change their attitude in an ironic commentary on the action: erect, or arched together to form a triumphal arch, or teetering drunkenly. With Jouvet in the central rôle of the debauched geography teacher it was an auspicious start for his new company and ran to over two hundred performances – roughly twenty times the average for productions at the Vieux-Colombier.

In all Jouvet was to stage nine of Romains's plays, but the most popular by far was his second production, *Knock ou le triomphe de la médecine*. The comedy concerns a scheming quack who takes over a dormant country practice and makes a fortune by persuading even the healthy that they are sick. Again, Jouvet designed and directed the production, arranged the lights and played the central rôle, all with his habitual meticulous intelligence. The rôle of Knock was an ideal vehicle for his comic talent: dry, precise, extraordinarily detailed and expressive (he possessed large, mobile rictus muscles), adding up to a nuanced composite parody of the medical profession's foibles. His performance in the previous comedy as Trouhedec, whom he played like a marionnette with a mop-like wig and a high squeaky voice, had been criticised for being too caricatural. In *Knock* he had a part that produced irresistible comic effects without any over-acting. Before the production opened Jouvet was sure of the text's dramatic qualities; he felt the audience would appreciate the medical satire and that it would certainly be a literary success, but he had little confidence in its box-office potential. He was also worried that it would be too short to satisfy the audience and persuaded Romains to write a one-acter to fill the evening out. In the event *Knock* turned out to be the greatest popular success of his career. It was revived time and time again, nearly every year until 1950, subsidising many less popular productions, staving off insolvency, and running to a total of nearly 1,500 performances! It was, as he wrote in *Témoignages sur le théâtre*, the talisman whose magic never failed in twenty five years.

This was just as well, because the company suffered its share of flops, particularly in the early years. The Comédie des Champs-Elysées was located some distance away from the popular theatre districts and unlike the Vieux-Colombier or the Atelier, whose devotees could be relied on through thick or thin, its public was fashionable and fickle. Romains's *Le Dictateur* (1926), a controversial play about despotism with obvious relevance to Mussolini's Italy, and *Le Mariage de Monsieur le Trouhadec* (1925), an inferior sequel to the first Trouhadec comedy, were both badly received. Zimmer's *Le Coup du deux décembre* was savaged by the press and had to be withdrawn. And during the disastrous five-day run of Crommelynck's *Tripes d'or* (1925) Jouvet remarked that there were more bailiffs waiting in the corridor than spectators in the auditorium. On the other hand Sutton Vane's *Outward bound* (1926) stands out as one of the hits of this period. A mystical, unsettling tragi-comedy, it also helped to counter the impression that Jouvet was only capable of handling stylish but lightweight comedy.

While Jouvet pursued his policy of promoting contemporary writing with mixed results, one of his unquestionable achievements was to have introduced Jean Giraudoux to the stage. From the opening night of *Siegfried* in 1928 it was clear that a major new talent had been revealed. The septuagenarian Antoine announced: "M. Giraudoux's arrival is an event which will have profound repercussions on the modern dramatic movement."[39] Giraudoux was already known to connoisseurs for his brilliant essays and reputedly precious and obscure novels. But it was Jouvet who helped him to discover his real vocation and bring it to maturity.

When it became known that Giraudoux was working on an adaptation of his novel *Siegfried et le Limousin*, his reputation for erudition and elaborately wrought prose led many to fear the worst. Giraudoux's sophisticated aesthetic, his taste for gratuitous association, irony, antithesis and all figures of rhetoric, seemed unlikely to transfer profitably to the more economical medium of drama. Indeed, his original draft for the play *Siegfried* was voluminous, over-populated with some three dozen characters, and in Benjamin Crémieux's opinion unplayable. But under Jouvet's guidance he re-wrote the play not once but a number of times, streamlining and clarifying the story, reducing the number of characters by a half and eliminating undramatic material. The resulting script was dramatically efficient yet still retained the brilliant Giralducian stylistic envelope.

On the opening night Jouvet, who was as usual gloomy about the play's chances of success, was heard to remark: "It'll not make a penny, but it will be the crowning glory of my life to have produced this play."[40] In fact the première of *Siegfried* was not merely one success among many, it was instantly seen as the most important theatrical event of the decade. Crémieux, like Antoine, hailed it as a watershed. He wrote: "*Siegfried* marks a date, a point of departure, a new hope. It marks the theatre's escape from naturalism and psychology into poetry. . . It marks the renaissance of style in the theatre. . . Never since Musset has a French playwright approached the stage with as much ease and grace."[41]

These are large claims to make of any writer but the hyperbole is justified if one realises that, except for Claudel, Giraudoux was the first great writer of the century to choose the theatre as his primary medium of expression. In this he effected that long-awaited reconciliation between literature and the stage that Antoine, Lugné-Poe and Copeau had dreamed of. Giraudoux's work, reflecting a preoccupation with fundamental human issues, is the product of a cultivated humanist mind nourished on the classics, mythology and the Bible. His is essentially a literary but also poetic theatre, a theatre of verbal magic where impossibly articulate characters express themselves in subtle poetic language, and whose brilliant surface is created by a delicate use of irony and wit. What *Siegfried* signified to contemporaries was the arrival finally of a writer worthy of a stage which twenty years of scenic reform had purged of commercialism and "l'esprit de boulevard".

Jouvet went on to stage nearly all of Giraudoux's subsequent works, acting in most of them as well. They included *Amphitryon 38* (1929), *Judith* (1931), *Intermezzo* (1933), *La Guerre de Troie n'aura pas lieu* (1935), *Electre* (1937), *Ondine* (1939) and a number of others. During the Occupation, when Jouvet and his troupe were on tour in South America, they gave the première of *L'Apollon de Bellac* (Rio, 1942). During Jouvet's absence Giraudoux had only one play staged in Paris: *Sodome et Gomorrhe* at the Théâtre Hébertot in 1942. On his return to France Jouvet mounted *La Folle de Chaillot* (1945), the last play completed by Giraudoux before his death towards the end of the war. Every première of a new play by Giraudoux was a major Parisian event, and though there were occasional failures such as *Judith*, the Jouvet-Giraudoux team was regarded as the most dazzling phenomenon of the French stage in the 1930s.

This writer-director partnership is often cited as the very model of its kind, and rightly so. That Jouvet helped to make Giraudoux into a great playwright is certain. Giraudoux himself acknowledged Jouvet the director, and especially Jouvet the actor, as his personal muse. In writing his plays, he said, the as yet shapeless and mute idea of a character would take on the appearance and voice of Louis Jouvet. Also, it was from Jouvet that Giraudoux, already an incomparable stylist, learned the nuts and bolts of the playwright's craft: how to jettison passages, however cleverly written, that did not contribute to dramatic development; how to effect a dénouement; the trick of the double exposition, one at the start of the play and another five minutes into the play for late arrivals.

Giraudoux, in return, gave Jouvet the most rewarding material for his company and his new style led Jouvet to develop a heightened sense of poetry as well as exploring new techniques. Acting in Giraudoux's plays required a new approach to dialogue, an urbane technique where no unwarranted emphasis was allowed to interrupt the seamless flow of language or to obscure any of its nuances. For these plays the actors were not afraid to stand still and speak, confident that the audience had only to *listen* to be convinced. Jouvet himself, with his dry and somewhat toneless voice, was a perfect medium for Giraudoux's irony. A classic example was Hector's Speech to the Dead in *La Guerre de Troie n'aura pas lieu*, an ironic funeral oration to the fallen warriors. It was spoken by Jouvet in sure taste, in expressionless and almost inflexionless tones, without a hint of pompous rhetoric.

Jouvet's encounter with Giraudoux in 1927 was perhaps the product of chance but in retrospect it takes on a quality of inevitability. Jouvet's conception of theatre *demanded* a Giraudoux. In a historical study of stage machinery, he traced the development of theatre through its various forms up to the modern era, that of the "Italian order" represented by the enclosed stage or, as Jouvet liked to call it, the *boîte à illusions*. The advent of the proscenium arch and stage machinery, he concluded, had made of the stage "a box of illusions whose only possibility of attaining nobility is through the nobility of its poets".[42] Jouvet himself was a past master of the box of illusions, but he needed poets of the highest order to give it meaning and validity. Giraudoux was just such a writer, one of the very few who, to borrow Cocteau's formula, managed to combine the rôles of poet *in* the theatre and poet *of* the theatre.

Along with Giraudoux, the other writer who inspired Jouvet to the peak of his achievement was Molière. His interpretation of *L'Ecole des femmes* set a standard by which future productions of Molière were to be judged, thanks to the freshness of Jouvet's approach to Molière and the perfect finish of his production. Jouvet did for Molière's high comedies what Copeau had attempted with his Italian farces, he freed them from the accretions of fossilised tradition and academic commentary which they had accumulated over the centuries, so that they appeared freshly minted.

To begin with, he dismissed from his mind the countless theories and opinions advanced by critics about Molière's supposed ideas, philosophy and intentions. Jouvet was familiar enough with these, having studied them exhaustively, but concluded that second-hand opinions based on literary or ideological criteria could offer precisely nothing to guide the actor coming to terms with a character or a director facing the play as a theatrical text. Theatrically, too, a *tabula rasa* was needed to sweep away the traditional gags and stage business which were supposed by some to have originated with Molière and which were perpetuated either by laziness or misplaced veneration. In fact most of them were probably apocryphal, but even if they were not, as Jouvet pointed out, what mattered today was finding means of expressing the play's essential situations in ways appropriate to modern audiences, rather than trying to preserve the external forms through which they had been expressed in the past. Handing down playing traditions from generation to generation resulted in the plays being treated as pretexts for a series of scenes rather than as organic entities. Jouvet said that when he was working on *L'Ecole des femmes* he was constantly asked: "How are you playing the speech on infidelity? and: How are you playing the *Maximes*? and: How do you play Agnes's 'Le petit chat est mort'? Everything is labelled, put into boxes with a title and a tradition. My answer was to say: 'I don't *play* any of that. I play the play, the story the play tells'."[43]

Jouvet saw – and in this he was in advance of critical opinion – that the only relevant fact that can be stated with any certainty about Molière is that he was a practising man of the theatre. For today's theatre practitioners, the Romantic picture of his plays as confessional outpourings, the scholars' inquiries into his sources, and so on, are irrelevant and obfuscating. Above all, he saw that the idea of Molière as a moraliser "hectoring the world, influencing manners and customs, expressly setting forth a philosophy or adhering to any system of morality whatever", showed a complete misunderstanding of the nature of Molière's theatrical enterprise. He wrote: "Who would attempt an enterprise as adventurous, as perilous, as consuming, as art, merely in order to give others a lesson? For the man who knows what it is to entertain people and to count the costs at the end of the day, there is only the choice, when he thinks of such a conception of dramatic art, between a Christian indulgence and a mild hilarity."[44]

This fresh approach was first seen in *L'Ecole des femmes* in 1936, a production which Jouvet had been preparing for many years. He approached it, as he did all his productions, through the story and the text and achieved an interpretation that was outstanding for its clarity and unity. It was played as a blend of high comedy, farce and poetry, with an air of gaiety pervading the entire performance. Jouvet himself played the central rôle, a part he had taken in his youth at the Théâtre des Arts. Breaking with the traditional conception of Arnolphe as a stupid, peevish and unattractive guardian, he embodied a bouyant, elegant and self-assured younger man. With Jouvet's elastic features and expressive mannerisms, Arnolphe's frequent asides drew delighted laughter, both when he was gloating over his successes and in the pained realisation of his set-backs. It was not a moralising lesson in humility but an exhilarating comedy of discomfiture.

Instead of disguising or weakly apologising for the contrivances of the plot, Jouvet played it for what it surely is – pure and perfect theatrical convention. So, for the dénouement where a long-absent father returns from America, he gave Enrique a spectacular theatrical entrance in a sedan chair carried by Redskin porters and attendants, to an accompaniment of stately harpsichord music by Couperin. Christian Bérard's set was conceived in a similar spirit of theatricality. It was neither aggressively avant-garde nor realistic but elegantly stylised. With its plain classical lines finished in primary colours it evoked perfectly the spirit and period of the comedy, and with its machine-driven walls permitting rapid scene changes in view of the audience it allowed Jouvet to deal with the problem of place without interfering with the play's continuity.

This production was one of the greatest successes of Jouvet's career. With 446 performances in Paris and 229 abroad, it restored a hitherto second-ranked comedy to a central position in Molière's repertoire. After the war Jouvet also tackled *Don Juan* (on tour, 1947) and *Tartuffe* (Athénée, 1950). These were highly personal interpretations, much influenced by Jouvet's growing obsession with religious matters. They were powerful and controversial productions which departed from tradition to introduce disturbing new ways of looking at the plays. His *Tartuffe* was closer to tragedy or melodrama than comedy. It presented the hypocrite not as repulsive or grotesque but as an enigmatic and seductive sceptic, similar in many ways to his Don Juan. Popular though they were, neither of them commanded the universal approval of *L'Ecole des femmes*.

Of all directors Louis Jouvet was the most unswerving in his fidelity to the text. Working with Romains and Giraudoux he made practical suggestions which helped to fashion the text in the making but he would never meddle with a finished text or bend it to accommodate a trick of staging. It was axiomatic in his view that the theatre owed its prestige to its writers. He categorically denied the director the status of creator. Only poets and composers aspire to vocations, he said; their interpreters – actors, directors, musicians – have a *métier*: a craft. Giorgio Strehler recalls Jouvet telling him: "You are not Mozart, nor Molière. But without you, without a theatre, a director, without interpreters, Mozart and Molière are but pieces of paper; valuable, interesting, but still only paper. It is you who bring them to life. But *never* permit yourself to think you are they."[45] The director's legitimacy, indeed his *raison d'être*, thus had to be predicated upon the most scrupulous respect for the playwright's intentions.

Jouvet also recognised, of course, that there could be no such thing as a purely impersonal rendition of a text, that any production inevitably reflects the director's own bias, but this only re-inforced the need for total integrity if the play was not to be deformed in the process. In Jouvet's case the notion of fidelity held a literal meaning. Whereas most directors would follow what they honestly perceived (whether by intuition or reasoned analysis) to be the play's "theme" or "central idea", Jouvet believed the play's essence to be lodged in the words of the text. His productions therefore started from an analysis not of what the characters are, nor what they represent, but what they *say*.

If the interpreter's rôle is to act as a direct bridge between the playwright and the public, as Jouvet believed was the case, the dialogue naturally becomes the element on which performance must be centred. For whatever suppositions one may make about the play's inner essence (Stanislavsky's "sub-text", etc.) it is in the words of the text that the author sets down his intentions. In these words are crystallised not merely literal meaning but also the vision and sensations experienced by the playwright at the moment of creation. This gives the text, for Jouvet, something of the inviolable integrity of a musical score, and also sets it above the non-verbal means of expression which the director contributes to a performance.

The principal burden is thus assigned to the actor, and more specifically to diction. The actor's aim must be to speak the text in such a way as to communicate not simply its immediate *meaning* but, more importantly, the creative *breath* that suffuses it. Jouvet considered that all good (*i.e.* theatrical) dramatic dialogue was charged with a physical pulsation which we refer to loosely as rhythm. *Knock*, he said, has this imperious quality. He described that play as a "pneumatic text whose pulmonary flux establishes in the actor a categorical physical state which makes explanations and exegesis superfluous; it results in a con-comitant nervous state engendering rhythm and movement, and bringing the actor to full possession of the character".[46] Jouvet taught his actors to breath the text ("respirer le texte" as he put it), for if the performer can discover and reproduce the original "breathing" of the writing, it is as if the playwright himself is present in the theatre and the performance becomes not so much a re-presentation as a re-creation.[47] Jouvet once described how he would direct rehearsals of Giraudoux's plays with the author sitting beside him: "His breathing would follow the text in an even or uneven rhythm, following the actors' steady or unsteady cadence. . . and from the more or less even rhythm of his breathing I could gauge the correctness of their delivery."[48] When the actors discovered the original breathing in the text, then the play realised its full potential as a conduit of "énergie humaine", the invisible force that unites the creator and the public.

Jouvet's emphasis on the text is apt to give the impression that he sponsored a literary theatre, a contention which, although true in a certain sense, needs some refinement. In a period when so many directors were attaching greater import-ance to the non-verbal, more affective and, they argued, more properly theatrical values of lighting, space and music, Jouvet was certainly drawn irresistibly towards writers who were liter-ate and articulate. Like Giraudoux, who once described style as the playwright's "secret weapon", he based his approach on the conviction that the subject matter is nothing without style and that great theatre is above all good writing. To that extent his was indeed a most literary theatre. But if by literary we mean something fundamentally un-dramatic then the term no longer applies. In fact, the approach described above was one which pre-supposed texts of real dramatic quality, because a faithful rendering of any text in its integrity will infallibly show up any dramatic weaknesses in the play. Inferior texts, if they are to withstand the test of performance, demand more licence from the director in the way of moulding, selecting, highlighting, glossing over weak points, than Jouvet would allow himself. This was said at the time to be the problem with his production of Romains's *Le Dictateur*. Here, argued John Palmer, was a classic case of Jouvet's scrupulous attention to every detail leading to the play's real subject being smothered under a mass of incidentals:

> Every line of the text, every situation, every character is emphasised, presented for itself, given equal value. We see a Cabinet Minister at work during a crisis, efficiently and impressively dealing with a situation, and so much emphasis is laid on these externals that the spectator may be pardoned for failing to realise that the real drama is, not how the dictator will settle the crisis, but what is happening to the mind of the dictator himself.[49]

Palmer, an admirer of Pitoëff's essentialist approach to theatre, attributed the production's failure to Jouvet's inability to look behind the textual detail. But one might argue instead that it revealed the weakness of a play which, for all its literary qualities, was imperfectly conceived as drama. When, on the other hand, Jouvet's method was put at the service of genuinely dramatic texts – *Knock*, for example, not a literary masterpiece but a highly perfected dramatic vehicle, or the plays of Molière and Giraudoux – it was apparent to everyone that what they were witnessing was not a literary occasion but theatre of the highest order.

Although the text had a uniquely privileged place in his theatre, Jouvet was acutely sensitive to the non-verbal elements of performance. He would go to infinite pains to obtain exactly the right dye for a costume or the most impressive sound effect for, say, the ship's siren in *Outward bound*. The quality he sought in these things was not realism but a theatricality which permeated all his productions. He particularly appreciated the theatrical qualities of light, though whereas Dullin would be guided by intuition, Jouvet made it the object of years of detailed study. Dullin's lighting was fluid, moody and often warmly coloured with pinks and yellow. Jouvet's was characteristically crisp, bright and sparkling. For the incidental music which featured in many of his productions he collaborated with Auric and Poulenc, two members of *Les Six* who also worked with Dullin.

At first he designed his own sets, which became progressively more decorative. Like most of his generation he abhorred pictorial naturalism but he also turned away from abstractionism and functionalism. His designs aimed to suggest by using simple means. He developed a form of selective realism, of which the interiors for Acts II and III of *Knock* were an early example, where carefully selected real objects were placed in a stylised, clearly theatrical, environment. The taste for selective realism was apparent as early as 1924 in Romains's *La Scintillante*, for which Jouvet designed a set of great detail and precision including a bicycle shop with twenty bicycles and shelves full of shining metallic parts. He particularly liked to enhance his sets with small, bright objects of glass or chrome to catch and reflect the light. Giraudoux must have been thinking specifically of Jouvet's interiors when he wrote the speech in *Intermezzo* where Isabelle describes her room to the Spectre:

> Everything in my room is arranged so that there is always a glint of light on everyday objects, on a vase or a drawer knob, catching the sunlight or the fire by day, and by night the light of the lamp or a moonbeam. That is my snare, and I wasn't surprised to see your face at the window that evening. You were watching the reflections of the flames on the fire-guard.

For many of his later productions Jouvet worked with Christian Bérard, the most brilliant French stage designer of the period. Bérard had previously worked for the Ballets Russes and with Cocteau who introduced him to Jouvet when they were preparing the production of *La Machine infernale* in 1934. Bérard had a versatile genius which could capture perfectly the spirit of seventeenth-century high comedy in *L'Ecole des femmes*, the light touch of fantasy in *La Folle de Chaillot* or the heavy rococo of Genet's *Les Bonnes*. His sets were not only visually striking but also conceived with an impeccable sense of theatre.

As regards their perfection, Jouvet's productions have never been bettered, though some people have considered them *too* perfect. That may seem perverse, but it is true that a calculated perfection can remove the sense of risk and danger that the very greatest productions convey. According to one's point of view, Jouvet's were either the jewels in a golden age of theatre or else the ultimate flourish of a moribund idea of theatre: either way they represent a *nec plus ultra*. Traditional directors such as Jean Meyer, one of his students at the Conservatoire, and other members of the generation to whom Jouvet was known as "le patron", owe him an obvious debt, particularly in respect of his idea of directing as a *métier*. At the same time it is easy to see why he has fallen out of favour among more recent avant-garde directors. From the vantage point of those who want theatre to be a dionysian festival appealing to the senses his approach can seem cerebral, over-civilised and irrelevantly literary. All the means of expression which ought to constitute the very grammar and vocabulary of performance were reduced in his productions to embellishments added to a spoken text. Other directors, who pin their faith on a popular theatre brought into working class suburbs and factory canteens, can with some justification tax him with appealing to a select, even snob, Parisian public. Above all, to those inspired by ideas of a committed theatre, or at least one which is politically aware, Jouvet seems an ultra-conservative aesthete because his one and only commitment was to the art of theatre.

Giorgio Strehler, one of the leading European directors of today, makes an interesting assessment of Jouvet's impact. Hailing "le patron" as one of the great influences on his own early development as a director, he goes on to conclude:

His ambition was to dedicate himself totally to the theatre, to be consumed by the theatre, whence his idea that the man of the theatre is "like an empty receptacle, hollow, resonant, waiting to be taken up and used". The actor is an impersonal instrument who "taps" the truth of theatre. In all this there was the classic trap of "all the theatre and nothing but the theatre". Later I started to ask myself: and what about life? and man? and where is the human core of this man-receptacle, this anonymous vessel? Then Brecht arrived. . . [50]

It is a personal viewpoint, but one which aptly defines Jouvet's unique place in the historical process. It can not, of course, detract in the least from Jouvet's achievement in setting unprecedent standards of artistry and finish and in providing some of the most brilliant productions to be seen anywhere in the 1930s. Simply, and this should not surprise us, his preoccupations no longer coincide with those of today's theatre people. Much the same is true of Giraudoux whose immediate appeal has waned, as often happens to major writers for a generation or so after their initial success. When Giraudoux's work comes to be re-valued, as it surely will, Jouvet's standing will be correspondingly enhanced.

Georges Pitoëff

The most subtle of French directors, Pitoëff never enjoyed the acclaim that came to Jouvet. Jacques Hébertot, who installed him in his first theatre in Paris, referred to him as the Cartel's poor relation, which was certainly true in the financial sense and posssibly also because he was the least understood. He had a nomadic career in the pursuit of the stage which took him first from his native Georgia to St Petersburg where he set up his first theatre, named "Our Theatre", and thence to Geneva where he founded a second theatre in 1915. Neutral Switzerland at that time offered a refuge to an array of international artists: Stravinsky, Diaghilev, Isadora Duncan, James Joyce, Tristan Tzara who invented the Dada movement in Zurich. . . It was in Geneva that the playwright Lenormand, an acquaintance of Freud, befriended Pitoëff who was later to stage many of his "plays of the unconscious". In Switzerland Pitoëff also became involved with Adolphe Appia and Jaques-Dalcroze. Pitoëff acquired a European reputation and his progress was watched with interest by Copeau and Hébertot. Their support, and the indifference of the citizens of Geneva to the new company in their midst, led to his moving to Paris in 1922. There the company went from one temporary base to another: Comédie des Champs-Elysées (1922-4), Théâtre des Arts (1925-7 and 1928-31), Théâtre des Mathurins (1927-8), Théâtre de l'Avenue (1932), Théâtre du Vieux-Colombier (1933-4). In 1934 Pitoëff finally obtained a secure lease on the Mathurins where he spent the remaining five years of his life plagued by failing health.

In contrast to the quintessentially French Jouvet, Pitoëff was a cosmopolitan artist. As such he made a unique contribution to the French stage, though its benefits were not always recognised by his adopted fellow-countrymen. The Compagnie Pitoëff on its frequent foreign tours drew more enthusiastic support elsewhere in Europe than in France. Antoine was one who disapproved of Pitoëff being a foreigner. In 1925 he said of Pitoëff: "He is not one of us and he in no way represents our spirit or traditions."[51] And when the Cartel was formed two years later he wrote: "I will say immediately that the presence of Pitoëff in this phalange pleases me less... What we need above all, I think, is to form a solid front to resist the influx of foreign elements."[52] Considering Antoine's own record in launching foreign writers in France, this was indeed strange criticism.

Pitoëff retained a thick Georgian accent, which makes his success in rôles like Hamlet all the more impressive. But this was obviously not what occasioned Antoine's resentment of the foreigner. In Russia Pitoëff had lived through the explosion of avant-garde experiments that preceded the Revolution. He had begun his career acting in Vera Komissarjevskaya's progressive theatre in St Petersburg, had met Taïrov and been impressed by Meyerhold's theatricalism, influences which often showed in his own productions. He was by far the most stylistically eclectic of all the Cartel producers. This cosmopolitanism was also a feature of his repertoire. Its linchpins were Chekhov, Shaw, Ibsen, Pirandello and Shakespeare. Except for the latter, it was almost entirely thanks to Pitoëff's productions that these important playwrights were known to French theatre-goers between the wars. The same is also true of a number of lesser writers: in fact, the final count of Pitoëff's productions reveals, in addition to 75 French plays, 44 Russian plays, 14 English, 13 Irish, 12 Norwegian, 9 Italian, 7 German, 7 Swiss, 6 Austrian, 5 Belgian, 4 Swedish, 2 Spanish, 2 Dutch, 2 Hindu, 2 Rumanian, 1 American, 1 Polish, 1 Armenian, 1 Hungarian, 1 Latin and 1 Greek! One would hardly think such a wide-ranging repertoire required any apology, yet somehow Pitoëff acquired a reputation for ignoring French writers. Since the latter constituted more than one third of his productions, his case was easy to support numerically. What probably upset critics like Antoine was that Pitoëff disregarded the French *classics* almost entirely (Musset and Beaumarchais constituted the exceptions) and opted mainly for obscure playwrights who served his particular conception of theatre.

The type of play that attracted him can loosely be termed "poetic". With Pitoëff the Idealist reaction that generated the French Symbolist theatre at the end of the nineteenth century enjoyed a final fling. He believed that each play had an essence through which it was in touch with the ultimate, quasi-divine mysteries at the root of human experience. Like the Idealists he saw the quest for reality in art as a process of peeling off the layers of contingent reality to discover the kernel of truth hidden within. Classical psychology, therefore, did not interest him in the least, nor did historical milieu. His forte lay in giving expression to the poetic resonances of the characters in a play.

It was in this direction too that his controversial talent as an actor lay. He was not a "good" actor in any conventional sense: he was no technical virtuoso and he could be extremely monotonous. But contemporary accounts make it abundantly clear that he had an unsettling presence which made a deep impression on spectators. His best rôles, which included Hamlet, fell within a broad type that ranged from the madness of Pirandello's Henry IV, through the murky waters of psychoanalysis in Lenormand, to the subtler and sometimes formless anxiety of Chekhov's characters – troubled psyches out of harmony with the world they inhabit. But if public and critics debated the unpredictable *je ne sais quoi* that Georges Pitoëff brought to his rôles, they had nothing but unreserved admiration for his wife and partner Ludmilla. Her acting was simple and understated, radiantly sincere, and she had an exceptionally melodious voice. As a leading actress of the period – both Claudel and Shaw considered here the greatest actress of their time – she was an important factor in the company's success. Being so heavily dominated by two such distinctive performers, though, it could never pretend to excel as an ensemble company – a fact which Copeau, in a friendly but firm word of advice, deplored.[53]

Pitoëff's productions do not lend themselves to summary generalisations. They operated in an inspirational, and therefore slightly hit-and-miss, way. Within the broad limits outlined above he was more eclectic, less methodical than any director save perhaps Reinhardt. His only fixed principle was that "in directing there are as many styles as there are plays".[54] The idea was commonplace enough – Antoine, Copeau, Dullin, even Baty all voiced it – but Pitoëff was the only one in practice who approached anything like the adaptability it implied. As a result, although certain of his productions were more important than others, no single one of them could be said to be typical of him in the way that, for example, *L'Ecole des femmes* epitomised Jouvet. With Pitoëff it was the total range of his productions that constituted his statement of theatre.

The paucity of his theoretical writings is also striking when compared with his contemporaries. He mounted more productions than his fellow directors (an average of five per year compared with Baty's and Dullin's three and Jouvet's two) and wrote far less. The essentials can all be read in *Notre théâtre*, a slim volume compiled in 1949 to mark the tenth anniversary of his death. But from these brief writings emerges a vigorous, succinct assertion of the ideas that underpinned the catholicity of his productions.

These ideas are not given as being in any sense revolutionary. On the contrary he more than once implies that they fall squarely within the modern orthodoxy: the scenic revolution which was once considered avant-garde is now the accepted state of affairs. Nevertheless Pitoëff reveals significant points of divergence from the Copeau-led tradition, compared with which his concepts are markedly bolder. At first sight they appear to resemble Craig's. While Jouvet remained safely anchored in the idea of directing as a *métier* and the director as an interpreter, Pitoëff asserts the absolute autonomy of staging as an art form. It is one which draws, naturally, on a range of more familiar arts – architecture, painting, song, mime, dance – but for the man of the theatre these are simply raw materials. Directing can only be understood if it is recognised as an independent art form in its own right, not as a simple amalgam in variable doses of these other arts. And the man who master-minds it is, no less than any other artist, an absolute creator: "The director – an absolute autocrat in drawing together the raw materials, beginning with the play – creates spectacle through the medium of scenic art."[55] No-one else knows the secret – certainly not the playwright who, he says, citing Chekhov and Pirandello as examples, often has little understanding of its operation.

Pitoëff not only proclaimed the director's autonomy, he practised it. When he accepted a play from a living author it was on the express understanding that he alone would decide how to stage it. But Pitoëff was not claiming an irresponsible freedom to do just as he fancied: it was a creative autonomy that hinged on certain obligations.

In the first place, the untrammelled licence claimed by directors opens up real possibilities of imbalance if they identify staging too closely with décor, lighting, or any other single component. This indeed is what seems to have happened: "Haven't we seen the stage invaded by painters (especially in Russia) who use it like an art gallery? The architect too has taken over the stage. . . The architect has invented a new 'permanent' stage, so permanent that the only way to change it is to leave it behind and go somewhere else."[56] Pitoëff's answer – and this is where he differed fundamentally from Craig – was to focus everything on the actor. "How," he asked, "can the director have failed to recognise the first of his instruments: the actor? The actor reigned supreme upon the stage before the director was born. What possible value can all the stage accessories have if they are not used solely to reinforce the mysterious power of the actor? Stripped of all accessories and left to himself, the actor will still act and there will be scenic interpretation, albeit incomplete; remove the actor, leaving all the rest, and there will be no scenic interpretation at all."[57]

Normally Pitoëff was less guilty of over-accentuation of any one of the scenic components than any other director except perhaps Dullin. His lighting was modest – a few spotlights artfully positioned always sufficed – and his stage designs relied upon inventiveness rather than lavishness. Though they varied considerably in style according to the play being presented, their common purpose was always "to serve as a screen behind the actor".[58]

As he once remarked, it may have been more logical for the autocratic director to follow Craig's recommendation and compose his own spectacles. However, Pitoëff himself opted for playwrights, and this was where his second obligation lay: not towards the playwright himself but to the plays he writes. "The director's first duty: to enter into communion with the text," he prescribed.[59] One notes particularly his use of the word "communion". His object was always to seize the essence of the play, to penetrate the play's form and grasp the ultimate source of its inspiration. For Pitoëff the latter was always of a divine nature and it came to him not through laborious analysis but as a form of revelation. Like Jouvet, he aimed to interpret the play faithfully, but for Pitoëff this meant something very different from Jouvet's dogged fidelity to textual detail. In practice it meant that each of Pitoëff's productions was a statement by scenic means of what, *in his opinion*, constituted the irreducible essence of the play. Needless to say, this did not necessarily coincide with the public's idea of the play, nor the critics' nor even the author's. So that, although he never settled into a consistently personal style, his productions often revealed a personal if not idiosyncratic interpretation.

Pitoëff never sought to gloss over this obvious fact, merely pointing out that since every worthwhile play lends itself to a variety of interpretations, and since in the theatre itself it is the director who creates, it was an inherent condition of theatrical endeavour. No genuine creativity is possible without some element of risk: "How should the director stage a play? In the first place he is not *obliged* to do anything. He is free, absolutely free. At the worst, he risks giving a false view of the play. That happens. Who does not make mistakes? But if his scenic interpretation corresponds to the play's essence, the production will succeed."[60] And if the worst comes to the worst, the playwright has the consolation of knowing that the production is ephemeral but the text survives to be presented anew.

Pitoëff held that stage designs should be simple and unobtrusive to prevent them from competing with the actor for attention. Whatever the idiom adopted – and with Pitoëff it could be symbolist (Wilde's *Salomé*, Claudel's *L'Echange*), expressionist *(Romeo and Juliet,* O'Neill's *The hairy ape)* or abstract *(Hamlet)* – his designs always made a stylised visual statement of the play's essence. Sometimes they were so extraordinarily apt that it was hard, having once seen them, to think of the play in any other terms. In Dumas's *La Dame aux camélias,* for example, the entire proscenium arch was transformed into an oval gilded picture frame and the play enacted behind it like a succession of sentimental cameos frozen in time. For Pirandello's *Henry IV,* instead of creating the impression of a magnificent imperial palace, as everyone expected, he gave an all-too-obviously cardboard two-dimensional set. Antoine waxed indignant about what he called this non-existent *mise en scène*: "it's unthinkable," he declared, "that anyone should present a Parisian public, which has taste, which is willing to go along with anything provided some visible effort has been made, with such a pathetic, penny-pinching spectacle".[61] What Antoine failed to see was that with this flimsy set Pitoëff had imaginatively expressed the theatrical nature and precarious foundations of Henry's self-delusion – so precarious, in fact, that at the end of the play when Henry is tempted to step out of his madness the cardboard palace started to collapse like a pack of cards.

Occasionally Pitoëff's attempts to present a play in a unified perspective ran disastrously awry. For O'Neill's *The hairy ape* (1929) he took his cue rather too literally from the stage directions to the first of the play's eight tableaux and visualised the entire play as taking place in the steel entrails of a steamship. The proscenium arch was disguised to resemble a ship's funnel, with the audience as it were peering down into the stokehold. In this stokehold the various tableaux were enacted: prison, Brooklyn Bridge, 5th Avenue and all. As if this were not sufficiently baffling, the funnel effect (which incidentally curtailed the sight-lines) also had the actors, who naturally walked upright on the stage floor, appearing at right-angles to the funnel!

At its best, however, Pitoëff's "communion" with the text inspired productions which were not merely alternative interpretations but powerful revelations. His version of Shaw's *Saint Joan* was exactly that. This production was the greatest success in his twenty-five years on the stage. It ran to over one hundred packed performances at the Théâtre des Arts in 1925-6 and was received rapturously at the Globe Theatre in London in 1930. *Saint Joan* illustrates perfectly Pitoëff's ability to take a complex play with multiple possibilities and to organise his own production around a single unified vision. In recent years the play had appeared in a variety of guises. Taïrov at the Moscow Kamerny Theatre had stripped the play of all its mysticism in order to launch an un-Shavian satirical attack on fifteenth-century society. The production in Berlin, meanwhile, by a friend of Reinhardt, had concentrated on authentic reconstruction of the historical milieu. There had also been Sybil Thorndike's robust and rational Joan in Lewis Casson's London production. And hovering behind all these there was the Saint Joan of Shaw's own preface: the "sane and shrewd country type, a born lass", the "woman of policy" who was a Napoleonic realist in war, a pragmatic fifteenth-century nationalist and a pre-reformation Protestant martyr!

Pitoëff side-stepped all these issues and went directly to the heart of the play as it appeared to him: "I want the spectator to be aware of one thing: that Joan is a saint. . . What I want to dramatise, above all, is the spiritual force that radiates from the heroine."[62] Everything in his production was subordinated – some would say sacrificed – to this central concept. The whole play was enacted in a skeletal triptych formed of a gothic arched frame with half-arches abutting at each side and angled towards the public. Backed by an open sky for exterior scenes or curtains for the interiors (black in the judgement hall, red and gold for the epilogue in the King's bedchamber), or flanked by railings for Reims cathedral, this motif allowed for dramatic variety whilst preserving the all-important thematic continuity. Ludmilla's interpretation of Joan was an outstanding personal triumph. She was completely possessed by the rôle, which was either instrumental in or coincidental with her own religious conversion. The many facets of Shaw's heroine were rigorously subordinated to the mystic. Her slight, willowy form and her habitual air of innocence and inner peace also served this unified conception of character. While her body and mind moved in the secular world, she signalled at every moment that her true drama was being lived in an inner world where her "voices" were more real than the people around her.

Ludmilla's interpretation and the production as a whole were not easily reconciled with the historical figure of Joan or with Shaw's rational explanation of her saintliness, and some critics remained unconvinced by Pitoëff's singular vision of the play. Antoine observed: "It required all of [Ludmilla's] luminous, burning sense of will to persuade one to accept this boyish sapling as our national saint."[63] For Norman Marshall the production "demonstrated the dangers of a tidy-minded producer seeking a single, unifying theme to bind together a great, sprawling, argumentative masterpiece."[64] As for Shaw, who had been longing for years to carry off a success of this magnitude in France, his letters to Pitoëff show him to have been jealous of the man who secured it for him. While paying homage to Ludmilla's genius ("really, she should divorce you," he wrote) he damns the production in wildly extravagant terms. Shaw did not actually see any of Pitoëff's stagings until 1930. But since he knew it to be infallibly true that an actor who also directs is incapable of doing either thing well, he was unshakable in his low opinion of Pitoëff.

But those who accepted the production on its own terms found in it a coherent distillation, if not of *the* essence, at least of *an* essence of the play. John Palmer compared it with the recent London production by Casson and was in no doubt about which was dramatically more effective. Of Casson's he wrote: "One scene followed another, intelligently acted, perfectly clear and logical, but the total effect was that of a series of charades which, put together, gave us the result: *Saint Joan*. The author's ideas were in all essential respects carried out. But never once did we have the feeling, which only the great producers give, that the play was a world in itself."[65] In contrast, Pitoëff's production succeeded because instead of dutifully presenting a play of complex ideas he by-passed the intelligence to appeal to something more compelling, a sympathy with the heroine's stage destiny. In the process he gave the play a unity which arguably is lacking in the text. As theatre it undoubtedly worked. It was successes like this that justified Pitoëff's claim that the director serves the playwright better when he *completes* the text theatrically rather than slavishly respecting its every detail.

Pitoëff produced nine of Shaw's plays but only *Saint Joan* had any great impact, and that perhaps rested partly upon the intrinsic appeal of its subject matter to French audiences. Beyond this there was not much mutual understanding between Shaw and the French. Shaw had considered this very question in an article in *Comoedia* in 1924 where he deplored the vanity and stupidity of the French public. "It is pitiful," he went on, "because an appreciation of my plays has become a proof of civilization, and up to the present France is almost at the bottom of the form. Nothing, however, can be done. I have educated London, I have educated New York, Berlin and Vienna; Moscow and Stockholm are at my feet, but I am too old to educate Paris; it is too far behind and I am too far ahead."[66] As for the French, their indifference may have been caused partly by the woefully inept translations by Augustin Hamon, a sociologist whom Shaw stubbornly insisted on nominating purely because he happened, like himself, to be an International Socialist. (For *Saint Joan* Pitoëff had the text revised by Lenormand to render it playable and resolved to ride out the storm which would inevitably break when the secret came out). But there must also have been deeper, less easily remedied reasons of national character impeding Shaw's acceptance in France. Notwithstanding the occasional success, his reputation there has rarely exceeded that of an interesting Irish Protestant oddity.

In contrast, Pitoëff's legendary production of *Six characters in search of an author* led to the enthusiastic adoption of its author Pirandello and initiated a whole new trend in French theatre. This was in 1923. It was Pitoëff's first major success at the Comédie des Champs-Elysées and it made the reputation of both the writer and the director. Pirandello was one of the most important and original discoveries of the 1920s, though he was not unknown before then. He had, in fact, been writing for twenty five years but it was *Six characters* that projected him on to the world stage. The première in Rome had provoked a noisy scandal in 1921. Reports of Feodor Komissarjevsky's production in London and Pemberton's in New York reached Paris the following year. The French translation, by Benjamin Crémieux, had been offered to Copeau who decided inexplicably that it was insufficiently interesting. Pitoëff snapped it up and immediately wrote to the author to set out his ideas for the production. There followed an argumentative exchange of letters. Pirandello, made apprehensive by Pitoëff's enthusiasm, wanted to tie his hands. Pitoëff, convinced as usual that questions of staging were his domain, would have none of it. Meanwhile he went ahead rehearsing the play as he wanted it to be. The two men eventually met when, at the request of Jacques Hébertot who feared the worst, the author came to Paris, watched a rehearsal incognito, then declared himself completely won over.

In staging the play Pitoëff followed Pirandello's stage directions closely, with one important exception: the Characters' first entrance. The formal innovations, like the undressed stage which shocked some of the public, should therefore be credited to the author. Pitoëff's distinctive contribution was the nightmare quality of his interpretation of the play. Antoine said that watching it was like being in the grip of "a collective cerebral hallucination".[67] There is a vein of grotesque humour in *Six characters* but it was the underlying tragedy that Pitoëff emphasised. Some later critics have accused him of being the source of an enduring tradition in France of productions which, they claim, give undue emphasis to the philosophical in Pirandello's plays at the expense of their theatrical playfulness. But Pitoëff was probably justified when he claimed his interpretation was faithful to the ultimate source of the play's inspiration. Pirandello himself said that he wrote it in order to "exorcise a nightmare", by which he meant the nightmare haunted by the painfully real ghosts of characters clamouring for existence.

For Pitoëff, the play of paradox in *Six characters* was not to be treated as an intellectual or even theatrical game but as one which probes the pathos of mortal man aspiring to some permanence. He explained: "These six characters are the creation of human imagination. . . Obviously, to us *we* are real, whilst they are only fiction. That is our point of view. But for the characters, it's the opposite: it is they who are immutable, eternal in their immaterial reality, whereas men only touch and breath a fleeting, ever-changing reality, an 'illusion of reality in the empty comedy of life'. Which is more real? Which is real? man or his creations? Shakespeare or Hamlet? God created Shakespeare, Shakespeare created Hamlet; but the reality of Shakespeare's existence no longer exists; the reality of Hamlet is *eternal*. That is the conflict."[68]

In his production he used the costumes (flamboyant for the actors, sombre, almost funeral, for the Characters), the make-up (ghostly white for the Characters, rather than the masks called for by the author), the acting styles and the groupings on the stage, to reinforce visually the distance between the actors' world and that of the Characters. His use of the scenery lift for the Characters' first entrance was inspired. It was the feature of the production most fiercely contested by Pirandello until he saw it in operation. The author had wanted them to make their way to the stage through the auditorium, *i.e.* from the world of the spectators. Pitoëff rightly believed that since the Characters had their existence in the theatre – and in a sense belonged there more than the actors who embody them temporarily – it was from the world of the stage that they should materialise. Their slow ascent, huddled together in a pathetic group in the lift cage, bathed in a livid greenish light, created an awesome vision, "equal in force and horror to certain moments of Greek tragedy" said Lenormand.[69]

Pitoëff was not the first to stage Pirandello in France – Dullin beat him to it by four months with *The pleasure of honesty* – nor did he have exclusive rights to his later plays. But he acquired the reputation of being the Sicilian Sorcerer's exponent in France with productions of *Henry IV* (1925), *Each in his own way* (1926) and *Tonight we improvise* (1935). He inaugurated a vogue of Pirandellism that is still not exhausted. The vogue was really more like a craze until well into the 1930s. Pirandello had more productions in Paris than any living author, Giraudoux included. His techniques of theatre-within-theatre, multiple perspectives on a given situation, flashbacks etc. and his themes, especially his exploration of the actor-character, illusion-reality dichotomy, were openly imitated by some lesser writers and produced echoes in several others: Anouilh, obviously, but also Ghelderode and Achard, Lenormand and Salacrou. After the war Pirandello posthumously achieved the rare double of being recognised as a classic at the Comédie-Française while simultaneously retaining his avant-garde appeal. Among later playwrights, Ionesco, Sartre and Genet show most clearly Pirandello's continuing influence.

By introducing Chekhov to France Pitoëff brought another lasting influence to bear on the French stage. Surprisingly, this major European playwright who had been at the centre of the Moscow Art Theatre's repertoire since the turn of the century, was hardly known to French audiences until the 1920s. Steeped as he was in the two cultures, Pitoëff was uniquely qualified to repair the omission. He translated and directed *Uncle Vanya* (1921), *The seagull* (1922) and *The three sisters* (1929). He also adapted *The cherry orchard* but died before it could be produced; it was eventually staged by his son Sacha Pitoëff in 1966. His translations managed to combine making the texts accessible to a French public and preserving their original character. He took great pains to adapt any over-specific or potentially confusing cultural references and to simplify the characters' Russian names. In spite of that he seems to have sacrificed not one bit of their distinctive atmosphere. Marcel Achard wrote of *Uncle Vanya*: "Everything in this production is irresistibly, inexorably Russian. The atmosphere is Russian, the characters Russian, the silence and the snow Russian, the décor Russian too."[70] Never mind if for modern readers his words recall Ionesco's spoof stage directions where a long English silence is broken by an English clock chiming seventeen English strokes: the impression of atmosphere recorded by Achard was overwhelmingly felt by Pitoëff's audiences.

An intimate knowledge of Russian provincial life helped to shape Pitoëff's interpretation of Chekhov. He understood instinctively the author's sympathetic, affectionate mockery of his characters. But more importantly, his own essentialist approach to theatre led him below the uneventful surfaces of the plays to the deeper eddies and whirlpools of unspoken emotions. He was not interested in Chekhov the realist play-wright, as Stanislavsky saw him, nor yet in the recorder of a disappearing social order: all that, he believed to be incidental. Having followed Stanislavsky's experiments at the start of the century, he later came to believe that the Moscow Art Theatre's naturalist productions belonged to a past age obsessed with outdated preoccupations. Seeing *The cherry orchard* at its Mos-cow première in 1904 he had marvelled at what he called an "epitome of realist production", but reviewing the same pro-duction with the same cast when the Moscow Art Theatre played at the Théâtre des Champs-Elysées in 1922 he was "astounded by its futility".[71] The real essence of Chekhov, he now believed, lay in his characters' inner lives. Chekhov, he said, "makes us love a society composed of insignificant beings who represent the great mass of people. But these beings carry inside them the seeds of faith, passion, genius and resignation. It is only from the outside that they are insignificant: within them burns a consuming flame".[72]

The important thing, as always, was to separate essentials from non-essentials, to disengage the timeless truth encapsu-lated in these characters. This explains his bold break with the realist or semi-realistic stage settings which directors generally consider essential for Chekhov, and which the author himself prescribed. For *The three sisters* Pitoëff simply said: "I thought four velvet curtains, two screens, two spotlights and a few chairs were amply sufficient."[73] And for *The seagull* those same basic elements of curtains and chairs were used again: at first, in 1921, to create a drastically simplified but still recognisable version of the set described by the author, and later, in 1939, an even more simplified version verging on abstraction. Pitoëff also did away with all the naturalistic sound effects which filled the air in Stanislavsky's productions. He used some incidental music, but relied principally on the words to create atmosphere. That, in fact, was the secret of Pitoëff's productions: he had the courage to play Chekhov's dialogue like a haunting melody sufficient in itself.

Cocteau, with his usual gift for epitome, characterised Pitoëff the man as "a spirit dressed up in a body". This is exactly how

Pitoëff most wanted his productions to appear. The spirit of the play was what counted above all. The body, of course, could not be discounted because the theatre's means of expression are concrete. Pitoëff never fell into the anti-theatrical excesses committed by the Symbolists in their excursion down the impasse of the disembodied stage. But neither did he allow his stage's specific forms to obscure what was universal and timeless in the plays he produced. The legendary poverty of his company – far worse even than Dullin's – no doubt contributed to the impression of economy his productions gave, but it was certainly not its principal cause. Dullin made a virtue of necessity – according to Barrault, "when his purse was full he would extol scenery; when it was empty there was nothing more true than the purity of a bare stage."[74]. Pitoëff's simplicity was always the result of an aesthetic choice, so that given a healthy balance sheet, he would probably have continued to stage plays in much the same manner.

His failing, which was also paradoxically his great virtue, was the single-mindedness with which he isolated the "spirit of the play": there is, for example, more to Chekhov than just "an atmosphere of words". His idiosyncracy probably explains why Pitoëff, although he preserved a most distinctive presence in his own life-time, never inspired any imitators or disciples. His most enduring contribution was in helping to dismantle France's cultural frontiers. The number of foreign writers he introduced to the French stage was in itself an achievement. More than that, Pitoëff was the first director to try to give audiences an idea of the distinctive national character of foreign playwrights. Antoine and Lugné-Poe had tried to gallicise their imports, in much the same way that productions of Molière in Britain tend to be anglicised. Whereas they had been content to adapt Ibsen etc. to their own stage practices, Pitoëff tried to re-think his staging in the spirit of Ibsen, Chekhov, Shakespeare or whatever. He awoke audiences to the fact that there existed a wider European theatrical movement, and this was a signal contribution to the French theatre where cultural chauvinism was an endemic trait.

Gaston Baty

For Copeau, Jouvet, Dullin and Pitoëff the non-textual elements of theatre were made to conspire towards a realisation of the text. But for a notable dissident, Gaston Baty, the text was no more important than any of the other components of theatre whose rôle was to conspire towards the realisation of Drama. In his pursuit of what he termed "théâtre intégral" he was the only member of the Cartel to challenge the assumption that the director's rôle is to serve the playwright. As early as 1920 he was asking: "By what strange abuse do people say that a writer is the 'author' of a play when all he has done is to supply the outline of what other people implement?"[75] Actually this worried the critics more than the playwrights, for whilst a small vociferous group of critics branded him the enemy of the text (and therefore of true theatre) writers with whom he worked, such as Lenormand and Bernard, all declared themselves fully satisfied with his productions.[76] To the public he became known as "the magician of *mise en scène*".

Unlike Dullin and Jouvet, he did not experience Copeau's influence. His approach to theatre was formed instead in Germany where the idea of the all-powerful *regisseur* took root much earlier than in France. As a student in Munich in 1907 he followed the work of Fritz Erler who was experimenting at the Künstler Theater with a simplified stage similar to Copeau's later *tréteau nu*. But a more decisive influence on Baty was Max Reinhardt whose productions at the Deutsches Theater he studied between 1908 and 1911. Reinhardt's work is not easily classified because he was an enormously eclectic director, receptive to a vast range of styles. His productions varied in scale from the gigantically spectacular to quite intimate chamber drama. Basically, though, they all sprang from a Craig-like concept of theatre, treating the text not as the principal object but just one component of a dramaturgy created by a *regisseur* orchestrating voice, movement, music and setting. The features of Reinhardt's productions that most impressed Baty were his dextrous use of stage machinery (which Copeau deplored) to speed up scene changes, and his brilliantly staged crowd scenes. Significantly, when Baty first went to work in the theatre in 1919 it was not to Copeau that he turned but to Firmin Gémier, a director noted for his large-scale productions who engaged Baty to work with him on his series of spectacles for mass audiences at the Cirque d'Hiver.

After a brief apprenticeship with Gémier in the immediate post-war, Baty formed a small company calling itself "Les Compagnons de la Chimère" in 1921. At first it played where it could: at the Comédie des Champs-Elysées, thanks to Hébertot's support, at the Mathurins, and on tour in Holland and Belgium. The need for a permanent base was pressing and in 1923, under-capitalised but with a utopian vision for the future, he bought a small vacant plot and built his first theatre. The legendary Baraque de la Chimère was a picturesque wooden building with a façade painted like a fairground booth – an improbable sight on the Boulevard Saint-Germain. Constructed in eight weeks it was demolished ten months later when debt forced its sale. Gémier, now in charge of the Odéon, offered Baty its stage but a more attractive offer soon came from Hébertot to take over the newly-converted Studio des Champs-Elysées. With Jouvet and Pitoëff sharing the Comédie on the floor below, Baty found himself in the most exciting theatrical complex of the period.

The tiny Studio provided an ideal laboratory for Baty's experiments. In four years he staged some thirteen productions, convincingly establishing his claim to be one of France's leading experimental producers. But by 1928, the year after the Cartel's formation, he was again looking for a theatre of his own. Baron Rothschild's Théâtre Pigalle, where he worked in 1929, boasted the up-to-the-minute technical facilities that appealed to Baty, but its large, somewhat featureless stage and modern character did not suit him. In 1930 he acquired the Théâtre Montparnasse which was to be his home until 1947. It was a medium-sized theatre, much in need of renovation but redolent of the theatrical past. With the very latest technical equipment judiciously installed without destroying the building's traditional character, it was an ideal stage for Baty's escapist drama.

Baty shared with the rest of the Cartel the same passionate dedication to theatre as the highest art form and the same

vocation of helping to effect a theatrical renewal, but he came
to the theatre by a different route. With Baty, theory preceded
practice. Alone among the four he was not an actor but a
scholar, art historian and theorist. He approached theatre firstly
in the light of his global vision of man's place in the universe,
and secondly in the light of his views on the origins and purpose
of drama. It was the conclusions he reached in these spheres
that provided the inspiration and philosophical justification for
all his theatrical experiments.

The conjunction of scholarship and faith was evident from
his first major study, *Le Masque et l'encensoir* (1921), a curious
work which merits attention both as theatre history and as a
call to arms. It is in the Middle Ages, when the liturgical drama
and mysteries achieve a high point of cohesion and balance
unknown since antiquity, that Baty looks for solutions to the
problems of modern theatre. The Middle Ages for Baty represent an age not only of faith but of cosmic order. Order, firstly,
in the doctrine of Thomas Aquinas whose thought remained
the primary influence on Baty from the days of his Dominican
upbringing. Instead of isolating humankind from the rest of
creation, Saint Thomas saw man and the animals and the inanimate world as each having their allotted place in the divine
scheme, each related to the other and all related to God. Baty
also sees the great gothic cathedrals and the vast cycles of
mystery plays as the architectural and dramatic faces of the
same integrated vision where science and faith, the spirit and
the clay, the word and the flesh, are held in balance, the one
complementing the other. In the Mystery play the stage, thanks
to the convention of the *décor simultané* or multiple staging,
represented all creation: heaven and earth and hell were constantly and simultaneously present before the eyes of the participants. And what was *seen*, the objects and actions on stage,
were at least as important as the words spoken: matter and
thought were fused in symbolic representation.

The subsequent history of theatre then presents itself as a
double process of decline: a shift from dramatic spectacle to
dramatic literature, bringing with it an ever-increasing domination by the spoken word, and the no less catastrophic disintegration of a once unified public, participating in a dramatic

celebration of shared beliefs, into the fragmented secular theatre-going public of today.

The rot sets in with the Reformation and the schism it operates between man and and the rest of creation. Martin Luther, detaching man from the Communion of Saints, projects him alone, "severed from the world of things, divorced from his fellow sufferers, his soul despising everything that lies beyond itself".[77] Then comes the Renaissance, flooding France with a cerebral art, impoverished, from Baty's point of view, because it celebrates form without content, matter without spirituality. Already the accent is on man. And Humanism, the third devastating current, brings a new breed of writers who "declare that only man interests them, not the universe, not the beauty of things and beings in whose midst he lives, but man alone".[78] The emphasis is now on the individual and the disintegration is nearly complete, but not quite: "The poison is not yet exhausted; after reducing the universe to this dust, it will now decompose each particle of the dust. The individual, even isolated from the world, is still living: he must be dissected. Here is his soul; there is his mind; and yonder is his body."[79] While the theologians take control of man's soul, the philosophers investigate his mind, and both hold his body in anathema. Cornelius Jansen shows men adrift like isolated souls marked for grace or salvation, in a world where flesh and matter are nothing but temptations to sin. Meanwhile Descartes confines the universe to the limits of man's thought: "He recognises only one truth: human reason. He rejects matter, things, the animals, the body. A healthy mind will only interest itself in material things to the extent that they permit scientific hypotheses to be verified."[80] For the theatre the implications of these ways of thinking are catastrophic. They lead to the triumph of classical tragedy which by a sweeping process of association Baty sees as Jansenist ("the rules are narrow, strict, absolute, and outside of them there is no salvation") and Cartesian ("drama is reduced to characters and characters are reduced to their thoughts"). Theatre had become a thinking, not feeling, art: in other words a literary genre, which *grosso modo* it was to remain across a wasteland of three centuries.

The diseases affecting modern theatre are thus identified: a narrow, egoistical accent on man isolated from the mysteries of creation; a substitution of literary values in place of integrated drama and spectacle; and its concomitant enslavement to the spoken word. Against this Jansenist-Cartesian tradition Baty said: "I try to serve theatre according to Saint Thomas."[81] His Thomist theatre, he explained, would resemble the "dream of an expressive universe", reaching beyond man to embrace all that exists, the animate and inanimate world of animals and plants and things, of ships and forests and mountains which also have a soul, and the great forces of the natural world, the sea, the wind, the sun, and beyond these mysteries to the still deeper mysteries of invisible presences, of death and infinity.[82]

"It's not a matter of talking about all these things but of making them *felt*."[83] Clearly, words alone would have a very limited usefulness in such a concept of theatre. Baty had already aroused the critics' hostility with an intemperate attack on what he called "the hypertrophy of the verbal element" in an article ironically entitled "Sire le Mot" (1920). The same critics were quick to see his productions confirm their suspicion that he was treating texts as mere pretexts for his own *mises en scène*. This was inevitable, since Baty was led to explore the non-verbal media of colour and light, music and scenery, as means of communicating all that words are incapable of expressing. Yet Baty himself always claimed to be a texto-centric director in the sense that the text was always his starting point and his aim was to realise in all its plenitude, using means specific to the stage, the world in embryo contained in the play. This much was true, though Baty's relationship with the text was clearly not that of Copeau or Jouvet nor even of Pitoëff. Like the latter he held *mise en scène* to be a creative not interpretative art. But whereas Pitoëff aimed to express the ultimate essence of the play, Baty's object was to use the play as a springboard to the world which lay beyond the play. He came to believe that beyond or above the play composed by the writer there was another drama which had been revealed to the author but of which the text was an incomplete shadow. At this point the director must take over from the playwright, the stage must take over from literature, to realise the "oeuvre rêvée", that is, not the literal play but the ideal play.

All these ideas were contained in a series of articles published between 1917 and 1921, and his subsequent writings were little more than reformulations of the same themes. Baty therefore came to the theatre already armed with a fully distilled theatrical doctrine and his subsequent life's work must be seen as a programme pursued with rare single-mindedness to realise his vision of an integrated theatre. His choice of plays bears this out. He naturally gravitated towards authors who gave maximum scope for the director to deploy the resources of the stage. In the 1920s this meant authors like Henri-René Lenormand and Simon Gantillon with their plays of the subconscious, and the "theatre of the unexpressed" represented by Jean-Jacques Bernard and Jean-Victor Pellerin. These writers provided many of Baty's most undisputed successes.

At first sight the fiercely anti-religious Lenormand would seem an improbable partner to Baty. But Lenormand offered something new in French theatre: in reaction to what he called the "Cartesian hero" with his rational motivation, Lenormand used the stage to show how human behaviour is controlled by subconscious impulses and external forces exerted by the material world such as climate. Add to that an original dramatic technique (original, at least, in French theatre) which discards linear action for a series of dramatic tableaux, and Baty's interest in Lenormand becomes self-evident. His first independent production was in fact Lenormand's *Le Simoun* (Comédie Montaigne, 1920). An unqualified artistic and box-office success, it ran to over a hundred performances and was revived many times in later years. *Le Simoun*, a "climacteric tragedy" set in the Sahara, depicts the successive stages of a man's incestuous love for his daughter fanned and exacerbated by the torrid climate. An outstanding feature of the production was its use of light and sound to make the oppressive heat and dusty simoom active elements in the drama.

Many of the features that attracted Baty to Lenormand were also present in the plays of Gantillon whose *Maya* (1924) proved to be one of the most enduring success of Baty's repertoire. *Maya*, whose title refers to the Hindu goddess of Illusion, is a good example of the type of escapist drama which post-war audiences sought and which Baty represented so well. The play has no plot nor even a dramatic progression, merely a sequence of isolated scenes linked by the presence of the central character. The heroine, Bella, is a prostitute and the setting is her room in a brothel where she receives clients. Baty created a set depicting the brothel with some degree of realism, but then used the lighting to dissolve it so that the real existed within a climate of unreality. In this way he tried to create a scenic poetry to express the point of the play, which is to evoke the eternal dreams that lie behind the banal transactions of life. Gantillon described Bella as "the plastic matter of man's desire: the caterpillar whose future wings are coloured by every man with the hue of his desire". By this he meant not simply men's sexual desire but the unconscious illusions they pursue in her. The play passed almost unnoticed in 1924 but its revival three years later was acclaimed a major theatrical event both for the originality of the writing and the poetry of its staging. It helped to win over some critics who had previously sounded warnings against the exhibitionist tendencies in Baty's directing.

Baty's was also the natural stage for the school of "silence", or more correctly "unexpressed", of which Jean-Jacques Bernard was considered the spokesman. In truth Bernard's style of writing sprang from an intuitive tendency rather than the application of any precise theory. His identification with the theory of silence came about almost by accident when he wrote a programme note for the production of *Martine* (1922). "The theatre," he wrote, "is pre-eminently the art of the unexpressed. It is not in what is said but in the impact of what is said that the deepest feelings are contained. Below the spoken dialogue is a hidden dialogue which must be communicated."[84] This unremarkable observation had obvious precursors in Maeterlinck, Strindberg, Ibsen, Chekhov and even in Marivaux's unspoken dialogue; but so tenacious were the rhetorical traditions of French theatre that it was still possible for a writer making such a statement to be seen as breaking new ground.

Bernard's theatre is not unlike Maeterlinck's in content, consisting in the evocation of "states of soul", but in a style closer to expressionism than symbolism. His best play, *Martine*, like Gantillon's *Maya*, treats a somewhat unremarkable, even banal subject of the kind favoured by nineteenth-century realist novelists – in this case the stirrings of love that a peasant girl about to be married to a farmer feels for the nephew of a wealthy neighbour, and her eventual resignation to what she accepts must be her lot. In fact *Martine* could well be the subject of a novel, but Bernard saw it as an eminently dramatic subject in that Martine's feelings are of such a nature that to articulate them explicitly would be to destroy them. They can only be hinted at, something which Bernard believed the theatre but not the novel can do: "the novel analyses, theatre synthesises, the novel explicates, theatre suggests."[85] Like Baty, Bernard was vehemently opposed to literature in the theatre and interested in utilising the scenic possibilities of the modern stage to the full.

A play which depends on silences rather than words, moods rather than psychology, impressions rather than action, presents obvious dramatic pitfalls. Bernard saw this as a daunting challenge but Baty saw it rather as a perfect test-case for his production methods. Bernard has recorded how, on reading the play, Baty exclaimed "At last! You have left me something to say."[86] All the director's skills were needed to make the audience aware of the unspoken feelings which pass through Martine. The set which he designed included a realistic interior which took its mood from subtle lighting changes, and an exterior featuring an apple tree seen at first in full bloom and later, as Martine's hopeless dreams are fading, without blossom. What Baty was aiming at was a theatrical equivalent of the "pathetic fallacy" where the inanimate world takes on a human state of soul. It was the technique in which he excelled, and with many plays it would be pleonastic but in *Martine* it was justified because of the unconscious and unstated quality of the heroine's feelings. "Such are the vagaries of the stage" wrote one critic; "one sets out to mix lights with music and scenery with a text; and suddenly the Unconscious materialises."[87] Here at least was one answer to the common charge that liberal use of lighting effects, inventive scenery and noises-off must necessarily result only in empty spectacle.

Baty's repertoire in the 1920s was dominated by plays such as these: good if not outstanding modern works reflecting the post-war tide of disillusionment with reality that also gave rise to surrealism. Where the writing was not of the highest order, there was always Baty's unrivalled genius as a purveyor of images to compensate.

In the 1930s, the high point of his career, Baty turned progressively from contemporary escapist writing to another form of escape, into the past, with productions of Shakespeare, Molière, Racine and Marivaux. These were bound to arouse the critics' suspicions: Baty's views on the spoken word in theatre seemed to be incompatible with the respect due to the classics. The unorthodox interpretations he gave only exacerbated the controversy which, far from avoiding, he seemed almost wilfully to be seeking. Possibly he was motivated partly out of defiance and a desire to show the director's power to influence a play, though he was always able to advance cogent justifications, supported by ample scholarship, for his choices. When staging *Hamlet* he spurned the versions normally performed in favour of the early version of 1602 which, he argued, was more concise, more theatrical, less "literary" than the later versions. He also justified the striking visual adornments of his production by demonstrating that the Elizabethan staging conventions were far richer and more spectacular than is often supposed. With *Macbeth* (1942), which he saw as less a tragedy of ambition than about the corrupting influence of a wife's love, he went further and played his own original adaptation in twenty tableaux. Perhaps his best attempt at a classic was his production of Musset's *Les Caprices de Marianne* (1935), one of the most seductively atmospheric of his career. Purists objected to the way he changed the setting from the sixteenth to the nineteenth century, but as a production this was poetic enchantment at its best.

Baty's starting point for *Le Malade imaginaire* (1929) was far more questionable. He invited the audience to lift the comic mask worn by Molière and to consider, not the farcical satire written by Molière but the real-life drama lived by Molière in 1673, the drama of a man beset by difficulties and near to death. Imagine, he said, that Argan is not a hypochondriac but genuinely ill. Then the whole play and all its characters must be seen in a totally new light: the comedy becomes an appalling, grotesque pantomime of callousness and indifference towards a dying man. Argan's consultation with his quack doctor Purgon was played in a funereal atmosphere, with the characters all in black and a figure of death hovering behind the patient's chair. Baty was not so naive as to underestimate the fury this interpretation would provoke. "At one time," he said, "I was afraid I would be sentenced to copying out 'I must show more respect for Molière' a hundred times."[88]

Whether Baty was a good producer of the classics is still a matter of opinion. In the context of his time he was the most daring of French directors. Unlike Copeau, who equated "originality" with exhibitionism, he liked to throw new light on the classics. His productions certainly did that in an original and occasionally stimulating way and demonstrated once again, as they were probably intended to, the creative power of the director. By deliberately challenging the critics' hide-bound and proprietorial attitude to the classics he helped to open the way for more adventurous interpretations. He was tactful enough to try to appease the critics on occasions. In a speech given before the opening of *Le Malade imaginaire* he explained that he was not proposing an approach that should be followed by others, still less that he was aiming to show the Comédie-Française how to play Molière. He said: "The best way is most certainly to respect the traditions. The King's players have handed down to the leading actors of the Republic the secret of performing their greatest playwrights."[89] This placatory note seems more prudent than convincing. Baty was far more persuasive when on another occasion he wrote about the Comédie-Française's "lifeless performances" and "lazy routine" masquerading as tradition.[90] It was the experimental producers, he asserted, who were unwrapping the mummified masterpieces and restoring them to life.

While Copeau, Jouvet and Dullin sought to purify the classics by returning to their theatrical sources, Baty was intent on exploring the by-ways, trying to bring out neglected facets of the familiar works. He called his production of *Le Malade imaginaire* a "variation in a minor key". His justification for doing this was that traditional productions, while safeguarding the essentials, must do so at the expense of the play's secondary features. Surely, he argued, it is permisssible for a director to

experiment by temporarily turning the spotlight on these neglected aspects. In this way Baty gave a useful reminder that the
theatre's vitality depends on it accommodating a wide range of
approaches. All the same, his experiments with the classics were
bound to remain just that: peripheral experiments rather than
finished achievements. Even when they were not exactly
wrong-headed they could never revolutionise the way a generation understood a great work of the past as did Jouvet's productions of *L'Ecole des femmes* and *Don Juan*.

Baty's finest productions, the culmination of his search for
"théâtre intégral", were his adaptations of novels like *Crime and
punishment* (1933), *Madame Bovary* (1936) and *Manon Lescaut*
(1938). Here he was able to mould scripts to his vision of man,
society and nature, while tailoring them perfectly to his own
staging methods. His adaptations, which he spent many years
perfecting, translated the narrative flow of the novels into a
succession of unforgetable tableaux – Raskolnikov's room, the
staircase where he murders the old woman, the "Comices
Agricoles" in *Madame Bovary*, the box at the Rouen Opera with
the proscenium arch modelled in perspective, and so on. These
productions were miracles of staging. *Crime and punishment* was
presented in some 60 scenes involving 13 different settings. To
achieve the necessary continuity he divided the stage into com-
partments, illuminating the different scenes in turn. For
Madame Bovary entire settings were constructed on mobile platforms so that as one set was trucked off to the wings, another
took its place. Baty was less interested in the characters and the
plots than the powerful moral themes they embody. Both plays
presented themselves to him as exemplary dramas of sin and
redemption – rather more plausibly in the case of Raskolnikov
than Emma Bovary! He was criticised by some for his interpretation of the stories, sometimes with good reason: Emma's
death-bed repentance was certainly never part of Flaubert's
scheme. However, such criticism, which is based on literary
criteria, seems to miss the essential point that theatrically these
were unblemished productions, the work of a great creative
director at the height of his powers, and executed with unrivalled pictorial and technical genius.

In his last years, after the Second World War, Baty grew

increasingly pessimistic about the state of theatre and withdrew into the world of puppets. On his own terms he had failed completely to bring into being the vision announced in *Le Masque et l'encensoir*. He had planned a theatrical renaissance to emulate the earlier golden ages of drama – the drama of ancient Greece, of the Middle Ages and the Elizabethan period – with the stage once again functioning as the focal point of the collective life and beliefs of the community. But this depended on a complete cultural transformation, a re-emergence of the overall order which had welded earlier audiences together, and no amount of scenic reform could accomplish that. By 1945 even the relatively restricted but cultivated audiences that had gathered around the Cartel were dispersed, the unified public remained as much an elusive and nostalgic ideal as ever, and Baty was unable to see the possibility of a new, wider public re-grouping around a more socially-orientated theatre – in which direction, as it happened, the best hopes for a popular theatre now lay.

The sense of personal failure is keenly expressed in *Rideau baissé*, a collection of his writings from 1921 to 1948 published as a farewell to the stage in 1949. In the preface he decries "the general cultural decline, the disintegration of the public, the polluting of something which ought to be held sacred by ideology and propaganda", all of which make it impossible to go on.[91] The postscript, *Finale en mineur*, is equally pessimistic about the theatrical public: "a gathering of individuals, separated one from another as they are by their culture, their convictions, their habits, not to mention their passions and their hates, this is not an audience: it's a crowd."[92] And so, having failed to reach his goal by the highway, he would now take to the side roads: "I have decided to ask from puppets what I can no longer hope to obtain from men." Although he bravely presented this as simply the continuation by other means of the same quest, the retreat into puppetry was really an admission of defeat for a director whose overall object had been to restore the balance between Man, Mind and Matter in an integrated drama.

When Baty, the last surviving member of the Cartel, died in 1952 the great years of the Cartel theatres were already a fading memory. The most innovative stages in France were now the

T.N.P. in Paris and Avignon, where Vilar was producing classics for the people, Barrault's Marigny theatre, and the tiny, impoverished studios of the Latin Quarter where the new absurdist drama, aided by young directors like Serreau, Mauclair and Bataille, was struggling to be born. Baty's escapist world seems very remote from all this, as indeed it was. Yet in certain respects his career makes a bridge between the most representative forms of pre-war theatre and the post-war avant-garde. His theatre was not organically different from that of Jouvet, Dullin or Pitoëff, but it contained significant differences of emphasis. Placing the director, not the author, at the head of the theatrical hierarchy, and breaking free from a quasi-obsessive preoccupation with textual fidelity, he showed that *mise en scène* could attain full creative status and still produce good theatre. And by leading the assault on the "hypertrophy of the spoken word" he opened the way for a more spectacular, less literary, and arguably less elitist theatre. In both these respects it was Baty, not the other members of the Cartel, who pointed to the future. This is not to say that what happened subsequently was a direct result of Baty's initiatives. In fact, the more revolutionary ideas of his contemporaries Artaud and Brecht proved to have a far greater impact on the post-war French theatre.

Total theatre – ritual theatre
3   – festive theatre

After the Cartel

The Cartel directors were progressive rather than radically
innovative; not original theorists but pragmatic men. Because
of this, rather than in spite of it, the years between the wars
were the first great age of director's theatre. In France this
mode of theatre had two outstanding strengths: first, it consisted of permanent companies working under a single director.
In spite of material conditions which were often far from ideal,
this system allowed them to achieve a consistency of standards
and style unmatched by any other mode of production, however
lavishly endowed. The benefits in terms of a sustained artistic
identity and regular following among the public were very
great. Secondly, these directors were the natural beneficiaries
of the spectacular revival of French dramatic writing that began
in the 1920s. In this respect they were reaping a harvest sown
by their predecessors from Antoine onwards. It must be obvious
that if playwrights are to be encouraged to write for the stage,
they have not only to see it as a worthwhile artistic medium
but also to feel they have a valuable rôle to play in theatre. Far
from suggesting that playwrights were superfluous, the
directors I have discussed aimed to provide such conditions.
That writers like Lenormand and Bernard, Romains and
Giraudoux, Salacrou, Cocteau and Anouilh, and many more,
found a natural home on the stage, often working in partnership
with a director, was one fruitful consequence of the way the
director's rôle evolved in France.

This is an appropriate moment to recall the enormous influence exerted by Copeau. The first directors, as I have suggested,
emerged to meet a perceived need for a specialist to control

the increasingly complex components of theatre. This in turn led to a re-appraisal of the function and value of each of those components. The conclusion reached, after a couple of false starts, was that the best way forward lay not in any one of the theatre's component arts (poetry, architecture, painting, dance) nor in any aesthetic system (realism, symbolism, expressionism or whatever), but in a sensible, harmonious balance of its con-stituent parts around the nucleus of a text. It was Copeau who first formulated and implemented this ideal. Dramatic art originates with the playwright; the director, absolute master of the stage, bodies forth the author's voice on the stage; only dramatic action has the right to determine stage architecture; plasticity rather than scenic illustration is sought; the accent is on the living presence of the actor, an intelligent fusion of diction and bodily expression. These were the priorities laid down by Copeau which bound the complex of theatrical endeavour in France between the wars. The emphasis varied here and there, but beneath it all lay this striving towards balance. Thus far, harmony between the component arts of theatre and harmony between stagecraft and dramatic writing are the dominant features of the director's theatre.

The Cartel traditions did not disappear with the death of its members but survived in varying degress in those who had worked with them. The most eminent of these included: Pitoëff's son Sacha; Copeau's nephew Michel Saint-Denis who had a distinguished career at the London Theatre Studio and Old Vic before returning to France as director of the Centre Dramatique de l'Est; and André Barsacq, Anouilh's director, working at the Atelier where he had earlier been Dullin's assist-ant. There were also Marcel Herrand and Jean Marchat, the leaders of the pre-war Rideau de Paris, who had taken over the Mathurins theatre on Pitoëff's death and between 1939 and 1952 continued his policy of presenting sensitive productions of foreign plays. Two other directors, Jean-Louis Barrault and Roger Blin, followed many of the Cartel's traditions, though both of these were also greatly influenced by Artaud.

The post-war theatre thus saw no abrupt departure from the practices of the Cartel directors, but was progressively modified and enriched by ideas coming from other sources. One of the most influential of these was Brecht. The Cartel directors embodied a progressive artistic movement which was nevertheless conservative in its relations to society. Although they were keenly aware of the need to broaden their social base they saw this in terms of cultural rather than political action. One subsequent tendency, which I shall discuss in Part 4, has been to re-think the relationship between theatre and society, bringing theatre closer to the sphere of political thought and action.

A contrary tendency which has gained ground since the 1940s is the idea of "total" theatre. This is a loose expression often invoked to enhance the credentials of any production relying heavily on a battery of sound and light to assault the senses. Properly used, in relation to directors as varied as Artaud, Barrault, Brook and Lavelli, it denotes an attitude to life expressed through theatre – or, more precisely, a form of theatre, usually of a metaphysical character, specifically dedicated to the expression of an attitude to life, as opposed to one where an attitude to life is implicit and emerges as a by-product. Anti-naturalist in character, it is another form of idealist theatre aiming at expressing the hidden world not contained in rational, verbal and material modes of apprehending reality. Hence Brook calls this tendency "Holy Theatre" and also "The Theatre of the Invisible-made-Visible". But contrary to the Symbolist theatre which aspired to a synthesis of poetry, painting and music, it seeks its means of expression in what is specific to the stage. It involves a director organising a perfectly controlled theatrical environment, bringing into play all the multiple resources of the actor and the stage and even of cinema. Although it may well be centred on a written text, it does not take the text as its object, since this form of theatre does not see itself as a vehicle of communication for playwrights. Because it finds its means of expression in the concrete and symbolic language of the stage, it is essentially the creation of directors. As such it corresponds more to Craig's New Theatre than to Copeau's. One can see it is clearly anticipated by Baty's "théâtre intégral". However, the main inspiration behind the vogue of total theatre in the 1960s was the posthumous legacy of Artaud.

Artaud

Artaud was a poet, playwright, actor, director, theorist and seer. He was an actor of alarming intensity, as one can see from his performance as Marat in Abel Gance's film *Napoléon*. As a director he founded two separate and distinct theatres, the Théâtre Alfred Jarry (1926-9) and the Théâtre de la Cruauté (1935). The latter, though pitifully short-lived, was more representative of Artaud and had a more profound long-term influence than the former. As a theorist he unleashed one of the most widely read works on theatre written this century, *Le Théâtre et son double* (1938), a thundering denunciation of all forms of theatre as currently practised in the Western world, and beyond that of the entire occidental civilisation it betrays.

Artaud arrived at this position after twenty years of the most varied artistic activity which started with his absorbing, then rejecting, the Vieux-Colombier tradition. His involvement in theatre began conventionally enough acting for Lugné-Poe, whom he soon abandoned, however, to work with Dullin at the Atelier (1921-3). Later he joined Pitoëff's company, taking small parts in several productions, where he proved unreliable, and he collaborated with Jouvet on a project for Strindberg's *Ghost sonata* which never materialised. What Artaud retained from these brief and often strained contacts is hard to say. For a while, at least, he found a source of moral and artistic inspiration in Dullin, of whom he wrote in 1921: "[his work] is based on a striving towards moral *purity*. Listening to Dullin's teaching one has the feeling of rediscovering ancient secrets and a whole forgotten mystique of staging. . . The Japanese are our direct masters and inspiration, and Edgar Poe too. It's *admirable*."[1] From Dullin and Etienne Decroux he gained valuable experience of physical expression based on oriental theatre and mime. But Artaud loathed the discipline of rehearsals, and what he regarded as the timid, restrained approach of these directors. One especially telling image, recorded by Barrault, is of Artaud playing Charlemagne in a rehearsal of *Huon de Bordeaux*, crawling towards the throne on all fours, and dismissing Dullin's suggestion that he try a slightly less stylised approach with a contemptuous "Oh if it's realism you want, well then!"[2] In his feverish quest for something more absolute Artaud became impatient with Dullin and Pitoëff. This is not to say his theories were a reaction specifically against them: in reality his reforming ambitions were more comprehensive in scope and came from more remote, speculative horizons.

Artaud's true roots lie less in the independent art theatres than in the avant-garde counter-culture that emerged in the aftermath of the Great War. The vein of anarchy and iconoclastic experiment stretching from Jarry, through Apollinaire and cubism, to dada and surrealism, was better able to accommodate Artaud's erratic brand of inspiration. This was essentially an extra-theatrical (and extra-literary) movement being pursued on a variety of fronts – notably poetry, painting and cinema – by artists for whom theatre was just one incidental form of action. There were those, like Breton, who hoped to annexe theatre to their cause, but this proved to be a vain hope. Dada-surrealism produced a small number of significant works such as Vitrac's good though sometimes overrated *Victor ou les enfants au pouvoir* and Tristan Tzara's equally original but virtually unknown *Mouchoir de nuages*.[3] Some did filter through to the "mainstream" independent theatres, thanks especially to Cocteau. But overall, until its belated re-appearance with Ionesco in the 1950s, surrealism's impact on the theatre remained negligible compared with its influence on other art forms.

One reason for this was that there was no director or company devoted to surrealism in the way that Fort and Lugné-Poe had provided a stage for Symbolism. It was to remedy the omission that in 1926 Artaud, Robert Aron and Roger Vitrac founded the Théâtre Alfred Jarry, potentially one of the most revolutionary projects of the modern theatre. By now Artaud had lost faith in his former Cartel employers, dismissing them as unsound, unworthy and irrelevant.[4] In the theatre's first manifesto he declared that nowhere in France was there a single example of "an absolutely pure theatre". The term pure theatre as Artaud uses it does not mean simply a theatre of theatricality but one involving the whole being and pursued unconditionally to its utmost consequences. For Artaud, it was no longer a question of renovating theatre but of renovating life by means of a theatre dedicated to real life – that is, to the subconscious, to chance and the irrational, concretely manifested on the stage. This brand of theatre, at least, would not leave the spectator intact. At the Théâtre Alfred Jarry the spectator had to be made aware that he was submitting to "a veritable operation in which not only his mind but his senses and flesh are involved. . . He must know we are capable of making him cry out."[5]

A vivid impression of what this might entail can be had from Artaud's short play *Jet de sang* which was intended for performancee in the theatre's programme for 1926-7. This cataclysmic and virtually unperformable work is remarkable not only for the violence of the satire directed against the mainstays of Western civilisation – love, family, religion – but also for its highly concrete images. Man's revolt against God is represented by a whore biting into her arm, causing a huge spurt of blood to submerge the stage. The script also calls for a collision of stars followed by human limbs of living flesh, doorways, colonnades and temples falling slowly to the stage to represent the collapse of civilisation.[6]

The intentions were in an authentic surrealist mould, but unfortunately, when the Théâtre Alfred Jarry opened, Artaud and Vitrac had been expelled from the official surrealist group, whose espousal of left-wing politics they disapproved of. The surrealist theatre therefore had to make its way without the support of the movement, and indeed had to contend with disruptive opposition from Breton and his followers. Without their support, and too marginal to attract the minimum number of subscriptions a theatrical enterprise needs to function regularly, it was unlikely to survive for long.

Four separate programmes were presented between 1927 and 1929 – six plays in all, and a total of just eight performances. Some of the presentations were simply dada-like acts of provocation. Hence, for example, the third act of *Partage de midi* (Comédie des Champs-Elysées, January 1928) which was played without Claudel's knowledge or permission and followed by a speech in which Artaud denounced the author as an infamous traitor. There was an equally scandalous performance of Strindberg's *A dream play* (Théâtre de l'Avenue, 2 and 9 June 1928), which Artaud genuinely admired, where he contrived to outrage both his guest of honour the Swedish ambassador, by presenting Strindberg as a victim of Swedish society, and the surrealist cabbale by having Breton arrested for causing a disturbance.

The Théâtre Alfred Jarry's most significant production was of Vitrac's *Victor ou les enfants au pouvoir* (Comédie des Champs-Elysées, December 1928–January 1929). This play is a satire on the bourgeois values of marriage, family, respectability and honour – familiar targets but attacked here with genuinely comic and sometimes unnerving panache. It involves a fully-grown nine-year old child prodigy whose precocious intellect views the deceptions of his elders with devastating lucidity. Quite unlike Artaud's *Jet de sang*, which is a raw transcription of a convulsively surreal vision, *Victor* introduces surreality into a recognisable middle-class milieu. In his production Artaud used a basically realistic interior set with unreal touches like a gigantic birthday cake, empty picture frames suspended downstage in mockery of the naturalist theatre's "fourth wall", and violent, unnaturalistic lighting. He urged the cast to play their parts to excess and stop at nothing: Victor with diabolic intensity, his parents as caricatural puppets, and Ida Mortemart, the enigmatic visitor, as the very incarnation of ideal beauty. The first performance was received with unease rather than tumult. The second and third, however, were given in uproar. Loyal surrealists, alerted to the fact that the play contained a beautiful lady who farted uncontrollably, came armed with stink-bombs, and the performances had to be suspended to allow the theatre to be ventilated. With these performances, uncannily reminiscent of Fort's last fling with *Cantique des cantiques*, the Théâtre Alfred Jarry came to an odoriferous end.

Artaud then devoted himself to his theories. As his ideas developed he drew away from surrealism, particularly with respect to the rôle of chance and improvisation in artistic creation. These were the crucial conductors of surrealist inspiration but Artaud favoured a more controlled approach. According to Robert Aron, even in his earliest productions he directed the actors very closely, prescribing every movement and inflexion for them to imitate.[7] And later, in 1935, he declined an offer by Barrault to work as his assistant on the grounds that "I DO NOT WANT a production of mine to contain a single movement of an eyelid that does not come from me".[8] His method may have been open to improvisation in the early stages but as the production crystallised everything was passed through a quasi-musical system of notation to achieve the necessary precision.

Where Artaud did remain faithful to the surrealist adventure was in his view of art (theatre) as an instrument for transforming life. The fundamental desire of the surrealists was not to change art but to change the world. For the official group this led to political action. For Artaud it implied provoking a new understanding of the hidden forces that control life. That was precisely what the Théâtre Alfred Jarry was intended to achieve. Later Artaud wrote: "I am not one of those who think civilisation must change in order that theatre may change; I believe that theatre used in a superior and infinitely difficult way has the power to influence the appearance and nature of things."[9] This was the most fundamental difference he had with those directors, the vast majority, who believed in theatre as an end in itself. Baty's reassuring promise, in his first theatre's manifesto, that "La Chimère does not make use of art, it serves it" was met by Artaud's counter-promise that "the Théâtre Alfred Jarry has been created to make use of theatre, not to serve it".[10]

"To make use of theatre": to what end? Artaud's main ideas were developed in a series of highly coloured articles, lectures and manifestos collected together in *Le Théâtre et son double* (1938). These writings are sometimes said to be obscure, though it is hard to see why. There is, admittedly, some blurring of detail at the edges, but the main lines are hammered out with such insistence that they are impossible to misunderstand. The cumulative impact of Artaud's style – emphatic, declamatory, constantly re-iterating key ideas – is rather like being hit with a sledge-hammer, highly effective, and similar to the sort of impact the theatre itself should achieve.

Little time is wasted on prosecuting the existing forms of theatre and art, which he assumes are too rotten to be saved. The cause of this he diagnoses as a fundamental separation of culture from life, itself a consequence of the separation of daily existence from the roots of life. The fault lies with Western man for having cut himself off from the deep forces of life and the primal impulses within man himself. Like Baty, Artaud sees this separation as a product of the humanist traditions originating with the Renaissance. Modern civilisation has condemned men to a solipsistic existence where, instead of being propelled by their actions, they are merely observers of their own thoughts and actions. "A civilised, cultivated man is one who is informed about systems of thought, who thinks in systems and signs and representations. He is a monster, the most absurd incarnation of this faculty we have of deriving our thoughts from our actions instead of fusing our actions with our thoughts."[11] Since in life itself men are insulated from everything of real importance, it is little wonder that art has degenerated into a narcissistic display of their trivial psychological dilemmas: "Judging by the state of our theatre, one would think that all that matters in life is whether we can make love successfully, whether we are going to make war or peace, how to come to terms with our petty moral qualms."[12]

What is needed is not a remedy for theatre but a cure for civilisation. Artaud's job now is to persuade us that the theatre, and perhaps *only* the theatre, is capable of effecting such a cure. "I propose to return in the theatre to that elementary idea in magic, picked up by modern psychoanalysis, which involves attempting to cure a sick patient by making him adopt the exterior attitude of the state to which one wishes to restore him."[13] The patient, in this case, is not an individual but collective. In "Le théâtre et la peste" Artaud develops a forceful analogy between theatre and the plague, which he considers to be a "psychic entity", a "spiritual disease" which affects society collectively. He describes in detail an outbreak of plague in Marseilles in 1720: the contagious breakdown of moral and social order, how under extreme conditions the mask of civilisation slips, giving way to collective madness, frenzy and gratuitous actions. The account is coupled with a clinical description of how the plague affects the individual: the organism is shaken to the core, the badness collects and comes to a head in a buboe which then bursts, draining and purifying the body. This is the convulsive, cathartic effect that theatre must seek to obtain: "It seems that collectively, by means of the plague, a giant moral and social abcess is drained; and like the plague, theatre exists to drain our collective abcesses."[14] When an outbreak of plague grips a town, people cast off the civilised constraints of order, reason and morality. In the same kill-or-cure way theatre will be "a beneficial experience because it forces men to see themselves as they really are, it rips off the mask, it shows men the dark powers and hidden forces, inviting them to confront destiny with a superior heroic attitude which they would never have had otherwise".[15]

If the forces released by this convulsive experience are dark ones, "that is the fault not of the plague nor of the theatre but of life".[16] In another essay, "Le Théâtre et la cruauté", we discover the grim metaphysical reality which Artaud wanted us to confront. The notion of cruelty is the most commonly abused aspect of Artaud's theory, often being equated with banal physical cruelty. As he explains repeatedly, he intended nothing of the sort. He chose the word deliberately, though perhaps ill-advisedly, to denote not a predilection for blood and torture but a natural force, a terrible ontological reality. The appetite for life is cruel because it is governed by implacable laws of determinism and survival. "Everything that acts is a form of cruelty."[17] "Effort is cruelty, living by effort is cruelty. Erotic desire is cruelty, death is cruelty, resurrection is cruelty, transfiguration is cruelty."[18] The Theatre of Cruelty intended by Artaud, far from seeking sensation in acts of violence, expresses a lucid, pure, detached submission to what he calls this "cosmic malevolence" (méchanceté).

All this implies the need for a new theatrical language and new lines of communication to be created in the theatre. Artaud argues, reasonably enough, that if theatre is to obtain a cathartic purging effect, if it is to "swoop down upon a crowd of spectators with all the awesome horror of the plague",[19] it must find means of attacking the human organism directly. Western theatre, which he constantly contrasts with the ritualistic oriental theatre, is a cerebral and verbal art calling for no profound involvement on the part of the spectator. Artaud was of course exaggerating. As we have seen, none of the leading directors was enslaved to the spoken word to the extent he implies. It might also be objected that Artaud under-estimated the capacity of the imagination (as opposed to the senses) to involve the spectator in an experience transcending everyday reality. But Artaud was aiming at something infinitely more savage and direct: "In our present degenerate state it is through the skin that metaphysics must penetrate our minds."[20]

The methods he advocated to achieve this are well known and in some degree self-evident. They call for the invention of a new "concrete" stage language deployed in space to create an environmental performance. The performance space will be simply the area contained within four walls, with the spectators in the centre and the action swirling around and among them. The audience will be hypnotically engulfed in vibrant concrete images created out of lights, colour, sonorisation, masked actors and effigies. The actor will be used like a mannequin in a hieroglyphic way, and his voice for its sonority in an incantatory way. The subjects will be drawn from ancient and modern myths showing men in the grip of natural and cosmic forces. The myth-maker is the director. In these ways theatre will be created out of everything that is specifically theatrical instead of out of that which is the least theatrical element in theatre, the text. This is a theatre of *mise en scène directe* which will get rid of the playwright once and for all and restore the stage to the director-high priest. For the most part these principles are stated in a summary manner, but one passage conjures up a particularly vivid impression of what it will resemble: "Cries, moans, apparitions, surprises. . . splendour of lighting, incantatory beauty of voices, bewitching harmonies. . . physical rhythm of movements whose crescendo and decrescendo mimic the pulsations of movement known to all, concrete apparitions of new and surprising objects, masks, puppets several metres tall, sudden lighting changes, physical action of light creating sensations of warmth and cold, etc."[21]

The Theatre of Cruelty manifesto, where the above passage appears, is precisely what its name implies: a statement of intent for a theatre which was meant to exist. Unfortunately the only practical demonstration Artaud was able to give was one unsuccessful production, *Les Cenci* in 1935. Written and directed by Artaud, it was supposed to illustrate super-human characters caught in a web of "cosmic malevolence", in this case incestuous rape, and inaugurate a new era in staging methods. The production was compromised from the start by Artaud's difficulties in financing it. His leading lady, whom he was forced to accept for the part because she provided most of the backing, was inaudible. Artaud's own performance as Cenci was not one of his best; he later admitted he had been overwhelmed by the immensity of the task and exhausted by the effort. Another serious obstacle was the theatre where the production took place. The Folies Wagram in the expensive sixteenth district was an ornately decorated palace only suitable, according to Artaud, to music hall. The setting, by Balthus, aroused interest but general reactions to the production ranged from indifference to hostility, and it closed after seventeen performances.

Les Cenci was only an incomplete and flawed test of Artaud's theory, and as Romain Weingarten remarks, "it is difficult to speak about a theatre that did not exist".[22] Even so, there must remain doubts about whether the Theatre of Cruelty could ever have achieved the sort of impact Artaud intended. The Balinese theatre which inspired his idea of a magical ritual was the encoded expression of collective experiences and beliefs, and as such was addressed to spectators impregnated with the meaning of its gestual code and able to understand the precise significance of an eye movement or a gesture of the hand. In a Western civilisation characterised by the fragmentation of individual experience and the dispersal of belief, the only counterpart would be crude and over-simplified in comparison. Moreover, it seems unlikely that *any* form of theatrical performance is capable of plunging modern Western man into the primitive state released by the plague. Perhaps what this amounts to is that in society as we know it theatre is *not* life, nor can we envisage conditions where the distinction between theatre and life would be abolished. Experience suggests on the contrary that Artaud's sensory methods are subject to the law of diminishing returns. The wave of Artaud-inspired productions in the 1960s produced some highly effective individual experiments but their cumulative effect ultimately was to dull the senses. In a way this goes to vindicate Artaud's belief that sophisticated audiences, however much they may relish a sensational aesthetic experience, are incapable of the unconditional response that would transform it into a higher metaphysical experience. What it cannot resolve, however, is the abiding paradox in Artaud that his theatrically-based revolution required the pre-existence of a public which only that theatre could bring into existence.

None of which detracts from the profound influence his ideas have had in post-war years. *Le Théâtre et son double* was republished in 1944 and was widely read and discussed. Beyond Barrault and Blin, who worked under Artaud in *Les Cenci*, a whole generation of directors and companies found their central point of reference in his writings. Peter Brook and Charles Marowitz in Britain, Grotowski in Poland, and the Bread and Puppet Theatre, the Living Theatre and the Open Theatre in the United States, are only the most conspicuous examples where his influence was decisive; in fact no theatre director of the last thirty years has remained unaffected by his ideas. In France Artaud's impact was indirectly reinforced by the visits paid by Grotowski's Laboratory Theatre and the Living Theatre in the 1960s. Huge claims have been made for Artaud the prophet, particularly in the 1960s when the cult was at its height, and as with all cults there have been excesses. His name was invoked in support of far too many exhibitionist performances of dubious therapeutic intent – abuses for which Artaud himself was no more responsible than Aristotle was to blame for the many second- and third-rate classical tragedies written by Racine's contemporaries. But now that the wave of undiscriminating adulation has passed, it is still possible to agree with Barrault's statement that *Le Théâtre et son double* is "without doubt the most important thing written about theatre in the twentieth century".[23]

This influence, incidentally, does not end with directors but extends paradoxically to playwrights too. A central feature of his global vision was the need to take theatre completely out of the hands of writers. This was the necessary corollary of his vision of a theatre of *mise en scène directe*. What has happened, in fact, is that the vocabulary of his "physical and concrete stage language" – the substitution of concrete imagery for verbal imagery, the exploration of the stage's spatial possibilities, the introduction of objects as agents of dramatic action, the use of ritual to create a powerful hyper-reality – has fruitfully been absorbed by writers intent on creating more spectacular, metaphysical, less psychological forms of drama. The absurdist plays of Adamov, Beckett and Ionesco, and the ritual dramas of Genet and Arrabal, show that Artaud's ideas found a rich seedbed in modern playwrights too.

In speaking of Artaud's influence, I should make it clear that there has never been any question of reconstructing Artaud's Theatre of Cruelty in its entirety – which in any case, as I have suggested, was more a visionary time-bomb than a practical programme. It is more a question of theatre people being, in the words Brook uses about himself, "directly stimulated by Artaud's thought"[24] – directly and ultimately indirectly since his ideas have been so pervasively absorbed that they now furnish a framework for thinking about theatre. Artaud has had this catalytic effect because he attacked the problem of theatre at its roots – like Copeau a generation earlier he started from a *tabula rasa* – and because he communicated in passionate terms a burning and exemplary belief in theatre's possibilities. He focused the debate more clearly than ever on fundamental questions concerning the specificity of the stage, questions which practitioners from Copeau to Baty had already addressed, although they themselves did not pursue them to their furthermost conclusions. In some ways he can be compared to Craig who also proposed a radically new type of theatre based specifically on the medium of the stage. Craig's ambitions, however, in keeping with the spirit of his age, were fundamentally aesthetic. Artaud, starting from metaphysical imperatives, went further, demanding that theatre should join forces with life and engage the spectator in a total experience: this too has become a major preoccupation of the experimental theatre.

Jean-Louis Barrault

Less original than Artaud, but infinitely more practical, the man who for nearly fifty years has been associated with a form of total drama is Barrault, who gave this definition: "life transmitted on stage by a *total* use of all human means of expression, by a *total* use of the entire range of expression of the human artist: song, poetic diction, prosaic diction, cries, breathing, silence, prosaic bodily expression, gesture, symbolic gesture, lyrical gesture, dance."[25] One particularly notes Barrault's emphasis on the human. The starting point for his total theatre, to which other instruments of performance will later be added, is a total actor.

This emphasis on the actor's art places Barrault in the tradition of Copeau, Dullin, Pitoëff and Jouvet, and marks a fundamental distinction with Gaston Baty's "théâtre intégral". Baty, a non-actor and a Thomist who denied man any privileged place in creation, aimed to dramatise the poetry of the universe with all the means at the director's disposal. Barrault, an actor and a humanist, has always defined theatre in human terms, both in the sense that the principal instrument of performance is the human actor and in the sense that its subject matter is a celebration of all that is human. He thinks of his art in terms of reaching out to make contact with men and women, to share his humanity with them, which is essentially the position of an actor. His favourite metaphor for acting is the act of love, implying a physical and spiritual exchange in which, he says, "each individual recognises and shares with the rest a re-discovered Collective Soul."[26] While his concept of theatre, within an overall humanistic perspective, is totally inner, his approach to acting is a physical one, calling for bodily address and technique. This down-to-earth approach has served him well, protecting him from the effects of his own intellectualising tendencies. Although Barrault can still succumb to dubious metaphysical abstractions he is constantly brought back to earth by a solid understanding of the actor and his technique. And if, as is often the case, his writings on theatre acquire the character of a mystical litany, with a marked predilection for words such as ardour, passion, grace, love, voluptuousness, intoxication, this too has its roots in the purely human art of the actor.

A general emphasis on man and a specific emphasis on bodily expression thus form the distinctive balance of Barrault's productions, and provide one of the few constants in a long and varied career. That he should have arrived at this position is due in part to his own outstanding gift for mime, but it also reflects the influence of the first of his masters, Dullin. Barrault became a pupil at the Atelier in 1931 at the age of twenty. Here he received Dullin's version of the Vieux-Colombier tradition, both in its vocational aspect – "The Atelier taught me the purest, most sincere working method. . . I breathed in an atmosphere of professional honesty"[27] – and its aesthetic aspect, combining the beauty of the text with a physical musicality based on bodily expression. To this "Religion of theatre", as he calls it, a specific technique was later added, though he learnt this not from Dullin personally but from the mime artist Etienne Decroux, another product of Copeau's school who had followed Dullin to the Atelier from the Vieux-Colombier. Decroux was a fanatical perfectionist who intimidated most of the pupils at the Atelier, but an excellent teacher of his art for those few who submitted to his discipline. His mime was a highly stylised art form, close to dance, requiring a rigorous understanding of musculature and breathing, movement, balance and counterpoise. His method demanded limitless dedication, exercise, diet and concentration. Decroux recognised and cultivated Barrault's innate gift, for that is what it certainly was. For two years Barrault seems to have fallen completely under his spell. They devoted several weeks to perfecting the famous *marche sur place* – the stationary "walking" of Baptiste in the film *Les Enfants du Paradis* – a particular and rather narrow application of a broader and very healthy concern for the physical details of technique.

Barrault's apprenticeship therefore began with a prolonged investigation into the art of movement in its purest form. He saw mime as one of the two poles of "pure" theatre, at the opposite extreme from pure diction, and distinguished two branches of mime, one which is an applied technique and the other, an art complete in itself, through which a transcendent metaphysical dimension is attained. He calls them objective mime – "gestures used to describe an action" – which is the counterpart of prose, and subjective mime – "gestures complete in themselves" – which corresponds to the alexandrine recitative. As an example of the latter he describes how a mime would express the theme of death: the body's violent struggle to resist, giving way to a long descent into the unknown, culminating in the ultimate transfiguration.

Both types of mime were employed in his first independent show entitled *Autour d'une mère* (1935), a "mimodrame" based on Faulkner's *As I lay dying*. More than simply an experimental performance, this was a public profession of faith, a manifesto-peformance intended to demonstrate "the entire range of expression available to the Human Being considered as an instrument of Dramatic Art".[28] The entire range of expression, that is, except speech, since the challenge Barrault set himself was to demonstrate that total drama can be created using only the expressive resources of the human body. From the novel depicting the life of a family at the time of the mother's death, he distilled a two-hour spectacle for fourteen masked but otherwise virtually naked performers appearing on an empty stage. The only speeches were two lyrical monologues delivered by the Mother after her transfiguration in death, and the only sound effects were created by the actors' rhythmic breathing and the different scraping or pounding noises of their bare feet on the stage. The "scenery" too was created by the actors who evoked cars, trees, animals, a river, fire and so on. The performance provoked mixed reactions, but on the whole was judged a success in having wrested the admiration of a sceptical audience who had come along predisposed to mock. Two now legendary scenes were particularly admired. One was where Barrault, playing both horse and rider, mimed the breaking-in of a wild horse, a virtuoso routine he had perfected during months of solitary rehearsal. The other was when, substituting for an actress who had pulled out at the last moment, he played the Mother in her death agony. With a bare torso and wearing only a flared black skirt and mask, he resembled a Mexican totem. As one of the sons, following her orders, made her coffin on the stage, Barrault's rasping breath synchronised with the noise of the saw in an awesome manner. Suddenly the breathing stopped and her hand, which had been raised, descended slowly in a draining motion which then spread to the rest of her body, followed by a progressive stiffening of the whole body. Artaud in the audience was mesmerised. In an article proclaiming *Autour d'une mère* a major event he wrote enthusiastically of

the irruption of magic when the horse-centaur appeared, the
sense of surprise and atmosphere pervading the show, and a
spirit of myth which he had thought to be extinct outside the
Balinese theatre. Artaud was characteristically critical of the
performance's general emphasis on the human anecdote, saying
that it described life instead of probing the remotest sources of
life. Yet it remained for him an exemplary demonstration of
the value of gesture and movement in space, and most important of all, it was theatre created exclusively from means specific
to the stage. He wrote: "It is in relation to the stage and on the
stage that this spectacle is organised; it has no existence other
than on the stage."[29] Artaud was probably right to see it as a
demonstration of possibilities rather than a complete realisation
of the new theatre. For Barrault too this initial investigation of
pure technique concentrating exclusively on the body was only
the first step towards a more comprehensive approach to performance.

As a result of *Autour d'une mère* he grew closer to Artaud and
other surrealists, the third major influence which completed
his formation. From Dullin he acquired a faith, from Decroux
a technique; through his involvement with the "libertarian"
wing of the surrealist movement he was led to explore the
psyche, the nature of reality, and eventually to find rôles for
his faith and technique within an overall attitude to life. The
years between 1935 and 1939 constituted a period of self-discovery and, he says, after the exclusively aesthetic preoccupations of the Atelier, an initiation to the lives of fellow-men.
Leaving Montmartre and the Atelier to strike out on his own
he took the top floor of a large building on the rue des Grands-
Augustins (later Picasso's studio) and with Jean Dasté formed
a theatre collective, Le Grenier des Augustins. It gave no regular performances and seems to have intended none, the object
being more to explore and celebrate life, read and exchange
ideas on art, and to experiment in an atmosphere of bohemian
freedom. The regulars included Desnos and Prévert, Tzara and
Vitrac, the young Jean Vilar and Artaud.

During this time Barrault "underwent" Artaud, he says,
"almost to the point of resembling him exactly".[30] He absorbed
Artaud's passion for Oriental theatre, his idea of the actor as

an affective athlete, and developed an awareness of, as he puts it, "horizons other than the extremely clear ones of the flesh as matter".[31] Artaud's highly developed sense of primitive magic and his theories concerning theatre and alchemy helped Barrault towards his own concept of total theatre, giving him in particular a greater insight into the function of space in performance.

Artaud had posited in a general way the correspondence between symbolic alchemy, seen as the spiritual double of a process which operates upon matter, and theatre, seen as the double of a hidden, archetypal reality.[32] All the components of the theatrical event, actor, audience, objects and sounds, were active elements in the process and the crucible where this alchemical operation occurred, the space where the performance takes place, stood for the Cosmic whole. It followed from this that the performance space, which Artaud refers to as a "magic space", cannot be regarded as neutral or indifferent but must be treated as another active element in the transformation process.

Artaud's hand is plainly visible in Barrault's "Petit traité d'alchimie théâtrale" ("Short treatise on theatrical alchemy"), as too is the difference between the two men's approach. Artaud's ideas were brilliantly original and provocative but not worked out in detail. Barrault, like a talented pupil, applied the findings of his own study of movement and breathing to these ideas in an attempt to codify the practical implications of the stage considered as a magic space. At first sight, admittedly, the highly theoretical "Petit traité d'alchimie théâtrale" gives the impression of a new cabalist Barrault who had abandoned practicalities for a heady brew of hermetic arts. Most readers would quickly grow impatient with what seems a capricious set of ideas enunciated as principles all derived from ternary associations: the basic ternary (masculine–feminine–neuter), ternaries of action (giving–receiving–retaining), of colour (violet–green–orange), of respiration (breathing in–breathing out–holding one's breath) and so on. The conclusions, however, do mark a clear progression in Barrault's ideas towards a fully integrated theatre of mixed means. It becomes apparent that speech is no longer considered an antithesis to movement but an extension of the range of expression of the human artist considered as a total instrument, and a medium, moreover, which operates on exactly the same principles as movement. All the arts are the product of a confrontation between two elements: breath vibrating the vocal chords, the chisel chipping at stone, the squirrel hair brushed against canvas, the bow drawn across a string – and the body in space. Barrault draws the conclusion that the human body cannot be isolated from the space it inhabits: "Theatre is the art of the Human Being" he states, as he has before, but now he adds: "In space."[33] And again: "The basis of theatre is the confrontation of Man and his surrounding Space." The way is now open for a genuinely total theatre; that is, a drama which remains centred on man and takes as its object total man, his thoughts, feelings, aspirations and history, but which also integrates man into the space he inhabits and the objects that surround him.

These ideas could easily have led Barrault to embrace Artaud's concept of *mise en scène directe* where the vocabulary of stage architecture, actors, objects, signs and sounds would replace the text. Barrault was probably better placed than anyone to make such a theatre work, since his concentration on mime had not been to the exclusion of the other instruments of performance. Dullin saw to it that his pupils acquired a solid understanding of all the nuts and bolts of theatre. Actors were expected to concern themselves with such things as lighting, costume, stage mechanics and carpentry, and Barrault applied the same cult of technical mastery to these as he did to the study of the body. His aim, however, was to marry these skills with great dramatic texts, for unlike Artaud he believed that only the vision and imaginative powers of a playwright can weld the resources of the stage into a coherent work of art.

Barrault's attitude towards the playwright was shaped by Dullin and the climate of the Cartel theatres generally. "A man of the theatre," he states, "only acquires his real face if he has the good fortune to unite with an author",[34] a remark obviously inspired by partnerships such as those of Jouvet and Giraudoux, Pitoëff and Pirandello, Dullin and Salacrou. He refers nostalgically to the Cartel years as a Golden Age, both for the artistry of its productions and the harmony in which *mise en scène* had evolved alongside great writing. If a return to the aestheticism of the Cartel was now neither possible nor desirable, the theatrical partnerships of the period remained a worthwhile ideal to emulate. Barrault desperately wanted "his" author, and in his memoirs we see successive attempts to "cultivate" Gide, who wrote the adaptations of *The trial* and *The castle*, Sartre, though in the event no project materialised, and Camus.

It was on Camus, who wrote *L'Etat de siège* (1948) at his instigation, that Barrault pinned his greatest hopes. Barrault had been working on an idea for a production based on Defoe's *Journal of the plague year* when Camus's *La Peste* was published in 1947. Abandoning his own project, he suggested to Camus, who had already written two moderately successful plays, that they work together to produce a play about the plague. Their common interest in the subject and their shared ideas about human solidarity seemed to guarantee a fruitful partnership. "I was overjoyed" wrote Barrault, "and already saw myself associated with Camus for a considerable part of my life. Camus was my 'chance'."[35] The production, however, was a failure. Barrault wanted to see the plague in Artaudian terms as a paroxysm of dark forces producing a redemptory effect – a view which can only be described as naive in the context of the immediate aftermath of the war against nazism. Camus, on the other hand, equated the plague with a form of totalitarianism and saw it as an unmitigated evil. This unresolved difference resulted in a production which was not merely ambiguous but confusing. Theatrically, too, there were weaknesses. In terms of technique Camus was attempting to break new ground but his philosophical and sometimes verbose style was at odds with Barrault's concept of a new form of drama exploiting all the possibilities of a concrete stage. *L'Etat de siège* was Barrault's first critical and public failure, but the bitterest blow was that it put an end to his hopes of a long partnership with Camus.

Barrault's efforts to graft his art to that of a playwright might be taken to indicate that he had reverted to the traditional concept of *mise en scène* as the vehicle for a text. Is his "total" theatre finally just a text liberally dressed up with a plethora of visual and auditory effects? Far from it, because in his ideas about how the various component parts contribute to the final production he makes a distinction between text and author. Whereas Jouvet took the words of the text to be the ultimate repository of the play's meaning, Barrault considers the text as the external correlative of something greater. He believed, rightly, that for any playwright with a sense of theatre the written text is not something complete in itself, nor even a purely verbal product, but a form of notation or score conceived for performance by the instruments of the stage. Theatre for Barrault is an essentially sensual art made of flesh, form and movement. For this reason, the text, while supplying an indispensable point of reference rooting the performance in reality, cannot itself be the ultimate object of performance. Roughly speaking, says Barrault, the spoken part of the text can be compared to the visible portion of a iceberg – important because it *is* immediately visible but *only* important because of the greater mass which supports it. In practice, of course, there can be no mathematical formula to determine the degree of importance given to a text: common sense dictates that the emphasis must depend on the play in question. Certainly no-one could accuse Barrault of undervaluing the verbal density and richness of the text in his productions of Racine and Giraudoux. His production of *Phèdre* was preceded by an exhaustive study of the nature of the alexandrine, the musicality of Racine's verse and the structure of the recitative.[36] At the opposite extreme, in productions like *The trial* where the entire dialogue can be spoken in an estimated fifteen minutes, mime, pantomime, shadow-play and scenic transformation come to the fore. Even in such productions, however, it is significant that Barrault did not rely on his own efforts as adaptor but sought the assistance of writers, nor was there any attempt at direct *mise en scène* as Artaud envisaged.

The reason, as I have said, is that unlike Artaud he came to see that only a playwright is capable of supplying the overall vision without which the director can generate only a display of visual and sensory effects. The same is true of the actor: without playwrights, actors are like instruments which no-one can play. Experiments to expand acting techniques and the arts of the stage will, on their own, lead nowhere: the hope must be that new playwrights will come along to exploit the possibilities made available to them. "As certain instrumentalists have acquired new techniques thanks to a composer who suddenly demands something new of the instrument, so the actor's technique can change only in response to new demands being made by a writer. Theatre practitioners may go round in circles tying themselves in knots, the future of dramatic art still remains entirely in the playwrights' hands."[37] Examples of what he has in mind would be Barrault's technically brilliant slow motion running and falling or, (a kinetic counterpart of Dali's floppy watches), his method of walking which gives the impression that the ground has gone soft. Without a context these are just virtuoso numbers, but integrated into Witkiewicz's expressionist distortions of reality (*The mother*, 1970) or Kafka's surreal nightmares (*The castle*, 1957, *The trial*, 1961) they help to create a revealing new dramatic style.

Barrault's twin ambition of joining forces with a major playwright and finding an original style of writing to exploit the language of the stage fully bore fruit in the 1940s in his outstanding productions of Claudel's *Le Soulier de satin*, *Partage de midi* and *Christophe Colomb*. Barrault has described Claudel unequivocally as the greatest dramatist of the century. If this opinion is justified – and there must be reservations about a writer whose plays to many people are more awe-inspiring than approachable – much of the credit must go to Barrault himself. Their partnership is the most spectacular example of a director literally rescuing a major playwright, converting his universally admired but unperformed texts into a living dramatic force.

Claudel had long been recognised as a literary colossus, with a high standing even among the surrealists in spite of his trenchant Catholicism. Desnos, when asked to name the greatest living poet, replied "Claudel, God help us!" But this reputation was of necessity based on literary judgement, productions of his plays having been few and far between. Lugné-Poe had produced *L'Annonce faite à Marie*, a scenically straightforward mystery play, in 1912. Copeau, who had produced *L'Echange* in 1914, planned to stage others but was forced to retreat when Claudel imposed impossible conditions. Baty also produced *L'Annonce* in 1921 but Claudel subsequently branded him as a saboteur and refused to authorise any new productions. Jouvet was preparing to stage *L'Annonce* in 1930 when Claudel, scandalised by the alleged immorality of other plays in his repertoire, suddenly withdrew his permission. Claudel's intractability was only one of the problems confronting would-be directors. His early plays, dating from the symbolist period, are vastly over-written with a surcharge of lyrical rhetoric obfuscating the action and themes. This weakness persists to some extent, though constant revisions in the light of Claudel's growing theatrical consciousness gradually led him to produce more workable stage versions. Meanwhile his best plays, *Le Soulier de satin* and *Partage de midi*, remained unstaged, the one because its vastness and complexity seemed to make it unplayable and the other, a theatrically more conventional play, because for personal reasons Claudel would not authorise its performance.

Yet their theatrical potential was enormous and of obvious interest to a director such as Barrault. Claudel's plays are dramas of spiritual conflict. Their essential theme, expressed in the preface of *Partage de midi* as the desires of the spirit pitted against the desires of the flesh, poses the question: can man possess the world and thereby fulfil himself? The answer is known in advance: he cannot, since only God can possess the world, but the plays' real interest resides in the tortuous paths that lead the characters to this realisation. To the extent that they embrace the spirit and the flesh, depicting man's struggle between the earth and heaven, and reveal the workings of a cosmic pattern of sin and salvation, these plays already suggest thematically a concept of "total" drama. Theatrically, too, they transcend conventional boundaries. Reading them, one is aware above all of an avalanche of poetry and some effort is needed to grasp the ambitious scenic vision, the Wagnerian fusion of form and content, that underly them. Claudel treats the stage as the entire universe. Settings, objects, natural forces and the elements play both symbolic and active rôles in the drama. As a diplomat posted to China in the early years of the century, Claudel had travelled in Japan and discovered Noh theatre which helped to form his ideas about the fusion of gesture and speech in non-representational spectacle. His growing fascination with performance, as opposed to dramatic literature, led him, in parallel with Barrault, to envisage a total fusion of idea, speech, gesture and music, a concept of total drama which achieved its fullest expression in *Le Soulier de satin*. This is a toweringly ambitious and, when it was written between 1919 and 1929, highly experimental synthesis of all Claudel's theological and theatrical beliefs. A work of multiple dimensions, more Shakespearean than French in form, it blends tragedy and burlesque, poetry and mime and even pantomime, shadowgraphy and ballet. A fascinating and distinctly modern feature is its self-conscious theatricality and the reflections it prompts on the nature of theatre, not only in the constant shifts in style and tone but also in the figure of L'Annoncier who guides the spectator through the performance.[38] The dimensions of the subject matter are equally vast, depicting a tragedy of star-crossed lovers against the back-drop of the entire universe, telescoping and superimposing centuries and continents, and inter-weaving the personal, the historical and the divine.

The production of *Le Soulier de satin* in 1943 remains one of the outstanding directorial achievements of modern times, as well as an exemplary instance of collaboration between poet and director. In order to stage it Barrault had to win over both the author, whom he wooed for three years, and the reading committee of the Comédie-Française where he was now a Sociétaire and which was perhaps the only theatre in occupied Paris with the resources and personnel to tackle a work of such magnitude. It was eventually agreed to cut and condense the play into a single performance lasting some four and a half to five hours, a delicate and painful operation carried out jointly by Claudel and Barrault. Throughout the rehearsal period the author demanded to be kept closely informed of Barrault's staging intentions, though Barrault dissuaded him from attending rehearsals in person. When eventually, ten days before the première, he came to watch a run-through, a new and closer working relationship began. Claudel became totally absorbed in the scenic life of his play. At the end of each day Barrault received copious notes on diction and phrasing jotted down by the author during rehearsals. It was evident that certain scenes were simply not working as they had been written. With remarkable pliancy Claudel agreed cuts, suggested alterations, and even re-wrote entire scenes overnight.

The success of the Barrault-Claudel partnership depended on a total accord between the playwright's theatrical vision and the director's approach to the stage. It might be wondered how a pagan sensualist such as Barrault could become the leading interpreter of an intensely religious, Catholic poet. Barrault's use of the stage had remained true to his original starting point, the art of bodily expression, but in his quest for total theatre he had made this the central component of a rich visual and auditory feast. In fact, it is not so much God that is celebrated in Barrault's productions as a passionate attachment to the created world – an approach to which Claudel's plays actually lend themselves very well. If Claudel the Christian (and his characters) know that earthly pleasures are transitory, this does not stop them being consumed with burning desire for the things of this earth. Because of this, if his plays are not to come across simply as theological theorems, any successful production must clothe the drama in a rich and sensuous physicality. Barrault and Claudel were both agreed on the absolute importance of the word and the gesture as the tangible correlatives, rooted in the physical rhythms of the body itself, of transcendent meaning. As Barrault discovered, Claudel's verse is quite unlike that of any other French poet. It is a physical pulsation based not on metre but on breathing patterns and rhythms. Like the individual words themselves, which Claudel defines concretely as "intelligible mouthfuls", the word-groups have their own physical presence which accords with the rhythms of the body and demand to be spoken with the entire body. Then, ranged beyond the human actor is the "grand spectacle" – the sumptuous décor and costumes, the machinery, music and lighting – which both men saw as not simply an adornment or frame but an integral part of the action embedded in the heart of the drama.

The production of *Le Soulier de satin* in 1943 was also a major patriotic event. Claudel's vision of salvation achieved through earthly suffering struck a special chord in the people of occupied Paris, and the very fact of its staging was an affirmation of France's undiminished cultural vigour. After the war Barrault went on to stage further plays by Claudel: *Partage de midi* (1946, 1961), *L'Echange* (1951), *Christophe Colomb* (1953, 1960), *Tête d'or* (1959, 1968) and finally *Sous le vent des îles Baléares* (1972), a remarkable series of productions which together revealed the scope of Claudel's dramatic achievement. Barrault's success in making Claudel into a living theatrical presence has encouraged other productions by other directors, though, with the possible exception of Vitez's recent *Partage de midi* (1976), none may be said to equal Barrault's in their richness and mastery of the scenic elements.

More recently Barrault has pursued his idea of total theatre in a series of productions based on his own adaptations of non-dramatic material: *La Tentation de Saint Antoine* (1967), which was a joint production with Béjart devoted to Flaubert, *Rabelais* (1968), *Jarry sur la butte* (1970), *Ainsi parlait Zarathustra* (1975), based on Nietzsche's writings, and others inspired by Saint-Exupéry, La Fontaine, Diderot and Voltaire. These *spectacles* as they are properly called, extend a line of work which began with *Autour d'une mère* and continued in productions of Kafka, Claudel and the *Oresteia*, all of them involving attempts to express the essence of human experience, as distinct from everyday life, with a symbolic use of the physical language of performance. The difference in the more recent spectacles is that, instead of a dramatic action, it is a single man's experience that supplies the human reality. Barrault's method is to compose a collage of text and dialogue, incorporating extracts from the author's writings, to illuminate and celebrate not his biography but his imaginative universe.

These productions have all suffered to some extent from a tendency to reduce the hero to an exemplary but over-simplified essence: Rabelais's zest for life, Jarry's iconoclasm and paralysing *fin de siècle* lucidity, Nietzsche's searing visionary qualities and so on. It can also be said that in his enthusiasm for the subject Barrault tends to assume a detailed familiarity with writings which the average theatre-goer does not have. His *Jarry sur la butte*, for example, deliberately excluded the popular, perhaps over-done *Ubu roi* and devoted itself to aspects of Jarry's philosophy little known outside a small circle of initiates and connoisseurs. On a technical level, however, none of the productions was without interest. Whatever his weaknesses as a writer of scripts, Barrault can always be relied upon to exploit the stage in an inventive, exciting way.

Rabelais was one of the most popular and noisy successes of Barrault's career, though it would be difficult to say how far this was due to the special circumstances surrounding the production in the unusual climate of 1968. In that year Barrault had been dismissed from the Odéon which he had run under licence from the Ministry of Culture since 1959. Unwittingly, and more because of the indecision of his political masters than his own doings, he had become a casualty of the social and political ferment that swept through France in May 1968. In the autumn, without a theatre, and the object of considerable public sympathy, he set about re-launching his company in the private sector with *Rabelais* as the opening production. Barrault had actually been preparing this production for two years and had planned to stage it at the Odéon, but in the new circumstances it inevitably acquired the character of a declaration of independence and was heralded by the press as a defiant riposte to the establishment.

Rabelais was conceived as a celebration of life and liberty, inspired by Rabelais's appetite for living, his irrepressible imagination and his humanist outlook. Barrault also wanted to bring out the parallels he saw between Rabelais's time and his own, both of which he saw as periods of emancipation for man, tempered by the reactionary backlash of authority. Theatrically, on every level, it was intended to break the mould of conventional theatre. Much play was made at the time of the fact that the production was mounted in a boxing stadium in the popular district of Montmartre, though in fact, despite its enormous popularity, it was not really "popular" theatre in the sense of theatre serving the needs and interests of a local community: the crowds who flocked to see it were made up mostly of the students and sophisticates who would have gone to the Odéon. Of greater significance was the scenic freedom that came with Barrault's enforced departure from the Odéon with its enclosed proscenium stage. At Montmartre the action was played on a cross-shaped stage made with platforms extending the boxing ring into the hall. Scenically the production was a triumph of vitality and inventiveness, with spectacular qualities similar to *Le Soulier de satin* and *Christophe Colomb*, though rather more formless and with a distinctly hippy flavour. Strip routines performed by dancers from the Crazy Horse Saloon, rock'n'roll numbers, psychedelic lighting effects and posters, combined with inventive miming to create a highly coloured impression of pullulating life. Barrault's ingenuity in staging individual scenes was undisputed. "How," marvelled one critic, "with eight ropes, dappled lighting on the ceiling, Polnareff's ravishing music, and twelve men swaying to the rhythm of the waves, does Barrault create out of nothing a ship sailing on the high seas?"[39] But even Michel Polnareff's score, underlining the action and linking the scenes, could not give an overall shape to the performance. The production's weakness, which is often the case with such adaptations, lay in the absence of authorial vision. From the five source books Barrault had culled a three-hour spectacle of great diversity but also inevitably episodic. While certain episodes such as the birth of Gargantua made a memorable impression, the effect overall was of a sprawling riot which was not easy to follow. Along the way, the force of Rabelais's humanist philosophy was somehow harmlessly dispersed in high-jinks, bawdiness and random volleys against figures of authority. Overall *Rabelais* was a *tour de force* of scenic inventiveness, but a triumph of staging over unwieldy and not wholly dramatic material – a phenomenon which would become increasingly familiar to theatre-goers in the 1970s as more companies took to composing their own spectacles.

These experiments in total theatre are the productions where Barrault is seen to be most fully himself, but they are only one facet of his work. His reputation is equally based on the artistry of his productions of familiar plays, impeccably staged but hardly avant-garde. The same man who brought Kafka and Claudel to the stage was also responsible for the post-war re-vival of Feydeau, establishing his farces as classics of the genre. In the forty years since Barrault broke with the Comédie-Française to set up his own theatre with his wife and life-long partner Madeleine Renaud, the Compagnie Renaud-Barrault has mounted some one hundred and fifty original productions of classical, modern and experimental plays. These were produced in a variety of theatres which to some extent identify the successive stages of Barrault's career. Between 1946 and 1956 the company rented the Théâtre Marigny, an elegant building on the Champs-Elysées. Here it acquired its reputation for high quality productions, though the audiences it attracted were select and fashionable ones. As well as a production style, the "style Marigny" as it came to be known, was identified with a distinctive artistic policy. One of its main features was the wide variety of plays presented in repertory. Shakespeare, Molière and Marivaux alternated with modern classics (Chekhov, Claudel, Giraudoux), contemporary writers (Sartre, Montherlant, Vauthier), ever-popular farces such as Feydeau's *Occupe-toi d'Amélie*, and experimental productions like *The castle* and *The trial*. Barrault had learned an important lesson in his first year with Dullin when he saw how the prolonged run given to *Volpone*, the Atelier's first major success, was interfering with the regular work of the company. From its beginnings the Compagnie Renaud-Barrault has practised repertory and continues to do so today – an enriching practice at a time when other companies are retreating into laboratories, cutting themselves off from public performance for long periods while pursuing theatrical research. Working in repertory requires high operating budgets and sustained effort, but the benefits are correspondingly high. It encourages versatility from the actors and allows the company to draw sustenance from theatre's classical traditions while also supporting new writers. It absorbs both successes and failures, enabling particularly popular productions to hold the bill at increasingly spaced out intervals and allowing the company to take artistic risks without staking its entire financial structure on a single production. Barrault tends to play down the extent to which his own theatre work has been subsidised by his cinema earnings. Even so, he is probably correct in believing repertory to be the "least bad" system for balancing the demands of art and business.

In 1959 the company's high international standing was acknowledged by Malraux's invitation to take over the Odéon as part of a comprehensive programme of cultural reform involving also the Comédie-Française and the Opéra. The offer was an unprecedented arrangement by which the second national theatre was given over to a private company – or alternatively, a private theatre company was nationalised by the state. The Salle Luxembourg, as it was then known, had a chequered history. Its original purpose, when it was built in 1782 for the Comédie-Française, had been to serve as a stage for new and original drama. Five years before the revolution it was the scene of the tumultuous opening of Beaumarchais' *Le Mariage de Figaro*. But the theatre's running costs were enormous and in 1829 it was sold into private ownership. Under successive directors it was dogged by ill-luck. Before the First War Antoine had succeeded in investing the Odéon with new vitality but his tenure was a financial disaster. No director, other than those who sacrificed their artistic standards to popular taste, had made the theatre commercially viable. Barrault's formidable brief in 1959 was to take this now dilapidated monument, re-baptised Odéon-Théâtre de France, and form it into a modern national theatre serving as a progressive wing to the more conservative Comédie-Française.

The terms of the contract were onerous and probably unrealistic, providing a level of subsidy which made it impossible to break even, but at least the arrangement was supposed to guarantee Barrault almost complete artistic freedom. Even so, artistically, his period at the Théâtre de France succeeded beyond expectations and was accompanied by an unexpected broadening and rejuvenation of the company's work. The first season, because of the speed with which the move took place, contained a number of revivals from the company's existing repertoire, though it was also marked by a prestigious opening production of Claudel's *Tête d'Or* and, more adventurously, the *première* of *Rhinocéros* by Ionesco – no longer perhaps a risky experimental writer but still sufficiently avant-garde to cause some officials to question Barrault's use of his subsidy. That production marked the end of Ionesco's initial period as an experimental playwright played only in tiny low-cost theatres in the Latin Quarter and his adoption by a wider public. For the company it signalled the start of an association with the "New Theatre" movement and was followed by productions of Beckett, Pinget, Duras and Genet, as well as other plays by Ionesco. As a natural corollary to this policy Barrault also made the Odéon into a forum for experimental production styles by inviting younger directors, including Jorge Lavelli, Roger Planchon, Antoine Bourseiller and Roger Blin, to mount productions there.

One problem arising from a wide-ranging repertoire is the difficulty of accommodating classical and modern plays, with their differing styles and demands, in a single performance space. Although the Odéon was cleaned and restored, its large and inflexible italianate design made it less than ideal for modern plays requiring a more intimate stage-auditorium relationship. A make-shift solution was to reduce the size of the auditorium by a canopy enclosing the orchestra and first balcony. Later, with the conversion of a gallery into a small studio theatre (the Petit Odéon), the Théâtre de France became a more flexible instrument allowing the large-scale productions of Shakespeare and the French classics to be presented in tandem with avant-garde plays. Barrault also brought a new idea to complement the straight dramatic performance by opening a theatre laboratory offering workshops on acting, play-writing, and stage design. But the most outstanding feature of all was the sheer number and variety of plays produced. In the *Cahiers de la Compagnie Renaud-Barrault* Simone Benmussa reveals the intensive pattern of work within the theatre in one week in 1961. While Obey's *Viol de Lucrèce* and Feydeau's *Mais n'te promène donc pas toute nue* were in performance, and with *Julius Caesar* in the final rehearsal stages, Jean-Pierre Granval, as guest director, was directing the first rehearsals of *Les Précieuses ridicules*. A fifth group, including Barrault, were at a first reading of Schéhadé's *Le Voyage*, followed the next day by a first reading of *The merchant of Venice* with Marguerite Jamois as director. Meanwhile plans for a poetry cycle were evolving with Henri Pichette as artistic director.[40] As a result of such adventurous programming, the fashionable Marigny public was soon joined by an enthusiastic, younger left-bank audience. Between 1960 and 1968 the Théâtre de France exuded a great sense of vitality, though the price of this was a reduction in Barrault's creative work as the adminstrative burden became more consuming, particularly after the adoption in 1966 of the Théâtre des Nations with its ambitious annual festival of international theatre.

All this came to a sudden end in the aftermath of May 1968, of which Barrault gives his own account in *Souvenirs pour demain*. It is typical of Barrault and Madeleine Renaud that, far from from being demoralised by an evidently traumatic experience, they seized the opportunity it gave them to make a fresh start. They decided that the company should become mobile. Political instability, as well as the need to match the performance space to the nature of individual plays, made it undesirable to work in a permanent theatre such as the Odéon or the Marigny. Barrault also renounced definitively the fixed frame of the proscenium stage. The converted Elysées-Montmartre, where the rumbustuous *Rabelais* and *Jarry* were staged, provided an opportunity to experiment with a more open stage space, but the acoustics and some sight-lines were poor. Taking the circus tent as a model Barrault then drew up plans for a wide, open stage at the edge of a circular or semi-circular arena, providing a more democratic seating arrangement. Unlike traditional theatres such as the Odéon, where the hierarchy of parterre, boxes, balconies and galleries stratifies the public socially, the new model must ensure that there are no privileged seats, and that none is more than 18 metres away from the stage. These principles were applied when the company took over the old Gare d'Orsay in 1972. An original theatre complex was created there, with an attractive octagonal main auditorium built of wood and designed to be transportable, a studio theatre, and a restaurant, all installed within the stone and iron shell of the station. In 1981 the company moved again, taking the wooden theatre with them, to its present site, a former skating rink in a rotunda on the Champs-Elysées.

After forty years of unbroken activity, the Compagnie Renaud-Barrault retains a place among the most vital and stimulating theatre companies in France. Its strength lies partly in Barrault's capacity for self-renewal, as demonstrated by the determination with which the company was reconstructed after the disaster of 1968, and, more generally, by its willingness to experiment with new theatrical ideas. One of the company's enduring attractions has been its leading actress. Before the war Madeleine Renaud was a brilliant young Sociétaire at the Comédie-Française where she seemed destined to become its leading classical actress, the interpreter *par excellence* of Racine and Marivaux. To everyone's surprise she has become one of the leading interpreters of difficult avant-garde rôles, with outstanding success as Winnie in Beckett's *Happy days*, as the the Mother in Witkiewicz's *La Mère* and in Duras' *L'Amante anglaise*. Meanwhile Barrault too, as director, has refused to be constrained by any narrow definition of theatre. Cutting across conventional categories of avant-garde, classical and traditional, he is just as much at home with classics like *Phèdre* and *Hamlet* as with experimental works of Kafka and Ionesco, and can score outstanding successes with Feydeau's farces and Offenbach's comic opera. For this reason he has sometimes been branded as an opportunist. In 1939 his decision to become a Sociétaire at the Comédie-Française dismayed many of his friends who declared him finished as a vital force in the avant-garde – though Dullin, who approved of the decision, saw it as a laudable attempt to "carry the struggle into the citadel itself".[41] Again, in 1959 with his appointment to the Odéon it seemed to some that Barrault would compromise artistic integrity for official position. It is possible to argue that this is indeed what happened. One could say that the staging of Ionesco at the Théâtre de France, and even the infinitely more risky staging of Genet's subversive anti-colonialist play *Les Paravents*, were simply classic examples of official culture extending its frontiers to take in the former avant-garde. But this is to assume that the only worthwhile contemporary art is avant-garde and anti-establishment, which may be a valid position for a critic, but an impossibly restrictive approach for a practising director to adopt. In fact, during his stay at the Odéon, as throughout his career, Barrault's lesson to the world was that there is no qualitative distinction between traditional and avant-garde, the only differences in theatre that matter being between good and bad.

Barrault's position today is unique, as the last representative of an idea of theatre formed before the war yet still holding enormous appeal for a broad cross-section of the public including young theatre-goers. Barrault himself, however, has come to feel increasingly out of sympathy with modern trends towards a politically involved theatre. His own art, with the aesthetic bias of the Cartel and the metaphysical orientation of

Artaud, has always placed a commitment to theatre and life above any narrower cause, but in *Souvenirs pour demain* he voices concern at what he calls "a spirit of propaganda", "intimidating conduct" and "men spending their time in unsolicited attempts to teach other men how to live".[42] More reflectively, in an article entitled "Conviction et malaise dans le théâtre" published in 1970, he analyses the climate and tendencies of the post-war theatre. In the "golden age of aesthetics" (Barrault's description of the Cartel years) the artist's mission was a personal one: his creativity was guided by his inspiration, his rôle was to testify to *his* experience, to share *his* dreams. This did not deny the social importance of theatre, which in an indirect way is considerable insofar as it truthfully reflected an individual's experience of the real world; but it meant that a diagnosis of social needs did not determine *a priori* the direction of the artist's work, whose authenticity (and hence ultimately its usefulness) was guaranteed by its freedom from extrinsic objectives.

Barrault believes that the post-1968 theatre, by adopting a more interventionist rôle, has forfeited its claim to universality. Rather than breaking down the barriers between men such theatre perpetuates existing ones and artificially creates new ones. "Political theatre," he declares, "is in reality class theatre attacking another class."[43] But, in his view, it is not the business of theatre to further an extra-theatrical cause in this way, nor to serve the interests of a particular class. Theatre being a pre-eminently human art, its aim must be to address all men, not a particular group or class, and if it relinquishes this aim theatre loses its universality and communication becomes impossible. "The primordial desire of the artist," he states, "is to be able to communicate with his fellow men. If he comes up against a refusal to communicate, what can be done? We have come to the heart of the malaise."[44] Barrault experienced an alarming symptom of this breakdown of communication in May '68 when his attempts to engage in dialogue with the *enragés* who had occupied his theatre – the fanatical leaders of students with whom he was basically in sympathy – were greeted with intolerant cat-calls and denunciations.

Before the war, the most absorbing issue for *metteurs en scène* and critics was the place of the text within the orchestration of the component arts of the stage. Since the 1950s the question of theatre's ultimate aim has been formulated in different terms. Now directors must take a stand either in the school of thought which sees theatre as an end in itself or in the opposing school which regards theatre as an instrument of social change. Barrault's position, in the non-utilitarian school, was settled in 1935 when he opted to become a pupil and disciple of Dullin. And although the events of 1968 undoubtedly gave Barrault a lesson in *déniaisement* from which he realised that theatre cannot function in isolation from contemporary political forces, his fundamental principles today remain unaltered. A great admirer of Vilar's *théâtre populaire* and one of the earliest to lend practical support to the committed director Planchon, he nevertheless remains constant in his faith in an older ideal of a theatre accessible to all and addressed to the common core of humanity in every individual.

The Latin Americans

When the ritual drama called for by Artaud finally conquered the stage in the 1960s it was a group of Latin-American directors who were responsible for many of its most exciting productions. One of the first heralds of the new trend was a production in 1963 of Rotrou's *Saint Genest* by the Peruvian director Rafaël Rodriguez. Rather than the text itself, an obscure baroque play of the early seventeenth century, it was the style of Rodriquez's production, with its provocative mixture of violence, ritual, fantasy and skilfully orchestrated anarchy, that attracted attention and gave a foretaste of later productions by Victor Garcia, Jérôme Savary and Jorge Lavelli.

One reason for the Latin-Americans' presence in Paris was the existence of the Université du Théâtre des Nations, an international theatre school created in 1961 as part of the cultural *politique de grandeur* being pursued by Malraux and De Gaulle, the same policy that brought Barrault to the Odéon. The centre, based in the Théâtre Sarah-Bernhardt at the Châtelet, offered free classes for young professionals of every nationality. Among its students in the early 1960s were the directors Garcia, Lavelli, Alberto Rody and the cartoonist-playwright Copi from Argentina; another young director, Ramon Laméda, from Venezuela; and two Mexicans, the playwright Carlos Fuentes and director-film maker Alexandro Jodorowsky. Also at the Université du Théâtre des Nations at this time were two young French directors, Jérôme Savary (who had also lived for a number of years in Buenos Aires) and Jean-Marie Patte. Out of this melting pot a powerful new current of stagecraft emerged from the confluence of French ideas inspired by Artaud, whose time had now come, and the Latin-Americans' dynamically mixed culture with roots in the Indian – highly stylised and hierarchical – and the Spanish, nourished on the spectacle of the *fiesta* and *corrida* and the religious rituals of the Catholic church.

The arrival of men like Garcia and Lavelli in Paris coincided with a sea-change in French theatre. The theatrical phenomenon of the 1950s was the ascendancy of the so-called theatre of the absurd, a movement originating in Paris but producing shock waves throughout the world. In that decade the vein of metaphysical writing explored by Beckett, Ionesco and Adamov and many lesser sub-absurdist writers had come to dominate the avant-garde almost to the exclusion of anything else. By the early 1960s Beckett and Ionesco were well on the way to being modern classics, a status soon to be confirmed by the Nobel prize for the one, election to the Académie Française for the other, and productions of both by the Comédie-Française. The avant-garde of the 1950s, which was essentially a playwrights' avant-garde, seemed thus to have reached a stalemate. With the rich vein of absurdism apparently approaching exhaustion, theatre-goers looked for, and to some extent found, originality in a fragmented spectrum of tendencies: the epic-style Marxist theatre of Gatti or Adamov in his later manner, the poetic theatre of Romain Weingarten, or the "New Theatre" proposed by novelists such as Pinget, Duras and Sarraute. In fact, although these were not without interest, they were all developing tendencies already present in either the existentialist or absurdist theatres of the previous decades, and none enjoyed more than a modest *succès d'estime*. The Latin-Americans, in contrast, offered something strikingly new and more in accord with the climate of the period. After the nihilism and reductionism of the metaphysical theatre in post-war years, played under the shadow the Cold War and the atom bomb, the various forms of spectacular baroque theatre practised by the Latin-Americans found a willing and responsive audience.

While not in any sense constituting an artistic school, nor even a loose professional association like the Cartel, and in spite of markedly different outlooks on life, Lavelli, Savary and Garcia base their approach to theatre on similar premises. What they share is a concept of theatre as ritual, visceral rather than cerebral, a feast for the senses celebrating both the outward spectacle and inner mysteries of existence. The vision of life communicated in their spectacles differs considerably — Savary's productions are robustly satirical, festive and anarchic, Garcia's are anguished and neurotic, coloured by what Unamuno termed the Spaniard's "tragic sense of life", while Lavelli's are more soberly mystical. But in staging their productions each of them assumes the rôle of Artaud's "master of sacred ceremonies" to construct his own theatrical universe where the creation of a climate, often violent, takes precedence over the expression of an idea. These qualities made them the ideal interpreters of the playwrights with whom they first made their mark: Arrabal, Copi, Genet, that is to say, dramatists whose plays favour the explosion of richly provocative spectacle where ritual, ceremony, cruelty and delirium are major elements. For similar reasons they have also revived with considerable success obscure and forgotten plays of a baroque character such as Oscar Panizza's *The council of love (Le Concile d'amour)* and Witold Gombrowitz's *Yvonne, Princesse de Bourgogne* and *The marriage*. More recently Victor Garcia, in partnership with Spain's leading tragic actress Nuria Espert, has made himself the foremost interpreter of Garcia Lorca, while Lavelli and Savary have turned increasingly to opera and the classics, in Savary's case with some very surprising results.

It is entirely natural that Garcia, Lavelli and Savary have been thought of as the heirs of Artaud. These men themselves, however, have wisely taken their distance from Artaud whom they recognise only as a prophet of a tendency which coincides with their own practices rather than as a direct influence. Garcia named Genet rather than Artaud as his major inspiration, while Lavelli claims to have been influenced by the theatrically staged mass spectacles of the Peronist revival in Buenos Aires. Their relationship with the Theatre of Cruelty is therefore different from that of Barrault, who experienced it as an immediate influence, or Brook who studied Artaud's writings and concluded that they must be received in their entirety, as a way of life, or not at all. The Argentinians, in contrast, entering the theatre at a time when Artaud's name was on everyone's lips and his sway over the avant-garde was starting to be reflected in practice, absorbed his ideas more by a process of osmosis, ideas which furnished a context for their own work rather than a direct stimulus. Certainly none of them seems to have been markedly affected by Artaud's precise idea of cruelty, nor even to have made extensive borrowings of the specific practices he advocated.

Yet, when their debt to Artaud is placed in perspective, the Latin-Americans can still be said to have come closer than anyone else in France to translating the general spirit of *Le Théâtre et son double*, if not its specific formula, into practice. Essentially, Artaud founded his hope for theatre on two developments: first, a return to ritual, that is to a magical and incantatory action which would speak to the senses and the emotions. Once the theatre had been purged of its logical-discursive aspects, it was ritual that would replace the descriptive and psychological content of theatre with a hyper-reality, abolishing at a stroke the barriers between spectator and spectacle, theatre and life. Secondly, and following from this, Artaud saw the need to break theatre's traditional dependency on the spoken word, the text, and the author. In both these fundamental respects Artaud anticipated the Latin-Americans' spectacles. Garcia and Lavelli, with their violent or mystical rituals, come closest to Artaud's concept of the director as a "maître de cérémonies sacrées". All three see it as axiomatic that the director is the supreme creative power in the theatre.

Victor Garcia

A small, intense, erratic man from a northern province of Argentina, Garcia was possibly the most daring and original creator of baroque spectacles in the 1960s and 1970s. At university he studied architecture and medicine, specialising in psychiatry, two interests which were strong influences on his work in theatre, though he gave up formal studies after four years to pursue interests in painting, dance, music and, eventually, theatre. Garcia disliked talking or writing about theatre but in his rare interviews he professed a feeling of hopelessness for what would appear to be an absurd and irrational activity: "The theatre is dead," he once declared. "I'm doomed to work in it, quite by chance, but it is hateful to me. I reject the bourgeois theatre in all its forms. I have no idea what should take its place... If I were a pure man I'd give up the theatre once and for all, it's rotten to the core... On the other hand, guerrilla and street theatre are useless, and all oppositional theatre too."[45] Having rejected his Catholic upbringing, and unable to find meaning or purpose in political action, it would seem that a hopeless, despairing quest for personal salvation was what led Garcia to create some of the most striking theatrical experiences of modern times. However, Garcia's professed pessimism is belied by other statements where he expressed a belief in the healing power of theatre, and by the intense dedication he brought to his productions. Moreover, one senses something of the showman's posturing in Garcia's public utterances, as well as the impatience of an intensely practical man who would far rather be working in a theatre than talking about it.

Garcia's studies in architecture and psychiatry showed in his use of the stage which he treated as an architectural space mirroring the inner space of the subconscious. It was a latent space where strong emotions and obsessions could be transcribed physically. Its language is the concrete one of scenic writing, which Garcia used to great effect to achieve a visceral impact operating through the senses, though the starting point and key to his productions was the scenic space itself. "The important thing," he said, "is to find an architecture. I dislike talking in traditional terms, stage left, stage right and so on, I prefer to talk in terms of horizontals, diagonals, north, south. . . I think, now, I have managed to master space; in a single second I can present a kaleidoscopic vision seen from several different angles."[46] Garcia's claim to be the master of the stage space is fully borne out by productions which show not merely a command of line but the much rarer ability to conceptualise complex constructions and movements in three dimensions.

Spatial experiments were at the origin of one of Garcia's earliest spectacles, a production of Arrabal's *Le Cimetière des voitures* (Dijon, 1966 and Paris, 1968). Garcia was invited to mount this production by Michel Parent who, as organiser of the Festival Dramatique de Bourgogne, had initiated a series of experiments in theatrical simultaneity. The idea was to explore various forms of theatre, for example concurrent actions and multiple performance spaces, in pursuit of a theatrical aesthetic which corresponded to the complexity and simultaneousness of experience in the modern world. *Le Cimetière des voitures*, the fourth and last of these experiments, was performed by a cast of local amateurs in a hanger normally used for the Dijon gastronomic fair. Here Garcia was able to design and built a multiple-stage, semi-environmental performance space. One acting area consisted of a rising platform running along three walls of the hall. Enclosed within this, irregular groups of seats were set at different levels: these seats could swivel to enable the spectators to follow the action through a full circle. The main acting area, in the form of an L on two levels connected by a ramp, was placed diagonally in the centre of the hall, and to one side of it there was a smaller, steeply raked free-standing stage. The boldest feature, however, was the disposition of the old cars in which a lot of the action was to take place. These were suspended in mid-air from a superstructure of scaffolding and could be raised or lowered by chains and pulleys.

Le Cimetière des voitures in 1966 was a double revelation. Not only was it Garcia's first major success, it was also the first production to realise fully the potential of Arrabal's unique dramatic world. A Spaniard by birth, Arrabal projects a surreal, often nightmarish vision of fantasies and obsessions. The distinctive quality of his plays stems not from a coherent dialogue but from a pattern of strange images which have their own irrational logic. His scenes are alternately solemn, bizarre, tender, violent, scatological, sometimes pushed to the extreme limits of what is bearable, and frequently take on a ritualistic character. Although intensely personal in inspiration, they have mystical qualities and at their best they can attain the level of myth. These plays demand a style of production unknown to theatre-goers and directors before the 1960s. Their guiding principle is baroque excess, in the images that proliferate as well as in the emotions they generate. This gives them great potential power, but unless they are presented within a rigorously disciplined and ordered framework, and with an authentic sense of ritual, they readily appear banal and self-indulgent. The earliest productions of Arrabal, although mounted by directors of great skill, had tended to short-change his plays, either by giving sparse absurdist interpretations on barren stages[47] or, in the case of *Le Grand Cérémonial*, by presenting a fantasised ceremony of love as a psycho-drama in a naturalistic style better suited to Tennessee Williams.[48] The result was to make what should have been an hallucinatory ritual resemble a pathological case-study.

Garcia proved an ideal director to exploit the volcanic potential of Arrabal's theatre as an irrational mode of exploration of the psyche. Sharing the same cultural background as Arrabal, Garcia was able instinctively to grasp the mysticism and anticlericalism of his play, and the sacred and blasphemous character of its rituals. Moreover Arrabal himself, recognising the essentially imagistic nature of his theatre, is fully in accord with directors, like Garcia, for whom the text is a spring-board for spectacles of their own invention.[49] This was just as well, because in Garcia's production the precise, quasi-mathematical structure of Arrabal's play was totally dislocated and the text itself was submerged in a powerful and theatrically brilliant spectacle.

One critic testified to the power of the production in terms normally used for religious rather than theatrical experiences. Artaud would have approved of this: "After seeing Arrabal's *Le*

Cimetière des voitures I remain haunted by it, shocked, fascinated, altered, to the point where everything unconnected with it suddenly seems diminished, obscured, discoloured. A prodigy! Before Arrabal, after Arrabal: the second part of my life began on the evening I saw the play."[50] An impressive bouquet indeed, but it should have been offered to the director because what audiences witnessed was not so much a production of a play by Arrabal as a "spectacle Garcia" inspired by the world of Arrabal's play. For one thing, a point not grasped by some critics at the time, it was not a single play but a collage of texts, Garcia interposing three quite separate (though thematically related) playlets into the principal text. All were played continuously in the set of scaffolding and wrecked cars described above. The performance began with *Oraison*, a bleak little dialogue between a couple standing below the suspended coffin of a child they have just killed, resolving to try to be good according to the scriptures. Garcia used this as an overture introducing the central themes of innocence, cruelty, goodness and religion. The action then broadened to *Le Cimetière des voitures*, an allegorical drama whose hero Emanou, a modern beatnik Christ-figure, is persecuted and crucified for trying to bring some goodness into the benighted world of down-and-outs living in a shanty town of scrap cars. In the middle of the main play Garcia placed *Les Deux Bourreaux*, a piece evoking the betrayal and execution of a father-figure. Arrabal's text is an ironic, melodramatic monologue, reeking of self-justifying religiosity, spoken by the mother who holds the stage with her two little sons while her husband's torture is evoked by off-stage noises. Garcia brought the implied action on to the stage with terrifying brutality. Leather-clad actors leaped athletically in and out of cars, slamming doors and boot lids, hammering with fists on the metal, and finally pinning the father down on a car bonnet where he was put to death. The spoken words were completely eclipsed by the physical action, producing a more direct but perhaps no less excruciating effect than that of the text. The interlude also prepared the way for the second half of *Le Cimetière*, which was played in an atmosphere of mounting violence and punctuated at increasingly short intervals by police on motor-cycles roaring round the hall in pursuit of their quarry.

Towards the end of the second act, after the arrest of Emanou, Garcia inserted a third short piece, *La Communion solennelle*. While the solemn ritual of a young girl being attired and made ready for her first communion was played on the central acting area, another action developing in counterpoint showed Emanou ritualistically beaten and prepared for execution. Arrabal's text ends bleakly, after the arrest and execution of the Christ-figure Emanou, with the unheeding inhabitants of the shanty town preparing for a new day, indifferent to the drama that has occurred in their midst. Garcia invented an entirely new ending where the crucifixion, with its implied futility, was followed by a resurrection, thereby completely overturning the pessimism of Arrabal's play but doing so with one of the most fantastic and awesome images realised by any director. Emanou, stripped naked save for a loin cloth, was chained face-upwards on a motor-cycle with his arms outstretched on the cross of its handlebars. A slow, wailing Way of the Cross procession dragged him round the three sides of the theatre, coming eventually to the centre where the motorcycle was fastened to chains and hoisted vertically into the air, in a theatre now silent except for the clanking of chains. Emanou's mortified body on its bizarre cross remained suspended above the audience, bathed in a ghastly green light, for some moments. Then the actors who had gathered below rose from their knees and with cries of joy and alleluiahs lowered the body and bore it aloft in a triumphal procession around the theatre.

As I have noted, *Le Cimetière des voitures* was mounted at the request of Michel Parent as part of a series of experiments in theatrical simultaneity. In practice the production involved only a limited form of simultaneity. Although the action moved to various locations within the building and was designed to be viewed from a variety of perspectives, it was for the most part performed sequentially, only *La Communion solennelle* being played concurrently with the scourging of Emanou. The justification for using a multiple stage therefore rested on the physical integration of the audience in the action, and it is true that in Dijon the production gained considerably in power from having the action performed behind, among and above the spectators. This justification was lost when Garcia mounted the spectacle in Paris two years later. The only theatre available was the little Théâtre des Arts, a conventional playhouse with neither the dimensions nor the flexibility, even after it was gutted, to accommodate the original concept. The result was that the main action was confined to an end-on stage extended by an apron surmounted by the scaffolding and cars, and a rather cramped runway around the other three walls. As in Dijon the spectators were given swivelling seats. However, except for the two processions in the final fifteen minutes – the only part of the spectacle to survive the move with all its hallucinatory power undiminished – the staging came to seem gratuitous in a way which was not the case in Dijon. Even so, this somewhat bowdlerised production was greeted as a sensation and ran for two seasons.

If his design for *Le Cimetière* already revealed an extraordinary capacity to develop an unfolding action in three dimensions, the environment he conceived with Wladimir Cardoso for Genet's *Le Balcon* (São Paulo, 1969) was an even more striking example of Garcia's architectural vision. Nothing resembling this sensational production, which ran for three years in Brazil, has ever been created in Europe. However, there are film extracts which give a stunning impression of Garcia's audacity. In the shell of a completely gutted theatre he constructed a vertical funnel of iron trellis-work extending some eighty feet from the basement to the roof. The spectators were perched around this, on many tiers of circular galleries, creating a voyeuristic effect as they observed the action taking place on a huge transparent elevator disc, in cages which also rose and fell independently, and on a helical catwalk which could be let down from the roof. Secondary images of the action were reflected up from an enormous parabolic mirror below, and the entire structure was lit by innumerable projections of white light from every possible angle. This amazing, vertiginous design for Genet's house of illusions remains without parallel, even for Garcia, though some of its features reappear in his more conventional designs, notably the complex lighting system and the use of steel and other non-yielding materials to create a hard, metallic, de-humanising environment.

Experiments with scenography, of which the two cases mentioned above are extreme examples, might appear purely formal. However, Garcia's mastery of the stage, and more generally of all the production materials, was in reality a technique intended ultimately to provide him with mastery over the spectator. In all his spectacles it quickly became evident that the performance was the context for a psychic conflict where the spectator was expected to submit to an excoriating process. Behind this approach lies a concept, ostensibly similar to Artaud's, of theatre as a therapeutic operation, and a belief that in man's present degenerate state it is only through the senses (the *skin* as Artaud said) that communication can be effective. Therapeutic is a term which probably applies more aptly to Garcia than to Artaud. Artaud's hope for theatre was that it would provoke a state of heightened consciousness in which the ultimate good lay precisely in that lucid awareness of certain unalterable realities: staring the forces of cosmic cruelty in the face would not neutralise them but would at least restore man to his wholeness. The healing process envisaged by Garcia, in contrast, is meliorist in a different sense, nearer to Freud than to Artaud, because it involves self-discovery and the unblocking of the subconscious. Although the methods adopted sometimes resemble atavistic exorcist rituals, the ideas behind them – overcoming inhibitions to release suppressed emotions, neuroses or fears buried in the subconscious – derive from modern psychoanalytic theory. Initially the stimulus is a subjective one – "I want to know where I'm going myself, track down the deceit and the fear and conquer them"[51] – but Garcia also extends the process to implicate his contemporaries. "If I create violent spectacles," he said, "it's because they reflect our world of violence and fear."[52] Like Camus who in 1944 identified fear as the dominant emotion of the age, Garcia too sees fear as modern man's principal demon, but he addresses the problem in terms appropriated from psycho-analysis: "Fear: the primordial, fundamental fear, the fear that is the root of all anguish, all aggressiveness, the fear of death. If, thanks to science and knowledge of the mind, man can become more aware of the universe, if he can understand death, he will destroy its mystery, and the principal cause of anguish will be destroyed too. . . Our entire existence will be transformed. Perhaps we will suffer from other neuroses, but the world will be perceived with dazzling clarity; we'll live in a hallucinatory state, the state that at present we can only attain through the morbid hyper-awareness provoked by drugs. I'm not making any judgement, just stating a fact: drugs make us forget fear but they don't destroy it. On the other hand, by analysing the mind rationally, if we have the courage of self-knowledge, we can achieve not a morbid hyper-awareness but a complete, balanced state of awareness; then the fear that holds us back will disappear".[53]

Garcia's overriding aim in designing *Le Cimetière des voitures* was to involve the audience as closely as possible in a collective emotional experience, an aim which fitted in well with Parent's enthusiasm for simultaneity. What Garcia only later came to see is that the *spatial* integration of actors and audience is only one way of involving spectators in a performance, and not necessarily the most effective one. As Garcia subsequently realised, the question of how an audience becomes involved in a spectacle is actually far more complex than a simple coefficient of physical proximity to the action. It seems, for example, that surrounding spectators with action, and therefore forcing them to twist and turn to follow it, may be closer to how we experience reality in life but in the theatre it appears contrived and can simply break the spell. Such questions were important to Garcia who aimed to introduce a relationship of domination and submission between himself and the audience, the rôle allocated to the spectator being what Arrabal called an "heureux coupable" or consenting victim. In productions after *Le Cimetière des voitures* Garcia's approach came to lay greater stress on developing images of sustained concentration and intensity, which may well be viewed from a constant vantage point, rather than physically engulfing the audience in an action. Hence his later policy of associating his scenography, whose creative power was amply demonstrated by earlier productions, with inherently richer texts such as those of Genet and Garcia Lorca, or even Arrabal's *L'Architecte et l'Empereur d'Assyrie*, a richer, more sustained script than the episodic *Cimetière des voitures*.

Another fruitful development led Garcia to pay more attention to the rôle of the actor. Garcia himself detested the self-exposure of acting[54] and his early productions were unmistakably those of a non-acting scenographer, displacing the actors in overwhelming mechanical structures and relying on the *mise en scène* as a whole to fill the audience's mind with sound and visual images. This they certainly did, but Garcia soon realised that a deeper and more sustained response can be provoked if the emotion originates in a human presence. His work with actors was aimed at intensifying their emotional charge and concentrated on the internal processes that energise the performance. To this extent it was similar to Grotowski's at the Laboratory Theatre. But whereas Grotowski's work involves a painstaking, quasi-mystical search for self-transcendence, Garcia's was directed towards a more brutal self-transgression. Rehearsals were highly charged affairs and could be traumatic for the actors. He expected the cast to be familiar with the text before rehearsals began and would not waste time (as he saw it) discussing it with them. Nor was much attention given to technique as such, since he assumed that his actors would find the necessary agility and stamina to express themselves provided the emotional motivation was present. The training was therefore psychological and spiritual and aimed at removing the blockages that impede self-expression. His first priority was to master the actors and break them in, using alternately brutal and cajoling techniques to disorientate them. He conditioned the actors by suggesting images with no direct reference to the text, and used bodily contact, massage and sensory rhythms to create a climate, gradually goading them into states of primitive emotion. To actors trained in conventional methods this could be highly de-stabilising, as Garcia propelled them into unfamiliar territory without the reassuring props of character, dialogue or acquired techniques to fall back on. A state of dependency resulted: "Then they fall in love with me, like a patient with his psychiatrist. I can be extremely demanding but I treat them tenderly. I reassure them; they are anxious because they are afraid of losing themselves. I take them in my hands and tame them. I aim to make them express something they didn't even know was inside them. When they discover a new personality, when they have lost their habits and mannerisms, then I set them free."[55] Garcia called this a "de-humanising" process because it robbed the actor of his habitual self. Its ultimate purpose, however, was to rid the actor of his persona in order to liberate the deeper self and make him more human.

After this initial conditioning, later rehearsals would focus more on the action. Here too Garcia did not allow the actors to work directly on the text, forcing them instead to refer constantly to the feelings provoked by their situation. The idea behind this was that the actors must be neither themselves nor the characters they play but receptacles for emotions born in the heat of the moment. From this arose Garcia's theory of movement as a gestual code for transposing emotions. He explained: "Movement must be as far removed as possible from realistic actions and must always be spontaneous and white hot. Movement is the product of an emotional stimulus. What interests me is the connection between the stimulus and the reaction; a movement should be rich in intentions, and it's the richness of intention that stimulates the audience."[56]

These ideas were implemented in his production of *The Architect and the Emperor of Assyria* at the National Theatre in London (1971) where the difference in emphasis with *Le Cimetière des voitures* was readily apparent. Admittedly the performance began, in darkness, with an aggressive sensory attack on the audience who were blinded by powerful searchlights raking the auditorium from the stage and deafened by the roar of an aircraft which finally crashed with an ear-splitting explosion. This was the means whereby Arrabal's self-styled Emperor arrives on a desert island where he meets his Man Friday partner, the primitive Architect. What followed this preliminary assault, however, was more dependent on inner intensity than external effects. On a completely bare stage dressed only with a myriad of bright white lights, and with the aid of just two props, a parachute and a fork-lift truck which assisted in their metamorphoses, two virtually naked performers gave a dazzling display of mythomania running through the gamut of human relations: mother-child, master-slave, doctor-patient, penitent-confessor, judge-accused, executioner-condemned man and so on.

Garcia saw the play in terms of a quest for identity and used it as a basis for exploring the neuroses and latent emotions below the surface of all men, an approach which disappointed some critics who sensed, rightly, that the play suggested an impressive allegory that was never developed in the production. It is true that Lavelli's production of the same play four years earlier was an altogether richer affair, a solemn ritual with mythic dimensions bringing Civilisation and Nature face to face, and one can be forgiven for preferring this, as a reading of the play, to Garcia's frenzied psycho-drama. But whatever one's views of Garcia's interpretation, the London spectacle was outstanding for the sheer energy of its emotional forces causing the play to beat with a physical pulse far stronger than any text. Ronald Bryden writing for *The Observer* found the play to amount to little more than a gallery of private obsessions, but added: "I can only explain my enjoyment of much of the evening as a response to its performances... Hopkins's Emperor is the best opportunity he's yet had to display one of the most formidable theatrical presences to emerge since Albert Finney and Nicol Williamson. Bullish, deep-throated, agile and sly, he's a dynamo of contained energy. When his pale blue eyes rake the audience, it's hard not to turn your own away."[57] It should be noted that Garcia, who speaks only a little English, was here directing through an interpreter, an arrangement which probably contributed to the marked displacement of the spoken word in the production. But even allowing for this, the production was consistent with Garcia's usual method of treating the script only as a guiding thread and concentrating on a physical language to communicate not the text itself but the emotional charge it contains.

The inherent danger in Garcia's approach is that, however theatrically brilliant the *mise en scène*, its success or failure remains entirely at the mercy of the actor's temperament and reactions. Garcia obviously liked to feel in total control of every aspect of the production, even to the extent of manipulating human emotions and using them, he said, in the way a composer uses notes in a musical composition.[58] Against this powerful ambition has to be set the fact that actors and actresses responded to his method with varying degrees of receptiveness.

According to Christiane Tourlet who followed the rehearsals at the Old Vic, Garcia's unorthodox approach proved to be particularly rewarding with Anthony Hopkins who eventually crossed the threshold of fear and self-doubt and became capable of a totally unselfconscious discharge of authentic emotion. On the other hand Jim Dale, playing the Architect, having on one occasion achieved a similar possessed state, later relapsed into inhibition, becoming resentful and unco-operative at times. Dale, said Tourlet, "showed a sense of inferiority with Hopkins, betraying a fear of the irrational."[59] Tourlet's account of the rehearsals sheds a retrospective light on the noticeable imbalance between the two characters in the performance. The Emperor clearly dominated the Architect who in turn appeared uncertain and ingratiating, which is possibly the opposite of what Arrabal intended.

Garcia unwittingly demonstrated both the strengths and weaknesses of his method in the most convincing way by mounting two productions of the same play with different casts. His first production of Genet's *Les Bonnes*, performed in Spanish by Nuria Espert's company, was a spectacularly resounding triumph; the second production, with an almost identical *mise en scène* but performed by a French cast, was a public and critical failure.[60]

The suggestion to stage *Les Bonnes* came from Nuria Espert who for ten years had pursued a courageous policy of introducing Spanish audiences to a modern repertoire, including Sartre and Brecht. She intended to stage a double bill consisting of *Les Bonnes* and a short play by her exiled fellow countryman Arrabal, *Les Deux Bourreaux*. At the suggestion of Arrabal, who had praised Garcia's production of *Le Cimetière des voitures*, she invited Garcia to direct the company. In the event the Arrabal play was felt to be too dangerous by the authorities who banned both plays on the eve of the opening night. Two weeks later the company received permission to perform *Les Bonnes* alone.

Les Deux Bourreaux, a play with obvious references to the Spanish Civil War, presented a clear political challenge. *Les Bonnes* is actually no less subversive but in a deeper, less obvious way, unrelated to any specific political context. As Genet himself made plain, the play is not a protest on behalf of servants;

it is intended, rather, to project a distorted image of oppression which is both a social condition and a state of mind. Yet, while we are obviously not meant to be persuaded that we are watching "real" servants, Genet places the ritual in a semi-realistic frame, in a domestic context which we recognise as an image, albeit dislocated and off-key, of reality. This lingering realism in *Les Bonnes*, roughly mid-way between the naturalism of Genet's first play *Haute Surveillance* and the purely imaginary action of his later works, has sometimes misled directors, and may indeed be one reason why *Les Bonnes* has often been seen as a lesser play than *Le Balcon* or *Les Nègres*.

Garcia's hyper-theatrical production, though not faithful to the letter of the play, perhaps came closer to its spirit than any previous production. Stripping it of every last vestige of realism, he constructed a pure self-referring ritual out of the maids' passions: the envy, loathing and above all self-loathing of oppressed people. Garcia wanted to present these passions in their purest and most universal aspect. He ignored the setting described by Genet – a cloyingly elegant Louis XV bedroom which Jouvet and Bérard had reproduced in a stylised form in the original (1947) production – and placed the action in a non-representational space evoking, perhaps, the form of an egg or a slightly futuristic chapel. (Garcia himself thought of it as a "huge metallic spittoon").[61] The stage floor tilted at an alarming angle towards the front. Upstage it was enclosed by fourteen vertical rectangular panels of polished aluminium, forming an open ovoid. As well as creating a hard, de-humanising climate, accentuated by the whiteness of the lighting, the aluminium gave a hall of mirrors effect, trapping the maids in a maze of distorted reflections. Each panel pivoted vertically, allowing the actresses to pass through to the wings at any point with a resounding metallic clash. Downstage centre there was a shallow circular pit lined with black satin – in realistic terms, Madame's bed, but in this ritualised production a gravitational point with the sacred character of an altar.

Like all Garcia's productions this was spectacle built around and upon the text and the result was an outstandingly visual and sensory performance. The dialogue was intoned and chanted or murmured hypnotically or screamed at fever pitch.

In parallel with the script Garcia developed a series of ritualistic set-pieces such as the ceremonial dressing of Claire-Madame, the opening sequence which lasted a full ten minutes. The emptiness of the stage, the absence of furniture and accessories, enforced an expressive physical style of movement that sprang from the actresses' contact with the stage floor on which they strutted, grovelled and scrabbled in a totally unconstrained display of emotion. Even when they were upright the steep angle of the floor ensured that naturalistic movement was impossible, so that the maids would be seen tottering precariously in a derisory imitation of Madame's bearing, or descending the slope in a rush of fury. The movements were contained within a complex *mise en place*, a studied geometrical pattern of laterals, diagonals and, above all, circular movements to heighten the impression of ritual. Overall, the result was an intensely concentrated performance with the outer form of a black mass but inspired from within by the maids' searing passions.

Its crowning glory was the final ceremony of transfiguration and apotheosis where Claire, dressed as Madame, commits suicide. In this it followed the pattern of Garcia's other productions, all of them involving a descent into a nightmare world of cruelty and oppression followed by images of his own invention to produce a liberating catharsis. At the end of *Le Balcon* the virtually naked actors all clambered up the sides of the iron tube leaving Genet's claustrophobic world of brothel and illusion far below as they climbed towards daylight and freedom. *Le Cimetière des voitures*, also playing against the logic of the text, went beyond the crucifixion to the resurrection and ended in a joyous festival. In *Les Bonnes*, too, the final image was a Christian one, as the author doubtless intended. "The highest modern drama," wrote Genet, "has for two thousand years and every day been expressed in the sacrifice of the mass."[62] Where other directors have seen Claire's suicide as a symbol of failed revolt and a futile act of self-mutilation, Garcia saw the entire play as preparing for the blissful, exultant moment of her apotheosis as she raises the poisoned infusion to her lips.

What is remarkable about this Spanish-language production is that wherever it was performed, in Belgrade or Vienna, Paris or London, Florence or Persepolis, it received the same high acclaim, showing how completely Garcia had achieved a theatrical language which made speech superfluous. Matthieu Galey wrote: "One only has to listen without understanding – in order to understand. Beyond the text, the ceremony's underlying intentions are made unmistakably clear, and perhaps even more so than if one followed the text word for word."[63] Galey went on to describe the production as an X-ray of the work, penetrating the text to reveal with greater clarity its internal structure and significance. Harold Hobson, who saw the show when it came to the Aldwych for the 1971 World Theatre Season, made an even larger claim: "in the eighty minutes of Victor Garcia's production of *The maids* we make more progress towards understanding Jean Genet than we have done in all the previous twenty years."[64]

It was a very different story when Garcia directed the play in French (Espace Pierre Cardin, 1971). Although the production was a close replica of the first it failed to generate the magic or heat of the original. With the same stage business, it nevertheless lasted some twenty minutes longer than the first, perhaps indicating a lack of tautness. Critics complained at what seemed an inordinately long, heavy-footed performance and – in spite of the fact that the text was now in French – a lack of clarity and purpose. The reasons for its failure are not mysterious. The production was compromised from the start by Garcia's lack of enthusiasm for the revival, reflected in infrequent attendance at rehearsals and more than usually capricious behaviour. Like many artists, Garcia lost interest in things once the original creative phase was over. With *Les Bonnes* the reaction was particularly strong because the rehearsals coincided with those for *The Architect and the Emperor of Assyria*, a taxing production capable on its own of absorbing all Garcia'a attention. For many rehearsals Garcia was content to leave things to his assistant director Michel Launay. A second problem lay in the casting. Whether Garcia's choice of actresses, old acquaintances from the Université du Théâtre des Nations, was simply wrong from the start, or whether something could have been salvaged if Garcia had taken a firmer hold, one cannot know. Whatever the reason, the chain of stimulus-reaction-stimulus on which Garcia depends to generate emotional energy in the performance and thence in the audience was never forged. Critics were most severe with Sylvie Belai (Solange) who appeared to be in a world of her own, giving an apparently mechanical and arbitrarily stylised display with no inner motivation, and fatally undermining her partner's otherwise creditable performance. Denis Bablet, comparing the two productions of *Les Bonnes*, wrote that in the Spanish performance "the two maids complemented each other perfectly. Each provided a vocal and gestual counterpoint to the other, the contrasts between them seemed to be a continual testing of an equilibrium that kept reasserting itself, and the two characters ended by becoming one." In the French production, in contrast, "the two maids confronted each other but there was never any dialectic exchange in their opposition. Instead of harmony there was a lack of contact, in place of dialogue, a refusal to communicate. If Michèle Oppenot gave her all, Sylvie Belai seemed to be in a different world. The relation between them was falsified, not only by the lack of a unified approach but because the mechanism of stimulus and reaction was disrupted."[65]

After *Les Bonnes* Garcia recovered his position with highly acclaimed productions of Lorca's *Yerma* (Madrid, 1970 and Paris, 1973) and Valle-Inclan's *Divinas Palabras* (*Divine words*, Madrid, 1975 and Théâtre National de Chaillot, 1976), both performed in Spanish with Nuria Espert's company. Until he broke with Espert in 1977 Garcia found a more stable context for his experiments working with actors who went along with his methods in a company which shared his language and culture. Such stability made failures like *Les Bonnes* less likely, but with Garcia the margin of error remained wide. As Nuria Espert, whom he once tried to kill, wrote of him: "The thing about Victor was that he always wanted to plunge the depths, to push things to the bitter end – and even further. It was true of his theatre productions and it was true of his life. . . In his productions, as in his life, he touched the skies and he plunged the depths."[66] And as the two productions of *Les Bonnes* underline, his highly personal interpretations of the plays he directed and his no less individual method of energising the performance allowed for no half measures between total success and total failure.

Garcia's death in 1982 at the age of 47 robbed the theatre world of one its boldest innovators. In one of his last productions, *Gilgamesh* (Théâtre National de Chaillot, 1979) based on fragments recording the life of the 28th century BC Mesopotamian ruler, and performed in Arabic, he experimented with an even more risky performance method. The actors' movements and positions were not rehearsed and fixed in advance but had to respond to the rhythms created by light and sound effects. Garcia himself controlled the spectacle's rhythm, introducing subtle variations and making each performance a unique event.[67]

It is a truism to say that the actors make or break a production but with Garcia's productions this was especially the case, for two reasons. First, because of the way Garcia ignored the text and built his spectacles around the play's inner action. The spectacle then became the vehicle by which meaning is communicated, perhaps supplemented by the text but more often supplanting the text, to such an extent that it was quite possible for the text to become indecipherable without there being any loss of meaning. Normally, when faced with an unconvincing performance in the theatre, the audience can at least fall back on "the play", *i.e.* the text, whereas in Garcia's productions, where the performance *was* the play, there was no comparable safety-net. And, secondly, because in squeezing emotion out his actors Garcia demanded something which neither talent, professional qualities nor technique can supply, and has to do more with inner resources. Tapping the actor's psyche as Garcia aimed to do, especially when starting afresh with a different cast for each production, must ultimately remain a hit-or-miss business. At its best, when the "white heat" Garcia talked about was generated, the result could be nothing less than electrifying. By the same token, when the vital spark was absent there would be nothing in the lifeless shell of the production to engage the audience in the spectacle. In other words, using terms not quite as Brook intended them, the result could be Holy Theatre or it could be Deadly Theatre.

Jérôme Savary and the Grand Magic Circus

Even more than Garcia, Savary makes the freest possible use of the liberties accorded to him in a theatre given over to the reign of the director. The theatre, he says, is "a language for yourself, not for putting on someone else's plays".[68] Accordingly, in his progression from Master of Ceremonies of the Grand Théâtre Panique in the 1960s to Ringmaster of the Grand Magic Circus in the 1970s, Savary eventually broke completely with dramatic writing to create a world of festive spectacle which has very little in common with theatre proper. Like Garcia his starting point was impatience with conventional text-based theatre which he described as "a touching museum of Balzacian society in its death throes".[69] His distinctive contribution to its renewal has been to bring the spectacle and showmanship of the circus and fairground to his productions. His is a theatre of greasepaint, false noses, trapeze artistes, percussion instruments and fireworks.

After training as a musician and painter Savary became involved in theatre at the Université du Théâtre des Nations where he acted in Garcia's student production of *Ubu roi* (1965). He also worked briefly as a designer for Jean-Marie Serreau, before concluding that stage design was an absurd, out-dated function.[70] His own first spectacle, *Les Boîtes* (1966) was a free-flowing episodic piece of staging using film, music and animals. Imagining that in order for it to be a valid production it had to be performed in a "proper" theatre, he hired the Théâtre de Paris for the production, a costly mistake that suggested to him the need for an alternative form of production outside the existing theatre network. His next production was *Le Radeau de la Méduse* (1967), composed by Savary himself and inspired by Géricault's painting of the life-raft carrying survivors of the sunken frigate Medusa. Savary staged the action on a raft suspended at a tilt above the stage and visible through a fish-net stretched from the balcony to the stage. The audience seated below could see only a writhing mass of bodies covered in slime and algae, and the net gradually filling up with bloodied limbs as the passengers fell to eating one another. This production was also a commercial failure.

In 1966 he met Arrabal, Topor and Jodorowsky and became involved in their *panique* "anti-movement", as they called it. *Panique*, named after the buffoonish god Pan, was the name adopted by Arrabal to distinguish his brand of theatre from that of the Absurdists. *Le Panique* was defined by Arrabal as "a way of being, presided over by confusion, humour, terror, chance and euphoria".[71] It was formulated as a non-dogmatic, all-embracing and unconstrained approach to art and life, and its main form of expression was the *fête-spectacle*. In Arrabal's case this stood for a ceremonial theatre that celebrates the confusion of life, mingling cruelty and love, lyricism and burlesque, the sordid and the sublime – "le ciel et la merde" as he put it. For the Mexican Jodorowsky, however, it implied a new performance art which he called the *éphémère panique*, an unscripted spectacle whose aim was to generate the collective euphoria of the fiesta. The programme of *éphémères paniques* which he staged in Paris (American Centre, 24 May 1965) when doves and butterflies were released into the air and live chickens decapitated, was based on scenarios by Arrabal and Topor but flowed into a formless happening generated by improvisation and chance.

Out of Savary's association with the "panicos" the Grand Théâtre Panique was formed in 1966 with Savary as its President. It boasted an impressive list of patrons including Buñuel, Mandiargues, Klein, Copi and Sternberg. In fact it never really existed except as a nominal entity which lent its name to two productions, one of Arrabal's *Le Couronnement* directed by Ivan Henriques in the tiny Mouffetard theatre (1966) and Savary's own production of Arrabal's *Le Labyrinthe* (Théâtre Daniel-Sorano, Vincennes, 1967).

It was in directing *Le Labyrinthe*, which began as a text-based production and evolved in stages towards a more circus-like spectacle, that Savary formulated his idea of festive theatre. Not that there would appear to be anything festive about Arrabal's play, a Kafka-esque nightmare of persecution set in a lavatory in the centre of a vast maze of sheets hung out to dry in a seemingly endless park. The central character's futile attempts to escape and his efforts to elucidate his predicament with characters who appear alternately solicitous and hostile, lead inexorably to his trial and condemnation for an unspecified crime. As a text it suffers from a too obvious and verbose dialogue, spinning webs of unreasonable logic in long speeches that could have come straight from Kafka. Nevertheless it contains some provoking images – the central motif of the maze, the disturbing figure of a fellow-prisoner inexplicably chained to the lavatory, the treacherous and amorphous texture of reality – which offer scope for the imaginative director. Savary not only seized on those but added many more of his own in a production which he described as a "Dionysian festival".

The spectacle imagined by Savary was nightmarish in its own way, but more in the style of a macabre pantomime. He injected a note of derision, turning it into an enormous, noisy farce of callousness and persecution. He also made it into an extravaganza of spectacle. There was already a dash of circus, with Savary himself conducting the show with the help of cymbals and drums on a platform suspended above the stage. The actors also carried instruments, using them to underline the action with snatches of Mozart or jazz or percussion noises. There were live fowl and a goat, and six new characters who paraded like mannequins or stood motionless, out-staring the audience. The lavatory featured prominently as an erotic object and the judge-cum-father figure became an obscene wine-guzzling figure swinging on a trapeze above the actors' heads.

But that was only the starting point. When Savary took *Le Labyrinthe* to London (Mercury Theatre, 1968) he began a process which eventually led to the text being totally discarded. The cast for the London production was recruited on the spot, most of them English or American. Since they did not all speak French, and because there was insufficient time for rehearsals, Savary outlined the plot and told them to improvise.[72] He also told them to act for themselves, not the public, so that instead of giving the impression of a performance addressed to spectators it would generate a contagious sense of freedom. Left to their own devices, the cast revealed unexpected talents which they incorporated into the show, reciting Shakespeare, juggling or breathing fire. Dorothy Knowles reported: "The performance differed from day to day, the actors cutting out what they did not like and performing only what they did like. On at least one occasion the actor playing the part of Bruno handed his rôle over to another actor half-way through the performance, and proceeded to exorcize his own demons by swinging out over the heads of the audience on a rope which hung down from the ceiling. A man with a hairy chest wearing a hat, a slip, and women's suspenders which held up long stockings, fired a toy pistol at the audience. A singer sang Spanish songs in the auditorium, and extras danced tangos on the stage and descended into the auditorium to drag spectators to their feet to dance with them in the gangways."[73] By now Arrabal's *Le Labyrinthe* had become entirely Savary's *Le Labyrinthe*.

There followed a tour of the United States where the company, now calling itself the Grand Panic Circus, played its increasingly spontaneous spectacle on university campuses and in New York, in a deconsecrated church. As the circus component developed to the point where it took over the show completely, Arrabal's name was dropped from the programme. The company also changed its name again, becoming Le Grand Magic Circus.

Le Labyrinthe, then, was not the realisation of a theatrical concept but the process by which Savary came to his idea of theatre. Or rather, the process through which he grew away from theatre. If he had approached *Le Labyrinthe* initially with the idea of revitalising theatre from within, by the following year he had decided there was nothing to be gained by salvaging a sinking ship. In an article dated 1968 he stated that theatre is still just as much as ever the lackey of literature, and protested about the difficulty of reconciling unscripted productions with the currently accepted notions of what constitutes theatre:

> You offer to mount a spectacle, they ask to see the text. You say there is no text or explain that the text is meaningless without the spectacle that goes with it, and they laugh in your face. And yet Artaud has never been more quoted, total theatre has never been more talked about than it is today. The fact is that, for today's writers, theatre is only 'total' if you leave the text untouched. So what it comes down to is that an 'experimental' spectacle is nothing more than a conventional play with crazy

décor and costumes tacked on, a percussion instrument in the wings, and a bit of blasphemy.[74]

Not that he would dynamite the old theatres. Let the audiences of "three wholesale grocers, a menopausal *grande dame* and two students who are too naive to see that theatre is about as relevant to modern culture as Tchiang-Kai Chek is to China" have their classics.[75] Meanwhile, in parallel to the "théâtre de papa", as he calls it, but outside the existing theatre system, Savary will get on with the job of providing festive spectacles for the people. Savary's criticisms extend beyond the text-based avant-garde of Beckett, Ionesco etc. to include experimental theatre groups like Grotowski's Theatre Laboratory and Beck's Living Theatre which, he says, are intellectual and elitist while pretending to be in favour of participation. "We, on the contrary, try to appeal to everyone: illiterates as well as the intelligentsia."[76]

The "Grand Magic Circus et ses animaux tristes" – the menagerie of sad-eyed animals representing humanity is composed almost entirely of humans – is no circus in the ordinary sense, though it makes use of clowning and acrobatics. Nor is it theatre, except insofar as its shows use a format resembling the English pantomime tradition, with a series of burlesque episodes loosely following a central narrative. Rather, it is a mixture of these, together with a dash of carnival and the travelling fairground and a dose of philosophy injected by its director. Savary is a satirical fabulist with an inclination for popular myths which he proceeds to turn upside down.

All these ingredients were present in the company's first spectacle, *Zartan* which was created (in English) in Toronto in 1970. A farcical parody in thirty two tableaux of Edgar Burrough's legend of the white man dominating the world, it told the story of Tarzan's "unloved brother", Zartan, the puny son of English explorers who is brought up by monkeys but escapes from Africa only to discover that it is life in the civilised world that really merits the description "law of the jungle". The plot resembled an animated comic-strip, a preposterous adventure involving romance and pathos, shipwrecks and wars, oil-rich Sheiks and naked harems, the Queen of England disguised as a fortune-teller, bankers, impresarios and a feminist colony on Coney Island. The spectacle made much use of drums, nudity and fireworks and was played at a furious pace. Like *Le Labyrinthe* it was narrated and "conducted" by Savary with his trombone and drums. Occasionally he would break the action to improvise a new gag or harangue the public with a pseudo-philosophical piece of orange-box oratory. If the pace flagged, a smoke bomb or a rabbit and some mice released into the audience would quickly restore pandemonium.

After Toronto the company began a tour which took it to New York where *Zartan* was played in the La Mama Theatre and in Central Park, then through North America and to Paris in the spring of 1971 (Cité Universitaire). After playing to packed houses every night for three months they began another tour through Belgium, Holland and Switzerland, to Yugoslavia and Iran for the 5th Shiraz-Persepolis festival. Here, where the Shah's regime evidently agreed with Savary's claim that free play is subversive to authority, they were banned from appearing in the streets. The open-ended format meant that the spectacle was evolving all the while. In America, for example, a new episode was added showing Zartan applying his knowledge of "savages" to help the American forces in Vietnam massacre the enemy. The cast was changing too. French speakers were recruited for the European tours, and the company's presentational, as opposed to representational, style of performance meant that their individual talents could readily be incorporated into the show. One can well believe Savary's claim that no two performances were ever the same.

Contrary to *Le Labyrinthe* which started as a text-based production and evolved into an improvised spectacle, *Zartan* and Savary's subsequent shows began life as textless scenarios. Such texts as have been published are merely a record of what emerged during the run. Savary indicates that it takes about a year for a show to be fully "run in". The first step is to construct an outline of the action and to place the gags, but in the Magic Circus the action is dictated not by the plot but by the performance space. "Generally speaking," he says, "we first study the area in which we will perform: the windows and doors, wherever they may be, near the rafters or the ceiling. We also study the theatre's surroundings: the exits, entrances, the courtyard, etc." The aim is to exploit the locale's features, using them like a conjurer's box of tricks for surprising staging effects. Only then is the play discussed, but at this stage too the emphasis is on action not ideas: "I am particularly interested in bringing out or in arousing man's *animal-like* nature. That's why we use screams, onomatopoeias, grotesque ways of walking. . . This is how we begin constructing our framework."[77] Savary's recruitment method is equally unorthodox. The Grand Magic Circus operates as a collective, more like a commune than a company. There are no auditions: anyone who wants to join can do so, though newcomers are given very small parts to begin with. Those who stay on gradually take on more responsibilities, but not exclusively as actors because the collective's tendency is to discourage specialisation.

The Grand Magic Circus owes little to theorising and everything to the personality of its director. The formula it has evolved is a tailor-made medium for Savary's showmanship, his taste for carnival and his anarchic and satirical cast of mind that attacks authority and humbug with derision. To the extent that it claims any philosophical justification it is the simple one that humanity has lost its sense of playfulness and fun. Savary says: "People are sad because they have lost their animality, their sense of play, their sense of participating in games. With modern civilisation and TV man has become a spectator. The people don't sing any more."[78] Without forcing them to participate, the Grand Magic Circus aims at least to re-awaken the spectators to what they have lost. Savary believes that for people imprisoned in the cycle of work and everyday life and who receive their culture passively on television this can amount to a re-awakening to freedom, the freedom of play and self-expression.

In an ideal world festivals would happen naturally and regularly, arising spontaneously out of the people's desire for spectacle. Savary, to his credit, does not pretend that this is what happens when the Magic Circus comes to town, nor does he subscribe to the spurious notion which was fashionable at the time the Circus was created, of abolishing the distinction between theatre and life. He recognises that the commercial contract with spectators – necessary because, after all, the company must live and meet its expenses, and until recently Savary received no state subsidies – falsifies the relationship. Their performances, therefore, cannot be seen as proper substitutes for natural play, merely a limited, temporary but perhaps educative glimpse of what Savary believes to be missing from life. Not surprisingly he finds it is children who respond most naturally to the invitation to play, and he actually draws a clear distinction between the company's two types of activity: on the one hand daytime sessions for children, held in streets, parks and playgrounds, and on the other hand evening performances for adults and family audiences. The daytime sessions are free. Make-up and costumes are available and children and actors improvise together. Savary believes these sessions to be the most rewarding because "we don't play for the people, we play *with* them".[79] Spontaneous play of this kind is rare in the evening shows: not because the performances are directed (though they are) but because of the commercial relationship which makes the players more like court jesters than equal partners: "How can you imagine that a person can play *innocently* with someone who is paid by him?"[80] So, he says, the best that can be hoped for in these conditions is that the public, after being entertained for a few hours, will come away with a re-awakened sense of its lost freedom.

After the huge international success of *Zartan* Savary went on to create some ten subsequent spectacles, from *Robinson Crusoé* (1972), based on the theme of solitude in modern society, to *Bye-bye show-biz* (1985), a slick parody of musical comedy giving a satirical potted history of show business from its origins among the cave dwellers in the stone age to the rock age. Along the way he has turned his burlesque mockery to melodrama (*Mélodies du malheur*, 1980), love (*Les Grands Sentiments*, 1975), Arabian tales (*1001 nuits*, 1978), Aesop (*L'Histoire du cochon qui voulait maigrir*, 1984) and Perrault (*Cendrillon*, 1973). The latter, a modern version of Cinderella where the carriage became a Citroen 2CV, was sub-titled *La lutte des classes (The class struggle)*, showing that Savary had lost none of his ability to derive surprising lessons from popular stories. His *Cendrillon*, which nevertheless contrived to have a happy ending, showed the disastrous consequences of waiting for a magic wand to wave away oppression and exploitation. "Perrault," explained Savary, "was a dreadful reactionary preaching mediocrity and leaving the poor with the illusion of some wonderful good fairy." And he adds: "Like the national lottery."[81]

With shows such as these, whether one calls them theatre or circus, Savary has certainly fulfilled his promise of creating a genuinely popular form of spectacle. The Grand Magic Circus draws spectators from all ages and classes, many of them almost certainly not habitual theatre-goers. Part of the attraction lies precisely in its iconoclastic approach to all forms of cultural sacred cows, an irreverent attitude which invites the complicity of sophisticated and unsophisticated audiences alike. Over the years its performances have become extremely polished and professional while still retaining some of the original beguiling impression of amateurism and spontaneity. The formula, however, remains essentially that of *Zartan*, and seems to be wearing rather thin. The outrageously flimsy linking of adventures and tongue-in-cheek philosophical debunking, and most of all Savary's own towering presence, give the shows a distinct sameness and can ultimately leave one feeling that Savary has lost his ability to surprise – or that we have lost our capacity to be surprised. The Grand Magic Circus's strength and weakness is that it is so entirely the creation of one man. At the level of conception his spectacles would often benefit from a less facile treatment of themes. At the level of performance it is Savary who holds the shows together as narrator and leading performer. He is metaphorically, and often literally, a one-man band. This he does with incredible energy and authority, though even his keenest followers might concede that his tendency to use the productions as show-cases for his own versatility, especially when it turns to demagogy, can be tiring.

These defects are widely recognised, and almost universally pardoned because of the extraordinary skill and inventiveness the company brings to its performances. Nevertheless there have been times when one has wished to see its talents applied to something more substantial. Savary himself reached this conclusion in the late 1970s and has started producing plays from the repertoire again, as well as collectively scripted spectacles.

In 1975 Ivan Nagel, the innovative director of the Hamburg Schauspielhaus, invited him to direct the resident company in a production of a German classic, Büchner's *Leonce and Lena*. Savary surprised those who feared the worst by treating the text of the delicate fantasy-comedy with irreproachable respect, though the production had the vigour and directness of approach that marks all Savary's work.

However, it was the production of Molière's *Le Bourgeois gentilhomme* with the Grand Magic Circus (Théâtre de l'Est Parisien, 1981) that really showed what could happen when the company's special performance skills were applied to a major text. Savary, who had recently been appointed to take charge of the Centre Dramatique du Midi in Nice, was evidently aware of the irony of the iconoclastic Grand Magic Circus coming face to face with establishment culture, a situation which was mirrored in the performance itself. There was nothing decorous or restrained about this production which made full use of acrobats and belly dancers, jugglers and clowns, rock music as well as classical chamber music. The action started with a group of buskers coming to perform in front of M. Jourdain's house. While Molière's play ridiculed M. Jourdain's attempts to acquire the respectable cultural trappings of a wealthy bourgeois, the street artists gradually invaded the house until finally taking over the action completely in the riotous final ceremony where Jourdain is supposedly admitted to the brotherhood of cultured people. But this was not, as some critics supposed, a simple piece of self-indulgence. The production demonstrated, as David Bradby put it,[82] the triumph of low culture over high culture in a vigorous affirmation of the popular sources of both Molière's and Savary's art.

Jourdain himself, played by Savary with a measured, resonant voice recalling General de Gaulle, was a complex figure, ridiculous in his excesses, yet a fundamentally sympathetic character with a real, if misplaced, desire for knowledge. Instead of simply making fun of M. Jourdain for his ignorance and inept cultural pretentions, this production called into question the culture he aspired to. Not everyone approved – Matthieu Galey compared it to Dali painting a moustache on the Mona Lisa[83] – but most people were overwhelmingly positive in their response to an outstandingly lively and colourful performance.

Savary's *Le Bourgeois gentilhomme* must be one of the most explosive productions of Molière ever given. His attempts to follow up its success have produced mixed results. *Cyrano de Bergerac* (Théâtre Mogador, 1983), though not such an ideal vehicle for Savary's talents as Molière's comédie-ballet, was a huge public success, running for two seasons, and received the Prix Dominique for the year's best *mise en scène*. Offenbach's *La Belle Hélène* (Opéra Comique, 1984) was enjoyable and accomplished but with less of the satirical bite that one has come to expect of Savary. Recently, he has turned his attention to promoting new playwrights; his present company which he calls the N.T.P.M. (the Nouveau Théâtre Populaire de la Méditerranée) offers grants and production possibilities to writers from the Languedoc-Roussillon region. Meanwhile, one must continue to hope that Savary will one day realise his ambition of producing Shakespeare with the Grand Magic Circus in the Palais de Chaillot: the result should be worth waiting for.

Jorge Lavelli

Compared with Garcia's frenzied psycho-dramas and Savary's unconstrained festivals, Lavelli's sombre rituals appear almost ascetic. Not that they lack passion: Lavelli's world is as emotionally turbulent as Garcia's but in his work the irrational forces, instead of erupting with violent intensity, are contained within a precise framework of ritual. His productions have none of the flamboyant showmanship of Garcia's and Savary's: instead, they are studied and demanding, reflecting the temperament of a subtle, meticulous director who uses his art as a means of imposing some artificial, temporary order on a fundamentally crazy world.

Lavelli's intention is to create a theatre as far removed as possible from the everyday world, mirroring the inner life and provoking a voyage of inner self-discovery. He has no interest in forms which reproduce everyday situations. The principal defect of all realistic approaches, he believes, is that they contain emotion in a rational framework and reduce it to an intellectual experience. His own aim is to arouse emotions such as fear, wonder, mystery, on a more elemental sensory level. To this end he has invented a highly original stage language, precise and complete in itself, comprising a system of "signs" written in space and time. His productions weave subtle, complex patterns, subordinating speech, music, gesture, movement and the other visual components of costume, make-up and lighting, to an overall sense of purpose. All these elements have precise contributions to make and, more unusually, each is given more or less equal value, resulting in productions which are altogether more balanced than either Savary's or Garcia's.

Of the three leading Latin-Americans Lavelli is the one who adheres most closely to the scripts he directs. His analysis of a play is based on a detailed study of the text but what he extracts from it is not literal meaning so much as its expressive rhythm: the interplay of strong and weak moments, the dynamic states of crescendo and decrescendo, the exchanges between soloists and chorus. And at the level of staging again, although the verbal expression of ideas is not his object, it is still the dialogue that controls the performance. Lavelli explains: "I am particularly interested in *forcing language to explode on stage*. This may seem a bit bizarre. But once language has been freed from its various limitations (stereotyped definitions) it can arouse certain feelings within the spectator's being. The words can be accompanied by very special gestures – altogether new and unexpected. In this way the stage space can be filled; it can be concretized, transferred into a living and malleable element intrinsic to the play itself."[84] Gestures and attitudes thus become more important than words in expressing feelings and states, though the gestures themselves originate in the dynamics of the text.

The syntax which binds his stage language together is rhythm, giving his productions a special kind of musicality: not in the usual sense of musical accompaniment but in his treatment of voice, movement and gesture too. Lavelli's approach to directing, with its emphasis on the expressive rhythms and tonal harmonies of a non-descriptive language, has always had a musical bias, making it unsurprising that he eventually gravitated to the opera where some of his most original work has been accomplished.

In the 1950s as a university student in Buenos Aires where he studied politics, Lavelli took up acting in the Independent Theatre Organisation, one of the few outlets for artistic experiment tolerated under the Peronist dictatorship. At this stage Lavelli seems to have regarded theatre as a refuge from reality, and for some years to come his work was devoted to research on a purely aesthetic plane, though in the late 1960s it derived new momentum from his realisation of its potential for subversion in the face of outmoded social and artistic institutions. In 1960 Lavelli received a grant from the Argentine government enabling him to study theatre in Paris for six months. He studied at the Lecoq mime school and mounted his first productions at the Ecole Charles-Dullin. The second of these caught the attention of Pierre-Aimé Touchard, then Inspecteur Général des Arts et Lettres, one of whose functions was to provide material support for promising young artists. With Touchard's assistance, he was able to mount a further production, Ionesco's *Le Tableau*, at the Université du Théâtre des Nations (1962). By now Lavelli was committed to life in the theatre and had decided that the situation in Argentina, where the period of radicalism that followed Peron's downfall had been succeeded by reaction and disillusion, made it impossible to practise his art there.

Lavelli's reputation was made with his first major production, *The marriage* (1963), projecting both director and author from obscurity to notoriety. The author Witold Gombrowitz, a Pole living in Argentina, was known as a novelist among a restricted public but *The marriage*, written in the 1930s, had passed almost completely unnoticed. As Lavelli has said, Gombrowitz, a first-time playwright with no previous experience of theatre and unhampered by its traditions, invented an unusually free form of writing. His play, which resembles a dreamed autobiography, is constructed in tableaux and has an amorphous but extraordinarily vivid texture. The plot is slight, the play's interest lying more in its atmosphere and in the characters who parade through it, surging up and fading from sight like figures in a nightmare.

What attracted Lavelli to this disturbing play was its climate of decadence and corruption and the unreal, dream-like quality of its action. His production used space, music and the actors to develop a climate of fascination and was based on a physical transcription of the text, which he described as being like a choral symphony. Before rehearsals began he plotted a *mise en scène* as precise as any musical score. The actors' movements, gestures and verbal intonations were noted, though not their psychological states. The movements were to evolve in geometric patterns of eerie processions following what Lavelli called "the crescendos and decrescendos, the pauses, intensities and varying rhythms of the dramatic action".[85] His difficulty at this stage was to persuade the cast to go along with a method almost unheard of in 1963, which involved the total abandonment of any form of psychological motivation and beyond that of all natural behaviour. Lavelli was especially interested in exploring intonation, breaking the last remaining link with realism and using the voice in an artificial way for its tonal and rhythmic qualities, like a continuous extension of the music which was specially composed for the production. He was using the performers more like musical instruments and hieroglyphs than people, and since Lavelli could not explain his method in any rational terms, the cast had to stumble on in the dark with little to guide them except blind faith in the director. It was only when costumes, make-up and a set were added in the final rehearsals that they eventually saw how their strange incantatory vocal sounds formed part of a coherent aesthetic whole. Everything in the production was as far removed from realism as it is possible to imagine, creating a grotesquely deformed but highly consistent imaginary world. Lavelli used a single set made from junk and old furniture to give an impression of decayed opulence, and used localised lighting to define specific acting areas. The stage was covered in a thick layer of dust and cobwebs. What shocked spectators most were the de-humanised larval creatures representing the characters. They were dressed in rags and were hideously disfigured with thick white make-up, enormous spots, crude red lips and coarse string wigs. The women had dessicated breasts painted on their costumes and the fiancée, Margot, was made even more grotesque with gigantic pink plastic thighs.

It seems very unlikely that such a provocative baroque spectacle could have reached the stage through the normal commercial channels. Instead, Lavelli presented it at the Concours des Jeunes Compagnies in 1963. The jury was evidently torn between its recognition of a distinctive original talent that merited support, and disapproval for the experiment: in a curious adjudication it awarded Lavelli the first prize while paradoxically urging him to use the five million francs to attempt something less unconventional. Lavelli, however, encouraged by favourable critical notices, chose to put the production to the test of a public performance (Théâtre Récamier, 1964). Here too it polarised opinion, one critic describing it as "a liturgy constructed with mathematical precision, a guignolesque Mass with enormous powers of enchantment",[86] another, Gabriel Marcel, sounding a warning against what he called the turpitude of a scandalous spectacle capable of depraving young spectators.[87]

Despite the admiration of a number of critics *The marriage* was not generally well supported by the public and it left Lavelli with heavy debts. However, the attention it attracted at least brought him early recognition and ensured that his work has been in demand ever since. Over the next five years he was able to mount nineteen new productions.

During the 1960s his experiments led in several directions. As well as a second play by Gombrowitz, *Yvonne, Princesse de Bourgogne* (1965), there was *La Princesse et la communiante* (1966), a spectacle consisting of two self-consciously scandalous short plays by Arrabal which Lavelli staged as an experiment in pure ritual. A more direct form of aggression was present in Peter Handke's *Offending the audience* (1966) and in a nameless Happening devised with Copi where a transvestite walking a mechanical dog, a mime enclosed in a large paper bag, and an artist making patterns by hammering nails into a plank, orchestrated a sequence of actions to the accompaniment of a few phrases endlessly repeated by Copi. Lavelli said that what interested him here was seeing whether, without a text and using only an idea as the starting point, a "theatrical moment" could be created. But concurrently with these rather limited explorations of theatrical techniques, Lavelli also directed a number of repertoire plays – O'Neill's *Welded* (1965), Claudel's *L'Echange* (1966), Vauthier's adaptation of Seneca's *Medea* (1967), Goethe's *The triumph of sensibility* (1967) – where character and dialogue play more conventional rôles. These productions revealed a quality which sets Lavelli apart from the other Latin-American directors, a sensitive respect for the text. Lavelli's stagecraft developed into a flexible instrument capable of accentuating the plastic *(The marriage)*, the action (Copi's Happening), or the dialogue, according to the intrinsic qualities of the text. In his production of Claudel's *L'Echange*, for instance, the musicality was rooted in the dialogue and Lavelli used the rhythms of speech and intonation to highlight the strong emotions contained in Claudel's poetry.

One of Lavelli's undisputed successes in this period was his production of Arrabal's *L'Architecte et l'Empereur d'Assyrie* (Théâtre Montparnasse, 1967). Arrabal has had the good fortune to be exceptionally well served by the Latin-American directors, each of them exploiting the plays in his own distinctive manner, but of the three it is Lavelli who has interpreted his scripts most faithfully. Unlike Garcia, who excelled at giving body to Arrabal's neurotic obsessions, or Savary who exploited the anarchic fantasy to make *Le Labyrinthe* a Dionysian festival, Lavelli has emphasised the ceremonial aspect of Arrabal's work. His productions come closest to Arrabal's own formula for "panic ceremonies" where the confusion of life must be balanced by a rigorous, quasi-mathematical construction, as precise and flexible as the application of set theory.[88] The concept is well exemplified in *L'Architecte et l'Empereur d'Assyrie*, a play whose formula – two mythomaniacs on a desert island enacting games – is simple, contained, yet rich in complex possibilities. Arrabal constructed the play almost like a game of chess, an analogy brought out implicitly by Lavelli's production in the precision of move and counter-move, and explicitly at certain moments such as when the Emperor was dressed as a Bishop on a chess board.

This production differed in almost every respect from Garcia's. Garcia, following his aim of dramatising naked human emotions, played the action directly on a bare stage devoid of descriptive references. Lavelli's production, in contrast, transposed the action into a theatrical framework of ritual and *jeu*. It was staged on a stylised desert island depicting a wooden hut and pallisade set on a mound, also made from planks of wood. The effect was both theatrical, inviting the audience to participate in an imaginary game, and exotic, hinting perhaps at a Robinson Crusoe – Man Friday or Prospero – Caliban encounter. Unlike Garcia's stark and strident production, Lavelli's was subdued and controlled, the latent violence not neutralised but contained in precise rituals and alternating with moments of tenderness and sadness. And whereas Garcia's version was hugely dominated by the Emperor's neuroses, Lavelli's highlighted the osmosis between two contrasting but complementary aspects of humanity, the primitive and the civilised. The power of Garcia's production was achieved through the brutal reduction of a multi-faceted play to an irreducible core. Lavelli's was more complex, less immediately graspable, but more richly suggestive. He saw the play as a web of interwoven themes: the characters' refusal to accept themselves as they are, expressed in their continual metamorphoses; the confrontation between the natural and the artificial in man; and the underlying fear of loneliness that binds the two men together in a love-hate dependency. All these themes converged in the final act of exchange where the Emperor, condemned and executed at his own request for killing his mother, is eaten piece by piece by the Architect-Judge. Lavelli played down the macabre – it hardly required emphasis – and presented this as a solemn and strangely tender ritual of communion, a final androgynous effort at unity by two characters seeking to transcend their human solitude.

After *L'Architecte et l'Empereur d'Assyrie* Lavelli's approach to theatre began to change as his perception of its social and political context became sharper and more critical. His research up to this point had been concerned with perfecting a theatrical language to express the fear, sensuality, violence and obscure longings of man's irrational state. The assumption behind such an approach is that theatre's function is to create its own independent reality, rather than reproducing a pre-existing reality, it substitutes for the everyday world an artifical one which obeys only its own laws and exists in the first degree of reality. Ritual, for example, is used to transcend the everyday: it serves to heighten the impression of an artificial order of reality, while lifting even banal situations to a transcendent plane. More generally, his productions reflect a desire to pass beyond the particular to the universal. Stripping the action of its contingent reality, they aim at the essential core of human experience, presenting emotion devoid of psychology and situations divorced from recognisable socio-historical contexts.

Productions such as these, which claim no extrinsic justification beyond the artist's freedom to create, have a private, almost introspective bias, and it is no coincidence that, as several critics noted, Lavelli's spectacles gave one the sense of witnessing the enactment of a private ceremonial, not the impression of a performance being addressed to a public. This is not to say that the spectators remain outside the performance, but it implies a view of art seen not as something demonstrative but as something exemplary, an expression of feeling which must originate in the artist's own experience. "The public," says Lavelli, "is an abstract notion. I can only imagine a spectator through myself. . . Basically, if a work is seen to be authentic, if one senses that it could not be other than what it is for the creator, then I don't see why other people shouldn't be moved by it."[89] His position is similar to that of Ionesco who, when accused by Kenneth Tynan of dwelling self-indulgently on the intimate, the personal, and ignoring "reality", replied: "In order to find the fundamental problem common to all men I have to ask myself what is *my* fundamental problem, what is my most deep rooted fear. It is by doing this that I shall touch on the fears and problems of others."[90] Lavelli similarly assumes that if the spectators are to confront images of their own experience, as indeed they should, this will only happen as a result of the authenticity of what is proposed.

Eventually, however, Lavelli came to recognise another form of authenticity: not the truthfulness of inner experience alone but an honest appraisal of the wider historical reality in which all individual experience is enmeshed. After 1968, and partly as a result of the political events of May, his work became less introspective, more receptive to a broader vision of things, and more critical in tone.

In the spring of 1968 Lavelli was working on the French première of Oscar Panizza's *The council of love* when the students of Paris took to the streets. For a few weeks it seemed as if the rule of authority had been broken by a collective libertarian tide protesting against the de-humanising efficiency of life in a modern industrial society and the alienation of the individual by impersonal, archaic institutions. For Lavelli, as for many artists, this was a period of re-appraisal when the conditions in which they created, the society within which they operated, and the relationship between their art and that society, all came under scrutiny. Possibly Lavelli had always realised that the rôle of an experimental artist is a fundamentally subversive one, both in the general sense that to belong to an avant-garde is by definition to reject the status quo, and, in Lavelli's own case, in the particular sense that adhering to the radical Independent Theatre Group in Argentina constituted an act of dissociation from the establishment. In 1968, after the brief euphoria of the revolution that never was, when the old order reasserted its rule as it quickly did, Lavelli was left with a heightened awareness of the social divisions and other defects of an ossified, stratified society which the student protest movement had vividly exposed. More pertinently, he also felt now that the artist's privilege of insulating himself from reality, withdrawing from an imperfect world into an artificial world of perfect order, is a self-delusion. There can be no immunity in theatre from the imperfections of the everyday world as long as theatre is practised in institutions which replicate the hierarchical structure, the contradictions and social divisions, of society at large.

All societies construct theatres in their own image; or more precisely, since theatrical institutions are ponderous and slow to change, theatres tend to reflect yesterday's society. That is why, as every progressive director intent on modernising theatre has eventually conceded, a complete theatrical revolution can never be accomplished by aesthetic reforms alone but depends on a wider transformation of society too. The question, though, is whether theatre can or should be used to precipitate such a transformation. To change art or to change the world?

Lavelli's response to the old question goes beyond crude alternatives. If he believes, first, that for the artist there is no real choice, since the artist's over-riding commitment is self-evidently to art, he also holds that art, even if it has no specific ideological basis – indeed, *especially* when it is free from narrow ideological directives – can help to change the world by changing people's perception of it.

On the question of political theatre Lavelli is quite specific. He has always held that political theatre is at best ineffectual, preaching to the already converted while leaving others untouched, and at worst self-indulgent. "Because it is political," he said, "it salves the consciences of progressive intellectuals. It reassures them the way Boulevard theatre reassures the petit-bourgeois." [91] For Lavelli, political action and art still remain separate alternatives: "If you are going to work in the theatre, you must do it sincerely and try to improve it as an art form. If not, then you take a rifle. . ." [92] On the other hand, if the artist's work is to have contemporary relevance it must be informed by a lucid and critical awareness of the society people live in. And since, as he puts it, "charity begins at home", the first task must be to put theatre's own house in order. The rôle he sees for theatre is therefore militant but non-political, or at least not directly interventionist. Its militancy is directed first against the micro-society that forms the immediate context of his work, namely theatre itself.

His attitude, which he calls an *ethic*, has crystallised around the notion of creative destruction. He envisages a systematic assault from within, leading eventually to the demolition of the entire theatrical edifice from whose ruins some new theatre may one day be born. What form it will take is impossible to foresee, but it must exist in a way which restores it to the community. Theatre claims to be a communal art form, yet at present, he says, it is the hostage of an institution designed to preserve the privilege of those who profit from it financially, the press which supports it, and the narrow circle of initiates who have mastered its forbidding social rites.

A central problem is that creative artists are not in control of the means of production. Between the artist and the public a massive administrative and financial structure has grown up:

"Everywhere, without exception, theatrical organisation is conceived and practised in an ascending order of responsibility; the artists, at the bottom, are valued on purely comercial considerations, reflecting a market value more or less dictated by the press."[93] And since theatre's organisation intimidates the artists, it is hardly surprising that the public too finds it intimidating: "Classified by an old witch with tickets of various categories, placed on a plan of the theatre by an expressionless undertaker, assaulted by the cloakroom lady's backward glance and assailed by the teeming wild-life of usherettes, set upon by programme vendors and chocolate sellers, greeted by pompously attired commissionaires, what reserves of masochism the spectator must draw on before he gets to his safely numbered seat!"[94]

Although the problems he describes are social and institutional, and strictly speaking distinct from questions of artistic creation, Lavelli holds that there can be no worthwhile revitalisation of theatre unless the whole complex of issues is addressed. The dilemma for the artist is that, on the one hand, theatre's wider problems cannot be resolved on a purely aesthetic plane, while, on the other hand, vested interests are so entrenched that there will be no impetus for change from above until, as he says, "a theatrical revolution shakes the entire edifice to its foundations".[95] Lavelli offers no facile solution, but senses that the process of destruction must originate at the base of the hierarchy. The artist's mission, he concludes, is to subvert from within. By gradually undermining the old traditions and complacency, by destroying outworn artistic forms and replacing them with fresh ones, a process of questioning is set in motion whose ripples radiate outwards through the theatrical institution and into society at large.

There were already signs of a more critical attitude to society in a second production Lavelli mounted of *L'Architecte et l'Empereur d'Assyrie* (Cologne, 1969). His original interpretation in 1967 had centred on the two individuals constructing an elaborate world of fantasy through which they eventually confronted their deeper personal reality. It highlighted the Emperor's neuroses, personal guilt and unfulfilled aspirations, against the implied background of his miserable life in an uncaring con-

sumer society. In 1969, in a starker, more allegorical production, the balance shifted from private ritual towards the play's
social significance, with the characters now seen as symbols of
Western civilisation and the under-developed Third World.
The self-styled Emperor who, at the start of the play is dominant and self-assured, the object of the Architect's admiration,
gradually discovered the meaninglessness of his superiorty, and
the crime he expiates at the end of the play was not the personal
crime of matricide but the alienation of man from his Self in
Western civilisation.

This new reading of the play was an interesting experiment
in relating private fantasies to the wider social context, but in
form it was hardly revolutionary. Lavelli's next project was an
experiment with far more radical implications, involving not
the re-interpretation of a text but an attempt to create a new
modern dramatic form. Bourgeade's *Orden* (1969), which has
been described as a militant opera, marked a significant stage
in Lavelli's career for several reasons. For one thing, its subject
matter was historical and political. Also, it was Lavelli's first
experiment in musical drama as a generically distinct art form:
not a play with musical accompaniment but a spectacle where
the action itself is conceived in musical terms and where ideas
are developed simultaneously in music, song and action. The
final reason why *Orden* was different from anything Lavelli had
attempted previously was that it involved him in a new creative
process with writer, composer and director all playing more or
less equal rôles in conceiving the spectacle. One of the fruitful
products of the questioning process of 1968 was the emergence
of less hierarchical creative methods. Some companies, like the
Théâtre de l'Aquarium, the Groupe T.S.E. and the Théâtre du
Soleil, have tried to do away with rigid distinctions between
authors, actors, directors and technicians and have developed
methods where the shows are devised collectively by all the
artists working together. *Orden* was not exactly comparable to
such experiments in *création collective* – it was rather the result
of three specialists co-authoring a spectacle – but it afforded
Lavelli an opportuity to participate directly in the work's
genesis.

Orden dealt with the rise of fascism in Spain. It depicted the complicity of Church, army and state, the notorious ferocity of the Civil War, and the continuing suppression of individual liberty under Franco's rule up to 1968. The spectacle was based on a text by Pierre Bourgeade published in 1968 under the title *La Rose rose*, a patchwork of quotations, slogans and impressions – not an intrinsically dramatic work but containing material which could lend itself to orchestration of song and chant. The idea of performing it came from the composer Girolamo Arrigo who was commissioned by the ORTF to set the text to music for performance at the 1969 Avignon Festival. Arrigo was joined by Charles Ravier the conductor of the Ensemble Polyphonique which was to perform the opera. It was at this stage that Lavelli became involved and the idea of staging the work as musical theatre took shape. Lavelli introduced another key member of the team, Pace, one of France's leading stage designers.

Lavelli's rôle in the production was two-fold. His task, as in all directing, was to translate ideas into plastic form, in this case transposing a fundamentally undramatic text into a sequence of appropriate theatrical tableaux. Here the challenge was not so much the absence of conventional dialogue, intrigue and character, since Lavelli was accustomed to moulding spectacles from tableaux, but the text's precise historical context and its overt political message. Lavelli's object was not to give a history lesson but to lift the action from its historical frame and make the subject relevant to today's public. He sought images of timeless relevance by constantly juxtaposing the human – the intimacy of the couple, the solitude of the prisoner and so on – against the march of historical events. More boldly, he aimed to de-politicise the action by staging it not as documentary drama but as a spectacular celebratory ritual, playing on the senses and emotions to prevent literal meaning from taking over.

Lavelli's other task as director was to effect a marriage of the component parts in a medium which, more than most, is a mixed art form. The principal defect of traditional opera, he felt, is that it sacrifices action and the actors to music and the singer, while in other forms of musical theatre, Brechtian opera for example, song is confined to a separate illustrative function.

Orden was an attempt to combine spectacle, music, action and text by blending them into a unified whole. The musicians, instead of being consigned to an orchestra pit, were brought on to the stage and integrated in the action. One of Lavelli's particular concerns was to develop the acting side of the singers' performances. "A singer," he said, "is not there just to sing notes, he must also possess dramatic qualities."[96] Whether he realised it or not, Lavelli was in fact developing an idea anticipated thirty years earlier in Artaud's concept of the "affective athlete" – an idea of the singer acting with his whole body, or an actor using his voice like a musical instrument as a continuous extension of his expressive range: in short, an idea of the performer as actor-singer-musician.

Orden represented something entirely new – the marriage of the lyrical and sacred dimension of opera with a modern subject in a way that helps people to relate to the contemporary world – and can claim to be one of the most significant developments in musical theatre since Brecht's experiments in the 1930s. It was acclaimed as the highlight of the 1969 Avignon festival and soon taken up by a Paris theatre, Les Tréteaux de France in Les Halles. There it was also well received, though in an enclosed space some of the atmosphere felt at the original open-air production in the Cloître des Carmes was inevitably missing.

For his next musical experiment, *Bella ciao, la guerre de mille ans (Bella ciao, the thousand years' war)* in 1972, Lavelli joined a team headed by Arrabal, who had been commissioned to write a new play for the T.N.P. by its director Georges Wilson. In fact, Arrabal too felt that the rôle of the author had been undermined by the movement of 1968 and decided to try an experiment in *création collective*. It was not a happy experience. Arrabal has described his rôle as that of synthesiser: "I limited myself to transposing all these people's ethical, political, social, philosophical ideas into theatrical images. I couldn't encompass all the nuances, all the ramifications of their ideas, but it seemed to me – to all of us – that we were on the right road to reform. On paper it was magnificent. At least, that's how it seemed at the time. Now that I have tried the experiment once, I'll never try it again."[97]

As Arrabal implies, *Bella ciao* exposed some of the pitfalls in collective authoring. Initially the team included everyone involved in the production – Lavelli and Arrabal, the designer Michael Raffaelli and composer André Chameaux, technicians, a score of actors and a Marxist pop group, Komintern, consisting of some fifteen musicians. This unwieldy team soon split into two groups, those like Arrabal and Lavelli whose concerns were artistic, and others who were motivated by political aims. It was also found that the process was placing too heavy a burden on the cast, who complained that it was impossible to rehearse and be involved in writing the play at the same time. Others followed them in opting out, until eventually Arrabal and Lavelli were left working with the two most politically committed members of the team, the communist stage designer and a militant left-wing actor, with the latter supplying the ideas, Arrabal fashioning them into dramatic material, and Lavelli directing the cast and the band. This was already a pale version of the utopian ideal of *création collective*, but there was a further blow to come. Some days before the opening, a representative of the Communist Party's cultural committee who had been invited by Raffaelli to watch a rehearsal declared it ideologically unsound. The designer was reprimanded by the party and promptly quit the production. Arrabal has presented this incident as a catastrophe which condemned the play. He said: "Given the nature of the spectacle, the right closes ranks, the Communist Party disapproves, so we're left with only the support of a few left-wing sympathisers. The mistake was in giving a share of the responsiblity to a party member, the designer, with the result that the party considered it was their play, and therefore it had to follow their line absolutely, or else be condemned irrevocably."[98] Whether the PCF's disapproval really had the least effect on *Bella ciao*'s reception seems doubtful, but it demonstrated to everyone concerned the dangers of confusing militant art with a political manifesto.

Bella ciao consisted of three inter-changeable sequences of sketches based on the themes of Culture, Capitalism and Repression. It was a flexible formula, part theatrical spectacle, part musical revue, using a blend of slogans, pop songs and cleverly staged routines as the vehicle for a display of militant fervour. The victim of its own formula, it rather resembled what Swift once called a nutshell in an Iliad, *i.e.* an elaborate package whose contents are deceptively slight. All that can be said in favour of Arrabal's unsubtle imagery is that it expressed his co-authors' political convictions unambiguously. The opening scene showed a decrepit personnification of Culture (who bore a distinct resemblance to André Malraux) presiding over a military parade-ground drill of his minions, passing in review all the apparatus of "bourgeois" culture: television, publicity, sport, "critic-cops", literary prizes etc. Other sketches showed a rugby match where Capitalists, divided into spuriously opposing teams of Conservatives and Traditionalists, grappled in a scrum around a gold ingot; and a *corrida* where the bull, a revolutionary leader, was taunted by Independent-Moderates and Moderate-Independents, and finally slain by four Repressives matadors. Overall it was a lively, fast-moving show executed with military precision, but disappointingly synthetic. Even after a rousing finale where the voice of repression was gradually swamped by a crescendo chorus of the revolutionary song "Bella Ciao", the remaining impression was of a cleverly staged spectacle exulting uncritically in the facile clichés of post-1968 Marxist cultural politics.

Orden and *Bella ciao* were two very different spectacles with a common purpose, to discover new forms of musical theatre of contemporary interest and relevance. In a search for a mixed form bridging the gap between lyric theatre and spoken theatre they re-joined a current which in essence was not dissimilar from Barrault's total theatre. Where others like Visconti, Zeffirelli, Peter Hall and Peter Brook, were working to reform opera from within and to bring it into the twentieth century, Lavelli's preference had been to side-step the formidable problems involved in modernising an archaic genre. Lavelli's reluctance to tackle operatic works is understandable enough. "I don't like opera," he once said, "it's dusty, intolerable,"[99] echoing the widely-held view of opera as a conservative, faintly absurd, relic of the past. The same defects that Lavelli attributed to the institutions of theatre pervade the world of opera, only on a greatly magnified scale with each production seeming to demand armies of artists, technicians and administrators, not to mention vast amounts of money. Yet the complexity and richness of opera, for all its pitfalls, pose an enormous challenge to creative minds, a challenge which Lavelli, with his growing fascination for musical drama, eventually found irresistible.

Between *Orden* and *Bella ciao* he had directed the first production of a newly written opera by von Einem based on Kafka's *The trial* (Vienna State Opera, 1970). It was not until 1975 that he eventually tackled a major work from the operatic repertoire. In that year, in a prodigious burst of creative energy, he directed Mozart's *Idomeneo* (Théâtre des Champs-Elysées), Gounod's *Faust* (Paris Opera), Campra's *Le Carnaval de Venise* (Festival of Aix-en-Provence) and Ravel's *L'Heure Espagnole* (La Scala, Milan). These were followed by six more major productions in 1977-8.[100]

Lavelli has described opera as being characterised by a "total divorce between its component parts, an interminable series of contradictions": contradictions, that is, between conductor, instrumentalists, soloists, chorus and technicians, between libretto, music and setting.[101] It is true that opera, because of its very complexity, is prone to imbalance between its constituent elements, but the contradictions Lavelli refers to are actually symptoms of a deeper malaise which is essentially a crisis of meaning and purpose. Opera can only function as a coherent art form when the competing interests of composer, librettist, conductor, designer and performers, are harnassed and subordinated to a common purpose, without which it lapses into weak drama embellished by pretty music, or else an impure branch of music with episodic illustration. Already in the 1930s Brecht had condemned traditional opera on the grounds that content or "message" was subordinated to the giving of pleasure, a criticism which could still be made when directors like Lavelli, Chéreau and other like-minded directors began to work in the opera in the 1970s. If opera has seen the beginnings of a tremendous regenerative process in recent years, it is because directors like Lavelli have confronted the medium's most fundamental problem, which is to transform a museum of past cultural glories into a living art form capable of expressing some aspect of what it is like to exist in the modern world.

In their attempts to give opera contemporary relevance, both

Lavelli and Chéreau have aimed to lift it out of its fuzzy conventionality – conventional character types set in pseudo-Romantic or classical periods – but the methods they use to achieve this are diametrically opposed. Chéreau's Marxist approach uses critical distanciation to bring the subject into sharp focus, presenting it in a specific historical context. Lavelli's operas, like his other productions, go in the opposite direction, playing on emotional states rather than individual psychology and often leaving the historical contexts undefined. This means that Lavelli is able to use music in a particularly expressive way, as Chéreau is not. Music, with its characteristic lack of specific reference, is too imprecise to serve as a vehicle for ideas, but a powerful medium for expressing conflict and qualities of feeling. Whereas the didactically inclined Chéreau looks for meaning in the libretto, Lavelli's method is to organise his productions as material incarnations of the drama's musicality.

Where the libretto is concerned his approach involves simplification and reduction, clarifying the often intricate intrigues and eliminating incidental detail to present universal human feelings embodied in archetypal situations. Lavelli uses the word "situation" in a Sartrian sense to denote the total set of circumstances that make up the context of an individual's life and the framework for his or her actions. Within the limitations of their given situation, Lavelli sees his characters as being free to choose, to act, to invent their destinies, and it is from the conflict of each character with his situation that drama is born. "Modernising" opera thus has a rather special meaning for Lavelli: it implies stripping the stories of the veneer of familiarity that obscures their meaning, presenting the old stories in an unfamiliar light so that the underlying situations can be seen more clearly. Of *Idomeneo*, for example, he wrote in the programme: "For Mozart, the ancient legend of the King of Crete tormented by a stupid vow is only a means of approaching the characters who are gripped by passion, riven with their consciences, confused by their moral standards, inspired by love, devoured with jealousy, and saved by youth and courage."[102] In Lavelli's production there was no baroque spectacle and no attempt to evoke ancient Crete. The stage, designed by Max Bignens, was simple and abstract – little more than an enclosed white space which could be transformed with other white screens and open cages moved in from the wings and flies. The characters were simply dressed and barefoot. The simplicity and clarity of this unusual approach in his first full-scale opera won many admirers. The critic of *Le Monde* wrote: "The drama unfolds not in a royal court but in the hearts of people who resemble us when we take off our fine evening wear, and the majesty of the drama is the majesty of human suffering."[103]

But not all his operas have been so abstract. In a controversial production of *Fidelio*, which he saw as a drama celebrating the fight for freedom applicable to any age, he imagined the action taking place in a stylised modern setting with metal cells, catwalks and gantries suggesting a prison. The intention was not to make the action seem contemporary but, as with *Idomeneo*, to find a context which would allow its timeless and universal relevance to be seen. For Gounod's *Faust* he ignored the vaguely late-medieval associations of the subject and set the action instead at the time of the opera's composition, in the mid-nineteenth century. He explained: "Goethe's Faust fascinates me, but I decided to ignore it in this *mise en scène*: Barbier and Carré's flimsy libretto is a very poor shadow of the original and doesn't contain much to inspire a composer. . . So I took Gounod as my starting point and suddenly everything became much clearer, more transparent, more logical; when the score was replaced in the context of its period its meaning and *raison d'être* became more obvious."[104] The choice was especially helpful in illuminating the rôle of Marguerite, perhaps the central character of Gounod's opera. Lavelli saw her as the prisoner and victim of a repressive, intolerant moral code, a situation made clearer to the audience by placing the action in the nineteenth century. Lavelli's choice brought audible murmurs of disapproval from some members of the audience at the Paris Opera, a public not noted for its progressive tastes, but others claimed the production as a regeneration of a worn-out classic. Jacques Lonchampt, in a review entitled "Blessed are those who see Faust", hailed it as "a resurrection of *Faust* which seemed almost unimaginable before Lavelli".[105]

Alongside his work in opera Lavelli has continued to direct plays, though less frequently than before. His projects have included a highly acclaimed production of Ionesco's *Le Roi se meurt* staged at the Odéon (1976) and the premières of two of Arrabal's best works written in the 1970s: *Sur le fil* (Théâtre de l'Athénée, 1975) and a semi-operatic spectacle *La Tour de Babel* (Odéon, 1979). Actually, to speak of opera and spoken theatre as separate activities in Lavelli's case is misleading because Lavelli, in the tradition of Wagner and Appia, treats opera not as a hybrid literary-cum-musical genre but as a branch of drama and applies exactly the same principles to opera and spoken theatre. In both cases his *mise en scène* involves an orchestration of attitudes, movement and spatial relations inspired either by the text or the music, the only difference being that in opera the framework in time and tempo is a given factor supplied by the musical score instead of being inferred from the text.

Although he has created an exciting and highly original style of theatre with productions of outstanding beauty and subtlety, Lavelli has so far failed in his aim of making theatre less elitist. There is undoubtedly much truth in his claim that theatre in today's society does not belong to the artists or the people but is a commodity controlled by market forces. Meanwhile, however, there is the paradox that Lavelli himself, a freelance director with no permanent links with a theatre or company where organisational or financial reforms might be tried out, regularly directs some of the most expensive shows in Paris. It is also fair to say that his approach to staging as a semiotic code requires some sophisticated deciphering by the spectators, and that this is not calculated to appeal to the masses. While rightly diagnosing theatre as elitist, Lavelli has eschewed what he would presumably regard as facile attempts to educate the non-theatre-going masses to the mysteries of theatre. In both these respects it is interesting to compare Lavelli with the directors discussed in the next chapter. These directors, starting from similar premises to Lavelli, concluded that an immediate programme to demystify and democratise theatre, rather than a millenary process of artistic subversion, was what was needed.

4   Théâtre populaire

People's theatre

The independent art theatres between the wars raised theatre
to a new level of artistry and integrity, in opposition to the
trivial entertainment offered by the commercial Boulevard
theatres. But their audiences were limited to a small and cultivated elite. That was Copeau's verdict in *Le Théâtre populaire*,
a booklet published in 1941, where he looked back on the
achievements of the independent theatres of the inter-war
years, and described it as a movement of little theatres. "What
I now understand," he wrote, "is that those little theatres were
just technical laboratories, conservatories where the noblest
dramatic traditions were nursed back to life, but which were
not true theatres because they lacked a public."[1] What they had
provided for their circle of initiates, he explained, were "luxury
pleasures" – pleasures of rare and undeniable quality, but
egotistic and ultimately insignificant. The need now was to
create a living theatre, one which would help the vast undif-
ferentiated masses to find purpose and meaning in their lives:
"For it must be living, that is to say popular. And to live, it
must offer men reasons for belief, for hope, for fulfilment."[2] In
Copeau's view this meant theatre would have to be either Christian or Marxist, the only over-arching faiths capable of uniting
an audience drawn from disparate social groupings. At least,
there was no longer any question of a theatrical renaissance
springing from formal scenic or aesthetic reforms.

Copeau was advancing these ideas during the German Occupation, at a time when those who looked beyond France's
divided and humiliated state were turning their thoughts to the
need for a movement of national and spiritual regeneration.

Like Marcel Carné's films *Les Visiteurs du soir* and *Les Enfants du Paradis* or De Gaulle's radio broadcasts from London, his essay was also a call to "la France profonde". But it would be wrong to see his advocacy of a "Théâtre de la Nation" only in terms of a response to the special circumstances of 1941. In fact, twenty years earlier when he closed his theatre in Paris and went to Burgundy, Copeau knew that the real problem was not an aesthetic one but that of building links between theatre and the vast majority of the population who would never even think of going to a playhouse.

Most of the attempts that have been made to create a people's theatre in post-war France owe something to Copeau's inspiration, though his contribution is only one strand in a complex pattern. The progress of *théâtre populaire* is closely – though not exclusively – bound up with the process of decentralisation. In this connection mention should be made of Gémier, Chancerel and Dasté who, like Copeau, took itinerant companies into the provinces, and of Dullin, one of the architects of the programme of decentralisation that led to the creation of seven Centres Dramatiques de Province between 1946 and 1961. Circumstances as well as individuals also played their part. The wartime division of France into "free" and occupied zones, and the censorship of theatre in Paris, meant that some of the most interesting young companies that had sprung up under the Front Populaire were now working behind the demarcation line. At the end of the war there were thus a number of young itinerant companies in the provinces, some of which would be transformed into national Centres Dramatiques.

The term *"théâtre populaire"* has been applied to, or appropriated by, people with very diverse aims, making it appear disparate and confused as a movement. For some it has meant making the classical heritage more accessible to working class audiences, while others have argued for a separate working class theatre movement outside the overwhelmingly middle-class established theatre. Copeau considered the first priority to be the creation of a modern repertoire relevant to the lives of the people;[3] others have concentrated on the organisational and institutional steps needed to democratise theatre-going. Some have seen it in terms of cultural dissemination, others as an

Different views of Theatre populaire

instrument of political agitation. Part of the difficulty lies in the ambiguity of the term "le peuple", which has been used to denote all the people regardless of class, or, more narrowly, the proletariat. Vilar, like Copeau, saw people's theatre in terms of one nation, one culture: "My theatre," he wrote, "is called the National People's Theatre not National Workers' Theatre. In France, a popular audience is not only a working class audience. Surely that's obvious, isn't it?"[4] In contrast to Vilar, the T.N.P.'s present director Roger Planchon would like to see it catering for more specifically working classes audiences.

The rôle of politics in *théâtre populaire* is no less problematic. Although people's theatre and political theatre are often equated, there is no direct or necessary correlation. At least, while the underlying purpose of people's theatre will always be political in a broad sense, to the extent that it involves the dismantling of cultural privileges which are largely class-based, its content is not necessarily political. As already mentioned, Copeau said that the National Theatre would be either Christian or Marxist, and attempts to build a popular theatre on a unifying religious base have been made by playwrights such as Henri Ghéon and companies like Les Copiaus and Léon Chancerel's Comédiens Routiers.[5] In France, unlike Russia and Germany, the practice of politically inspired theatre for the masses is a relatively recent phenomenon. Radical left-wing and agit-prop theatre did exist in France between the wars, albeit on a small scale, in ventures such as Léon Moussignac's Théâtre d'Action International and Jacques Prévert's more militant Groupe Octobre.[6] However, it was not until the belated discovery of Brecht in the 1950s and even more markedly around the time of the upheavals of 1968 that such forms really became prominent in France.

Beneath such divergent approaches, however, people's theatre in its various forms has a clear common goal: to widen theatre's social base by bringing it into the lives of the masses who for geographical, social or economic reasons have hitherto been deprived of it. *Théâtre populaire* can be thought of as efforts to bridge the yawning gap between elitist avant-garde theatre and low-brow popular entertainment by making good, worthwhile theatre available to all. In spite of the very different approaches they have inferred from it, this has been the shared aim of the directors who are discussed in this chapter.

Firmin Gémier and the first Théâtre National Populaire

The idea of *théâtre populaire* in the sense of a theatre of and for the people, is not a recent one. It has been an intermittent preoccupation for more than two hundred years – ever since, in fact, theatre was perceived to have lost its broad communal base to become the cultural preserve of an elite. It has often been said that the expression "people's theatre" is, or should be, a pleonasm, a view which harks back nostalgically to the origins of theatre and the mediaeval Mysteries when there was nothing exclusive about theatre, and dramatic performances were indeed celebrations for the masses. In a somewhat different sense, Shakespeare, Molière and Calderón, with their socially mixed audiences of gentry and groundlings, *la cour* and *la ville*, literates and illiterates, could also be described as "popular". It is only with the emergence of aristocratic tragedy, and more markedly with the consolidation of literary theatre as a minority class-based pursuit in the eighteenth century, that a distinction becomes possible between "theatre" on the one hand – literary, legitimate and elitist – and on the other hand non-literary "popular theatre", now relegated to the culturally "inferior" genres of melodrama, circus and vaudeville.

Perhaps the earliest self-conscious attempts to promote a people's theatre came during the French Revolution with the *fêtes populaires* celebrating democratic republicanism and with the suppression in 1793 of the Comédie-Française and its company, the Troupe du roi, and the reclaiming of the Théâtre Français for the sovereign people. Re-named the Théâtre de la République, for a year or so until Thermidor it acted as a forum for patriotic republican dramas celebrating the main events of the Revolution. For most of the nineteenth century, however, people's theatre was kept alive as an idea, rather than a reality, in the minds of writers like Jules Michelet, Octave Mirbeau, Louis Lumet and Romain Rolland. In 1848 Michelet spoke rhapsodically of his vision of the masses drawing civic and moral inspiration from theatre: "Show the people on stage its own legends, its deeds, its accomplishments. Nurture the people with the people. Theatre is the mightiest tool for education and bringing men together: it may represent the best hope for national renewal. And I mean an immensely popular theatre, a theatre answering the thoughts of the people, that would travel to the smallest villages."[7] Rolland, too, saw theatre for the masses in terms of a civic ideal. In an impassioned manifesto entitled *Le Théâtre du peuple* (1903) he analysed the reasons for the cultural alienation of the workers in an overwhelmingly bourgeois society and set out the aesthetic, economic and organisational requirements of a people's theatre. Rolland's vision was neither paternalistic nor one involving the absorption of the workers into middle-class culture, but was directed towards the raising of consciousness – not to promote antagonism but to unite the populace in an awareness of its common identity and destiny. Already it was being realised that the utopian ideal of "One Culture" would not be achieved solely by writers able to capture the preoccupations of the masses but required a programme of practical reforms involving the location and internal layout of playhouses, the timing of performances and the cost of admission. Rolland, for example, wrote: "The main thing is that seats must be equal. The brotherhood of man in art, which is the proper aim of popular theatre, will only be achieved – indeed, universal art of any kind will only be achieved – once the stupid domination of the stalls and boxes has been broken, and with it the class antagonism caused by the offensive inequality of placing in our playhouses."[8]

Rolland wrote these words at a time of widespread interest in the idea of people's theatre when numerous attempts were in hand to make it a reality. One of the most significant of these was Maurice Pottecher's Théâtre du Peuple at Bussang in the Vosges. This annual festival, which has survived to the present, was founded in 1895 with the intention of giving free open-air performances for up to two thousand spectators, presenting plays directly relevant to the lives of the people. Many of the plays based on the customs and folklore of the community were written by Pottecher himself. In 1899 he also published an essay entitled *Le Théâtre du peuple* where he argued the case for a theatre responding to the interests and needs of people in the provinces. This was effectively the first call for a systematic programme of theatrical decentralisation.

In Paris, too, there were a number of ventures in people's theatre at the start of the century. Two which opened in 1903 were Henri Beaulieu's Théâtre du Peuple in Clichy and Eugène Berny's Théâtre Populaire in the working class district of Belleville. The former tried to present contemporary plays whose subjects were thought likely to interest working class audiences, beginning with Zola's *Thérèse Raquin*. Rolland's verdict on this theatre, which survived for only one season, was that it suffered from *embourgeoisement* and that few real "people" were to be seen among its audiences drawn from the predominantly petit-bourgeois surrounding district. The Théâtre Populaire, on the other hand, adopted a policy of presenting old favourites of comedy, farce and social dramas, and offering very cheap subscriptions to members of trade unions and workers' co-operatives. With this formula it operated quite successful until 1910.

Apart from Pottecher in the provinces, the most vigorous promoter of theatre for the people was Firmin Gémier. Gémier, himself a man of the people with a taste for pageant coupled with a strong civic sense, and a director with a genius for staging mass spectacles, eventually became the first director of the original Théâtre National Populaire when it opened in the Trocadéro in 1920. Behind him he had a wide experience of people's theatre ranging from the staging of open-air pageants and a travelling theatre which toured the towns and villages of France, to vast spectacular productions in the arena of the Cirque d'Hiver in Paris.

Gémier had begun his career in the 1890s as an actor at the Odéon, the Théâtre Libre and the Théâtre de l'Oeuvre where he was the original incarnation of Père Ubu in Jarry's play. Becoming conscious of the art theatres' narrow horizons, he began to look for plays that were more involved with social realities and in 1902 he directed Rolland's *Le 14 juillet*. His desire for contact with the masses and his growing interest in theatre as a form of civic communion led him in 1903 to stage a hugely ambitious open-air spectacle involving 2,400 performers and 18,000 spectators as part of the festival celebrating the centenary of the entry of the Pays de Vaud into the Swiss Confederation. An even more fantastic undertaking was the Théâtre National Ambulant which he founded in 1911 with the intention of taking theatre to the people in the manner of strolling players, but on a hugely magnified scale. This was not merely a touring company but a complete mobile playhouse modelled on the Théâtre Antoine. It involved a fully equipped theatre with stage, proscenium arch and auditorium, seating for 1,600 spectators, big tops, workshops, generators and lighting rigs, dressing rooms and offices, all packed into thirty seven wagons towed by eight steam traction engines. Gémier thought of the Théâtre Ambulant as France's first national theatre, which in a sense it was, and he was intoxicated by the idea of the excitement this strange caravan would create whenever it pulled into a town. He said: "I am going to say something which will shock you: the theatre built of stone in a fixed location is a heresy. It is contrary to the vital principle, the fundamental idea of theatre. Can you compare a theatre with stone roots and stupid feet, jammed between blocks of flats, standing unobtrusively beside the pavement to let the crowds go past, can you compare such a theatre with one which erupts into a town with the noise of its eight engines, its wagons, trucks, workshops, and without warning plants itself in a square, on a boulevard, blocking the way, forcing the passers-by to stop, to look at its façade and read its posters. . . ?"[9]

The theatre gave its first performances, in a frenzy of public interest, parked on the Esplanade des Invalides, then set off on a tour of northern France. Gémier put his faith in a solid repertoire – Molière, Beaumarchais, Tolstoy and Balzac –- and extremely cheap seats. Its success at each halt was enormous, amply supporting Gémier's belief that there was an untapped demand for good quality theatre in areas where previously town-dwellers would have enjoyed occasional old-fashioned melodramas, and villagers nothing at all. Unfortunately the expense and complexity of the enterprise condemned it almost from the start. Moving the theatre by road proved impractical and Gémier had to transport everything by train, adding to the cost. By the end of the first three-month tour he was bankrupt, and although a much reduced version of the Théâtre Ambulant was re-launched the following year, it was clear that a democratic movement to bring theatre to the provinces would not succeed on any wide scale until government or municipal subsidies were made available for the purpose.

Gémier continued to plan for theatre on a large scale. After the Armistice he took over the Winter Circus in Paris and prepared to stage two massive productions. *Oedipe, roi de Thèbes* (1919) was by Saint-Georges de Bouhélier, a playwright whose earlier efforts to create a national repertoire had already interested Lugné-Poe. Inspired by Reindhardt's famous circus production of *Oedipus Rex* (1910), Gémier staged it on a gigantic scale including athletic displays by two hundred Olympic athletes. This was not simply eye-catching embellishment but a perhaps over-literal attempt by Gémier to recreate the spirit of the collective celebrations of ancient Athens when theatre, processions and athletic games were all combined in public festivals. Gémier's second spectacle at the Cirque d'Hiver was a Provençal nativity play which was announced as the first of a series of "Chronicles of France". The production, in which animals and dancers participated, was directed by Baty who had already assisted with *Oedipus*.

When, after many years of campaigning, several parliamentary reports and two parliamentary Commissions, the National Assembly agreed to the creation of a permanent Théâtre National Populaire, Gémier was the obvious choice for its director. His aims on taking up the post in 1920 were clear. In his mind the function of a Théâtre National Populaire was to be both popular *and* national, not sectarian but unifying. He saw theatre's unifying rôle in the celebration of what he called a civic religion whose principles – the individual's right to freedom, respect for others, justice, fraternity, peace – were capable of uniting all the people of France, regardless of class, religion or political party. "Every people," he said, "has a need to project an affirmation of its ideal."[10] The rôle of the Théâtre National Populaire was to provide a home for a unifying national drama projecting such a civic ideal.

Unfortunately its success was hampered from the start by the government's failure to provide Gémier with the resources he

needed. For one thing, the theatre he was allocated, the Trocadéro Palace, an ornate folly built for the Universal Exhibition
of 1878, was situated in one of the most fashionable and expensive districts of Paris – a hopeless choice for an egalitarian enterprise. Vilar was later to suffer from the same handicap when
the T.N.P. was re-launched in a different building on the same
site. Secondly, the Théâtre National Populaire had no permanent company and insufficient resources to pursue a continuous
programme of creation, which meant that its rôle was effectively
limited to presenting successful productions from the Odéon,
the Opéra and the Comédie-Française at cheaper prices. These
were well enough supported and probably attracted some spectators who would have been deterred from seeing them by the
high-brow atmosphere or the cost of tickets at the Opéra and
Comédie-Française, but it hardly corresponded to Gémier's
idea of people's theatre. Moreover, his own rôle as administrator left little scope for creative work. Even the ambitious
open-air spectacle he planned for the theatre's inauguration, a
triptych representing the spirit of the Republic, the Great War
and the heroic effort of post-war reconstruction, had to be
shelved for lack of money. The same fate befell another project
for an early experimental *son et lumière* spectacle involving some
40,000 people occupying a large part of the gardens of
Versailles.

   The setting up of the Théâtre National Populaire was an
important step in the right direction, but Gémier knew that if
it was to be more than a token gesture it needed more resources.
Accordingly, he began campaigning for control of the Odéon
as a way of acquiring a subsidised company to work on a repertoire for the Trocadéro and so give the Théâtre National
Populaire some meaning. Meanwhile, in 1920, he launched
himself into another and apparently paradoxical venture by
taking over the Comédie-Montaigne and installing Baty as its
director. This was to be an avant-garde literary theatre presenting a mixed repertoire of classical and new authors in an elegant
new auditorium. Gémier somehow saw this as different both
from the Boulevard theatres, as indeed it was, and from the arts
theatres like the Vieux-Colombier and Lugné-Poe's recently
revived Théâtre de l'Oeuvre. Gémier scornfully dismissed such

arts theatres as chapels for initiates, though in fact his own formula was hard to distinguish from Copeau's, even down to the creation of an "Ecole Gémier". This acting school was run for him by Dullin and it formed the nucleus of the Ecole de l'Atelier when Gémier lost interest in the Comédie-Montaigne in 1922. By that time he had the Odéon under his wing. The eight years of his management of the Odéon saw an intensive and varied programme, with the emphasis principally on new plays. As a *théâtre d'essai* it could claim a creditable record, but from the point of view of the creation of popular theatre for the masses, it was a failure. At the Odéon he had to contend with the conservative tastes of its *public de quartier* and the theatre's image as the second home of the classical repertoire, while any idea of mounting productions at the Odéon and transferring them to the Trocadéro proved unrealistic because of the vastly differing sizes, publics and purposes of the two theatres.

As early as 1926 Gémier passed the Odéon's artistic direction to his assistant Paul Abram and in 1930 he resigned from its management. Although he remained with the Théâtre National Populaire until his death, his sights were now fixed on promulgating an international theatre movement. The Société Universelle du Théâtre was conceived by Gémier as a federal body to which each country's national professional association would belong. Its aim was to advance the cause of theatre throughout the world, promoting international goodwill and understanding. It seems incredible that such an ambitious scheme should be undertaken by a single individual, yet Gémier travelled from country to country with missionary zeal and succeeded in organising an annual Congress and international theatre festival, the first of which took place in Paris in 1928. Gémier himself died in 1933, by which time the international movement he launched was well established. Although the Société Universelle du Théâtre did not survive the strains of war, the international theatre festivals were resumed in 1954.

Gémier's was only one of several initiatives to bring theatre to a more representative mix of people in Paris and the provinces. On the face of it none of them might be said to have given more than occasional demonstrations of the possibilities of a people's theatre without succeeding in establishing it as a permanent presence. As Copeau pointed out in 1941: "Looking at the fortunes of the so-called 'popular' theatre in France, the situation seems inexplicable. The objectives are clear and well expressed. The French mentality seems to find it perfectly easy to grasp the need for a healthy theatre dedicated to the nation, and to understand its aims and the conditions necessary for its existence. But the projects all fail. The ideas do not take root."[11] With the benefit of a longer term view, the legacy of Gémier and others who campaigned with him can be seen to be greater than Copeau thought. During the 1920s and 1930s an important principle was fought for and won: the right of the people to have access to theatre as a "public service", to use Vilar's expression: not a commercial commodity available to those who could afford it but a basic necessity which should be available to all regardless of income. The consequence of seeing theatre as a cultural service, obviously, was that responsibility for providing the necessary structures, theatres and money must fall to the state, and this too was accepted in principle. Although it was not until the 1950s that the Théâtre National Populaire became a central force in France's cultural life, it was on foundations laid in Gémier's time that its future success was built.

Jean Vilar

After Gémier, Vilar did more than anyone to advance the cause of popular theatre. More than a director, he was an outstanding *animateur*: a man motivated by an overall artistic policy in which moral and social as well as aesthetic considerations are intertwined. He was a highly competent director and a brilliant entrepreneur, but what made his work significant was not these skills as such but the way he used them to realise what he saw as the ultimate purpose and meaning of theatre. He said: "One has to ask *why* one is creating theatre. And, in consequence, *for whom*. Personally," he added, "I know why and for whom I am working: for the *wage-earners*."[12] His vision of theatre for the people led him to create two hugely successful popular institutions, the Avignon theatre festival and the T.N.P. Yet Vilar did not set out with the intention of taking up where Gémier had left off. It was only after several years of experimenting and reflecting on the problems of contemporary theatre during and after the Second World War that he eventually came to regard the democratisation of theatre as a moral and civic imperative.

Vilar's mentor was not Gémier but Dullin. His interest in theatre was ignited suddenly in 1933 when, as a student of literature, he happened to attend a rehearsal of *Richard III* at the Atelier. Vilar was struck by Dullin's interpretation but especially fascinated by seeing something he had until then considered only as literature being transformed into theatre. Immediately he enrolled in Dullin's school where he spent three years studying, acting in several small parts and working as assistant stage manager. He displayed none of the precocious brilliance of his contemporary at the Atelier Jean-Louis Barrault but, like all Dullin's pupils, he acquired a practical grounding in theatre skills, developing the foundations of what proved to be a considerable acting talent.

He hoped to stay with the Atelier as a professional actor, but his career was interrupted by military service in 1937-8 and the mobilization in 1939. After being discharged on medical grounds in 1940 he joined a small touring company under the leadership of an enterprising young director André Clavé. La Roulotte was one of a number of small semi-professional companies which travelled around France during the Occupation. It mostly visited small towns and villages where theatre was almost non-existent, peforming in village squares, parish halls or cafés. It was from such companies that Copeau hoped his dream of a popular theatre would grow to be a reality. For Vilar, however, La Roulotte was a stop-gap activity. His ambitions at this time were directed less towards cultivating a provincial public than fostering the modern repertoire on which he believed theatre's future depended. And, although the experience of performing with inevitably limited means for unsophisticated audiences was not lost on him, confirming Dullin's teaching that simple but sincere theatre establishing direct contact with the public was the most rewarding of all, he was impatient to create his own company. While Clavé continued his work in regional theatre, becoming director of the new Centre Dramatique de l'Est in 1947, Vilar left La Roulotte in 1943 and returned to Paris to form La Compagnie des Sept. This was a small art theatre in the tradition of the Vieux-Colombier and the Atelier, to which it was immediately compared. Thierry Maulnier wrote at the time that it brought back memories of the Atelier in its earliest days.[13] Vilar's policy was to promote innovative plays which would not find an outlet in the commercial theatre. After directing Schlumberger's *Césaire*, he became impatient with the dearth of original French texts and turned to foreign playwrights: Strindberg for *The dance of death* and *Storm*, and the Norwegian Sigurd Christiansen for *A journey in the night*. His last and most successful production with the Compagnie des Sept was the first French production of Eliot's *Murder in the cathedral* (1945) which had the distinction of being the first and only recipient of the Prix du Théâtre voted by the leading critics of the day. These plays were presented in spare, economical productions whose simplicity again recalled the Vieux-Colombier. At first the company performed in the tiniest of Paris theatres, the sixty-seat Théâtre de Poche, but as its following grew it was able to fill the larger though still relatively modest Vieux-Colombier and Noctambules theatres.

Vilar rapidly acquired a reputation as a sensitive and intelligent actor-director and his company could undoubtedly have gone on to make its mark as a small theatre of quality. But by the end of the war he was growing frustrated with directing tasteful productions of what he termed "confessional" drama for a public of cognoscenti. This, and his mounting irritation with the narrow horizons of modern writing, set Vilar thinking about the possiblities of a more open theatre for the future.

His earliest reflections on theatre's problems were contained in a series of talks and interviews mostly dating from 1945-6 and later collected in a volume entitled *De la tradition théâtrale* (1955). The title concealed an ambivalent attitude on Vilar's part towards his predecessors. He saw himself as standing in the tradition of Copeau and the Cartel, and paid tribute to their achievements, but one of his recurrent arguments was the futility of trying to emulate them. He was acutely conscious of the fact, as he saw it, that the aesthetic reforms initiated by Copeau had been carried to their logical conclusion in the years between the wars and believed that only a radical change of direction could take theatre out of its present impasse. He wrote: "After thirty or fifty years of *mise en scène* considered as a creative art, theatre has now reached a point of decline."[14] Years later, with the benefit of hindsight, he claimed that the decisive advance of the 1950s had been to liberate theatre from the confines of the picture-frame stage and place it on an open stage. He said: "The four great Cartel directors had reached a point of perfection both in the human and strictly technical dimensions of theatre. Their domain, rich or poor, bourgeois or otherwise, was the *scène à l'italienne*. I decided to avoid it."[15] This is of course a vast over-simplification, and misleading if it suggests that an architectural form is something to be adopted or rejected independently of other considerations. In Vilar's case the choice of an open stage, whose significance was as much symbolic as practical, was just one of the ways in which his vision of theatre as an artistic and social force was expressed.

As early as 1946 Vilar identified theatre workers' primary task as being to bring theatre to the material disadvantaged and culturally deprived sections of society. He stated: "I am convinced that in a better balanced, more equitable society the general public would adopt new and aggressive art forms and make them their own. But the people who come to our theatres are not representative of the general public, I mean the workers, the engineers, the soldiers, students and impoverished young people; they are, alas, the well-fed and the comfortably off, the black marketeers and the property owners." And he added: "Personally I would rather play to empty seats for my own pleasure than have to deal with a public whose only virtue is that they can afford 90 or 155 francs for a seat."[16] The price of admission had long been seen as a major obstacle to attracting working class audiences and would evidently not be remedied unless generous subsidies removed the need for theatres to operate at a profit. Another familiar target attacked by Vilar was the divisive, antiquated architecture of playhouses with their rigid separation of stage from auditorium and the segregation of the public in a whole hierarchy of classes according to the ticket price. "The popular masses," he said, "are shocked by the arbitrary division of audiences into social categories. Instead of unifying, present-day architecture divides."[17]

These were certainly real problems which would have to be tackled if the non-theatre-going public were to be enticed back to the theatre, but Vilar realised they were not themselves the cause of theatre's narrow appeal, nor would eliminating them automatically result in a more equitable distribution of theatre. The real problem went much deeper: it was that people did not feel the need for theatre. As Vilar said, people would willingly make sacrifices in pursuit of things they felt passionately about, and he pointed to the bullfights in the Midi which regularly attracted the poorest of rural workers in their thousands, in spite of seats which cost many times the price of a theatre ticket in Paris. The moral was easily drawn: "Our task, therefore, is to give people a passion for theatre."[18]

In essence this was what Copeau had argued in "Le Théâtre populaire" in 1941. But while agreeing with Copeau that the general object must be to make theatre more relevant to the lives of ordinary people, Vilar at this stage had no clear view of how it could be achieved. He did not share Copeau's faith in decentralisation, thinking (erroneously, as he later conceded) that there was not sufficient support in the provinces for permanently established companies and that occasional gatherings of the people for special festivals was the best that could be hoped for there. Essentially he believed that only playwrights could create a theatre to inspire the masses, but here too he was pessimistic. He complained that with the solitary exception of Claudel, modern writers were either writing inexcusably pedestrian dialogue devoid of poetic vision, or else, like Sartre and Camus, were too intellectual and philosophical to engage the interest of the masses.

Inevitably, then, Vilar was forced to think about the rôle of directors since it seemed to him undeniable, if regrettable, that the director occupied the key position in modern theatre. In 1946, in a lecture entitled "Le metteur en scène et l'oeuvre dramatique", he stated that the real creators of the previous thirty or fifty years had not been playwrights but directors. Vilar deplored this situation because he had no faith in *mise en scène* as an autonomous art and certainly did not expect to see any wider transformation coming about as a result of work in this field. On the contrary he stated: "What we need to get rid of as soon as possible is precisely this idea of 'the art of *mise en scène*' considered as an end in itself."[19] For Vilar, *mise en scène* was a secondary, interpretative art which drew its meaning from the play being staged. If its importance had become inflated out of all proportion, if it had come to be regarded as an art of primary creation, this was because of the paucity of good writing. But the huge claims made for the art of *mise en scène* by the likes of Craig had simply not been realised: forty years of intelligent creative work had manifestly failed to bring a wider public into the theatres or to return the art of theatre to a central place in the life of the community.

Here Vilar's thinking enters a vicious circle. On the one hand, the only legitimate creator in theatre is the playwright, but playwrights with a command of theatre are lacking. On the other hand the directors who have been virtually obliged to assume the playwright's rôle are incapable of compensating for the lack of authorial vision. Meanwhile, all attempts to innovate with more profoundly meaningful forms of theatre – Vilar cites Artaud's idea of theatre as collective ritual – are frustrated by a supply system which treats theatre as a commodity and will only handle products for which there is a known market. Vilar was only able to escape from this vicious circle by looking for a solution outside theatre itself. "What is needed," he concluded, "is to build a society, and then perhaps we can make good theatre."[20]

This provided a neat formal conclusion to the argument and was probably an accurate assessment of the best long-term hope for theatre. But millenary visions are of little practical help to a director intent on revitalising theatre in the here and now, and Vilar himself was certainly not content to wait for society to change. An opportunity to explore contacts with a new public came, almost by chance, the following year in 1947 when he was invited to give a single performance of *Murder in the cathedral* in the courtyard of the Papal Palace at Avignon. At first he refused the offer but as he continued to turn the idea over in his mind the obvious difficulties – the enormity of the leap from the small Paris theatres he was accustomed to, and the all too apparent technical obstacles – became an irresistible challenge. A few days later he approached the municipal authorities with his own more ambitious proposal for a seven-day festival involving three major productions and the construction of a stage and seating for three thousand spectators.

Vilar saw in Avignon an opportunity to attempt something which was impossible in the Paris theatres: a theatrical event which the participants would experience as a special festive occasion, but not in the debased sense of a social ritual, as in the capital, nor in the sense of civic pageantry of the kind organised by Gémier. He resisted the obvious equation mass public + historic setting = popular pageant, and thought in terms of bringing drama of the highest quality to a large untapped public. The accent was always firmly on drama which meant, for example, that the unique location had to be treated as a performance space and not an historic building. Rather than illuminating the old stonework, archways and doors he used lighting to isolate the action on the stage. To some it seemed almost perverse that instead of exploiting the incomparable architecture as a setting he sought on the contrary to distance the production from it, but in terms of Vilar's priorities it was a sensible approach. In this way the potentially overwhelming historical references were neutralised so that the courtyard's most general features – the dark walls forming an enclosure, the night sky above, which helped to induce a comfortable sense of unity in the audience – enhanced the occasion without taking attention away from the play.

The stage too was uncluttered with scenery. Vilar's instincts, like Copeau's, led him to place his faith in the virtues of a great text speaking for itself through the performers. Dullin's example had confirmed this, and his early work with La Roulotte and his productions in Paris also had the simplicity that he equated with honesty. At Avignon the size of the courtyard, with spectators seated up to thirty metres from the stage, would in any case have made elaborate decorative effects futile even if Vilar had sought them. Using an open platform some fifteen metres wide, with no proscenium arch or curtain, he developed a production style aimed at exploiting the directness of contact with the audience that this made possible. The actors provided the main conduit for the play, and Vilar encouraged them to give big, expansive performances. Their gestures were bold and striking, but the effect was one of exuberance rather than bombast, thanks partly to the youthfulness of the company. Vilar recruited an outstanding team of committed young actors and actresses, among them Sylvia Montfort, Jean Négroni, Jeanne Moreau and the young film idol Gérard Philipe who became its star attraction after he joined Vilar in 1951.

Most of his productions were given on the bare stage with no scenery and only a minimum of purely functional accessories. They relied entirely on the actors and area lighting to situate the action. Critics dubbed this the "trois tabourets" style after the production of *Richard II* where the only objects on the stage were three stools. But far from being austere, as some critics have suggested, these productions achieved a visual richness through an imaginative use of lighting and costume, and were sometimes positively sumptuous. Vilar and his designer Léon Gischia attached great importance to costume though naturally, given the size of the arena, it was colour rather than details that predominated. They used colour to seduce the eye, to differentiate the characters from a distance and also, in a simple emblematic way, to define the characters. There was a similar combination of the functional and the decorative in the way Vilar used light. His lighting rigs were quite basic but he used them boldly to create simple, attractive patterns and, on occasions, to create settings. In *Don Juan*, for example, dappled lighting situated the action of Act III in a forest and four vertical shafts of light represented the pillars of the Commander's tomb. In Kleist's *The Prince of Homburg* Vilar created a prison by projecting a curtain of light from above. Devices such as these run the risk of seeming mannered but with Vilar they were never used self-consciously for "arty" effects; he was simply utilising the language of the stage intelligently to project the drama to the furthermost rows of spectators.

In taking on the organisation of a provincial theatre festival Vilar brought imagination and high artistic standards into an activity where enthusiastic amateurism tended to be the norm. He saw it really as a continuation of the work he had been doing in Paris, on a far larger stage, of course, and for much bigger audiences, but governed by the same artistic principles. In contrast to the worthy but staid productions of old-fashioned verse dramas previously presented in the Papal Palace, he aimed from the start to establish the Avignon Festival as a dynamic centre for theatrical creation. The first programme in 1947 consisted of three French *premières*: a new play by Maurice Clavel, one by Claudel and Shakespeare's little-known *Richard II*. Certainly Vilar never patronised his audiences by feeding them familiar, undemanding plays. By putting the emphasis on creation he hoped to stimulate their critical awareness and create a feeling of involvement in an artistic adventure.

The success of the festival was immediate. Whereas the majority of critics had initially been indifferent or downright sceptical, by 1951 they were applauding Avignon as one of the most exciting and innovative stages anywhere in France. The audiences grew rapidly during the first three or four years, though Vilar himself harboured doubts about their social complexion. Ironically, the commercial factors that had alienated him from the Paris theatre proved to be an abiding problem at Avignon. With only limited subsidies he was forced by sheer economic necessity to go against his principles and charge prices nearly double what he had hoped and adopt a discriminatory two-tier price structure. It was not until 1954 when the T.N.P. took over the festival that he was able to charge what he considered popular rather than commercial prices. But from an artistic point of view the festival was an undisputed success. The 1951 season, the last before Vilar returned to Paris, was a most resounding triumph. It included two outstanding new productions: Kleist's masterpiece *The Prince of Homburg* and Vilar's most popular production of all, *Le Cid*, two plays of heroic individualism with the newly-recruited Gérard Philipe in the title rôles. By now Vilar's work was being acclaimed both nationally and internationally as an inspired example of quality combined with popularity.

At this time the French government was carrying out a major reorganisation of subsidised theatre in the capital. In the movement to bring theatre to the wider population, Paris had been outstripped by the provinces where the creation of permanent centres and troupes had been proceeding apace since 1946.

Between 1948 and 1951 a series of parliamentary commissions had been set up to report on decentralisation, popular theatre and the Théâtre National Populaire. Their findings confirmed that while popular theatre had made significant progress in the provinces, no successful formula had been found to reach a popular audience in Paris. The last of these commissions, set up to examine the long-standing problem of the Théâtre National Populaire and its building, the Palais de Chaillot, contained a far-reaching conclusion: "The success of the provincial Centres Dramatiques would indicate that theatre must go out to a popular public in working class districts, and that a popular public exists for classical and modern works of quality. The aim should be to effect a systematic penetration of the suburbs with a repertoire different from that of the present Théâtre National Populaire."[21] This paved the way for the re-launching of the Théâtre National Populaire with an increased budget and a clearly defined rôle, and Vilar's nomination as the director best qualified to revitalise it.

The T.N.P., as it now became known, had a subsidy which was not ungenerous, though never sufficient to realise all Vilar's aspirations. He had concluded years earlier that the theatre had to break out of the traditional Italianate order with its picture-frame stage, curtain, footlights, boxes and balconies, all of which were divisive. Ideally the T.N.P. should have been given a purpose-built theatre in one of the suburbs, but it had to operate from the Palais de Chaillot on the site of Gémier's old Trocadéro. The Chaillot had one asset, the size of its auditorium with seating for up to 2,900 spectators in a relatively democratic arrangement. In virtually every other respect it was an intractable monster. One of Vilar's first actions was to deal with the cavernous stage. He covered the orchestra pit with a wide forestage extending into the stalls, which supplied a more open performance area similar to the stage at Avignon and gave good visibility from all parts of the house. But nothing could be done to remedy other features of the building, its oppressive monumental style and its location in the expensive sixteenth *arrondissement*. These were simply handicaps that Vilar had to live with. Not the least of Vilar's achievements was the extent to which he succeeded in making students and workers feel the

T.N.P. was their theatre. He sought the co-operation of trade unions in setting up *Associations populaires*, arranging block bookings and laying on free transport. He also abolished the divisive practice of first nights and press nights, thereby implying that the public, rather than a coterie of opinion-makers, would be the judges of a play. By starting performances at a more convenient time for workers (8.00pm instead of 9.00), providing free programmes and cloakrooms and banning tipping, he helped to make theatre-going a pleasanter, more relaxed affair.

As well as bringing people to the Chaillot, he also arranged to bring theatre to the people. At first this took the form of mini-festivals and "T.N.P. weekends", a novel formula involving a package of theatre, recitals and meals at extremely low inclusive rates. The first such weekend was held in the industrial suburb of Suresnes and included a musical matinée concert, dinner and a performance of *Le Cid*, followed on the Sunday by meetings with the cast, lunch and a performance of *Mother Courage*, all for 1,200 francs or £1/3/0 (£1.15). Similar weekends and sometimes one-day visits concluding with a supper-dance, were held in other working-class suburbs and later at Chaillot. Such mini-festivals appealed to Vilar because they placed theatre in the context of a special festive occasion, and as a way of initiating contact with a new public, implanting a need which would grow into a sustained relationship with the T.N.P. The first weekend at Suresnes was an altogether exceptional affair. It was attended by government officials and dignitaries from the communist municipal council, famous artists and show-business celebrities, even royalty from Italy and Monaco. But later, when "le Tout-Paris" had satisfied its curiosity, the T.N.P. weekends proved genuinely popular and did a lot to help Vilar reach a previously untapped public.

Vilar's arrival at the Palais de Chaillot signified the convergence of the two most significant strands of theatrical reform that had been developing alongside each other since before the First World War: one current embodying the social ideals of Gémier, the other inspired by the most influential aesthetician of the modern French stage, Copeau. That convergence had of course already begun: Copeau had recognised its inevitability in 1941, and the appointment of Jouvet and Baty in the last years of their lives to take charge of Centres Dramatiques had been steps in that direction. With the government at last committed to voting the Théâtre National Populaire the resources it needed, Vilar was in a position to accomplish reforms that others had only been able to dream of.

Vilar announced that the new T.N.P. was to function as "a public service, exactly like gas, water or electricity."[22] By this he meant that the theatre was going to be given back to its rightful owners, the public, and with the unrestricted access, quality of service and low prices that people were entitled to expect of a public utility. Although he made it clear that priority had to be given to building up support among working class audiences, he also warned that it was not a specifically working class theatre but "a rallying point at the highest level for the greatest number". Like Gémier, his ideal was to unite people of all classes in a festive celebration of their common humanity. As he said: "We must try to unite in dramatic communion the shopkeeper from Suresnes and the magistrate, the worker from Puteaux and the stockbroker, the postman and the teacher."[23] Behind all Vilar's initiatives in the field of staging, repertoire, administration and publicity, lay the ideal of giving everyone the opportunity to enjoy "the pleasures of an art which since the time of the cathedrals and the Mysteries they have wrongfully been denied".[24]

If his policy vis-à-vis the public recalled Gémier's ideal of "theatre for the greatest number at the cheapest prices", his approach to *mise en scène* followed Copeau's example. Rejecting the scenic refinements of the Cartel theatres he revived Copeau's *tréteau nu*. Like Copeau, he based his approach on a moral attitude which equated asceticism with honesty: "I came to the theatre with the intention of restoring its aridity, its dryness, and in consequence it efficacy. That's not simply a style; it's a moral position."[25] There was no proscenium arch or front curtain: instead of confining the performance in an illusionist box, Vilar wanted to place it on an Elizabethan-style stage where the audience would confront it directly. The back of the stage was enclosed either with a cyclorama or, more typically, towering black curtains. When the play required it, a stylised setting would be used, but for many productions the only setting was an empty platform surrounded by curtains, or a free-standing construction of blocks or steps, more achitectural than decorative. These ascetic stage settings were complemented by striking costumes and simple sculptural lighting. In such a large theatre as the Chaillot, performances automatically became somewhat rhetorical: movements across the stage were bold and sweeping, delivery was loud and carefully articulated. These were the main features of what came to be called "le style Vilar". It was a heroic style which was sometimes criticised for its lack of pace, but at its best it could be enormously powerful.

For Vilar, *mise en scène* was essentially a matter of creating the optimum conditions for the playwright to communicate with the public through the medium of the performer. He tried to restore to the actors some of the creative initiative that the reign of the dictator-directors had taken away from them. The director had to be as "neutral" as humanly possible, both in his reading of the text and in directing the actors. In fact, Vilar disliked the title *metteur en scène* and preferred to be known as a *régisseur*. Although Bernard Dort dismissed this as simply playing with words, it did correspond to some reality in Vilar's method. He approached rehearsals with an extraordinary lack of preconceptions and tried simply to prompt the actors towards their own discovery of the rôle. One actress said it was more a *mise en condition* than a *mise en scène*.

In the question of repertoire Vilar was guided by his belief in theatre's potential as a unifying force. He was opposed to the idea that the bourgeois monopoly on theatre should be countered by a specifically working class theatre, believing that quality, not political content, was what gave the stage its status of rallying point for the people. Since he did not share Copeau's cultural nationalism, this meant that he was able to range far and wide, choosing classical or contemporary plays, French or foreign. He was quite capable of saying one day that his overriding priority was to support new playwrights, and maintaining the next day that the T.N.P.'s first duty was to present the classics, and no doubt he was sincere in both. The only plays he would exclude *a priori* were those he considered facile, trivial or badly written.

The new T.N.P. opened in 1951 with two successes from Vilar's existing repertoire, *Le Cid* and *The Prince of Homburg*. These were as popular in Paris as they had been in Avignon, but the new productions were less well received. Brecht's *Mother Courage* was a brave choice but it made only enemies. The appearance of an East German communist playwright in a French national theatre angered the establishment which began to query Vilar's use of public money. On the other hand, some of those who supported the choice were dismayed by Vilar's interpretation of the play. He fell into the classic trap of admiring Mother Courage's resilience and optimism. It was an understandable mistake, as Brecht's theories were unfamiliar in France and not properly understood, and the text itself is not unambiguous. But presenting it as an epic of heroic individualism made nonsense of Brecht's criticism of war and capitalism. Another new production, Molière's *L'Avare*, was fiercely criticised for its ponderous pace. Most disastrous of all was the reception given to two new works by contemporary writers, Henri Pichette's *Nucléa* and Vauthier's *La Nouvelle Mandragore*. These were original poetic dramas of the kind Vilar saw as vital to the creative life of the T.N.P., but both were complete flops. Their failure led Vilar to reconsider his artistic policy. He sensibly concluded that it was unrealistic to force the pace on two fronts simultaneously, recruiting new theatre-goers and initiating them to unfamiliar avant-garde techniques. Vilar always hoped that a time would come when the ordinary public could be reconciled with the most advanced forms of contemporary writing, and in 1959-61 he was to attempt, without much success, to operate a small experimental wing of the T.N.P. in the Récamier theatre. But in 1953, after two rather shaky seasons, he settled down to producing classics and plays by modern but not fiercely avant-garde writers such as Pirandello, O'Casey and Robert Bolt.

In the debate over the classics, just as in other areas, Vilar's stance was that of a progressive moderate. He objected strongly to the radical argument that the classics, being part of the middle-class cultural heritage, could have no part in people's theatre. He likened that position to cultural terrorism and pointed out that if followed to its conclusion there would be no theatre at all, popular or otherwise.[26] To those who argued that it was patronising to introduce the workers to the classics, he replied that what was really patronising was to tell the workers that the classics were not for them. His position was that if the classics were perceived as bourgeois cultural forms, this was not because their ideology was intrinsically bourgeois – an absurd charge to make against Shakespeare, Molière, Hugo, Corneille – but because they had been annexed by the middle classes. He assumed, therefore, that what had beem colonised could also be de-colonised. Stripped of the stuffy academicism and bourgeois assumptions they had accreted, presented in simple, unadorned productions, in theatres rid of the divisive rituals and snobbery of theatre going, they could once again be made accessible to all.

To prove this he did not hesitate, when directing an old school-text classic like *Le Cid*, to exploit the qualities that had made it popular in the 1630s: the unashamedly heroic vision of the individual confronting the world, its fast-moving melodramatic action, its lyrical beauty and its youthfulness.

Although Vilar was never a political militant he did move closer towards establishing a direct link between theatre and politics during his twelve years at the T.N.P. He had become involved in the popular theatre movement in the belief that witnessing a great dramatic work was an exciting and uplifting experience, a privilege which everyone should have the opportunity to enjoy. Bringing good theatre within the reach of the culturally disenfranchised seemed in itself to be a worthwhile and adequate objective. Gradually, however, the aim of straightforward cultural dissemination was replaced by a desire to make theatre play an active rôle in contemporary issues. Vilar now looked for plays that had an educative value in the broadest sense. This did not mean works of propaganda but plays to stimulate reflection and assist a better knowledge and understanding of man and the world.

Vilar also went further and stated that his ultimate objective was to *convince*, though his understanding of what this implied was much less radical than that of, say, Brecht or Planchon. He certainly wanted to direct audiences towards an awareness of contemporary problems, but this desire was held in check by the artistic scruples he inherited from Dullin and Copeau. If he regarded theatre as a progressive social force, his idea of *mise en scène* was a conservative one based on respect for the text. There was certainly never any question of the director consciously bending a text to suit his own conception of it. Every worthwhile play contained a lesson, but the director's rôle was simply to present the text clearly and honestly for its lesson to be perceived: "Convince, without subjugating the play. Illuminate it, not dress it up. Without vulgarising it, make it beautiful and accessible to everyone."[27] Since his directorial ideal was impartiality, his means of persuasion was the choice of repertoire. Vilar selected plays whose action and characters threw light on current affairs: not simply plays which raised general themes such as liberty and justice but works which could be seen as relevant to specific issues of the day. In 1961 he wrote in *Bref*, the journal of the Association du T.N.P.: "It matters little whether a play was written twenty centuries ago if it is a faithful mirror of our problems in 1960 or 1961. The Cuban problem is treated in Corneille's *Nicomède*. The problem of people's rights under the law is treated in Sophocles' *Antigone*. The problem of General de Gaulle and the 'rebel' generals is perhaps dealt with in Corneille's *Cinna* and Calderón's *The Mayor of Zalamea*."[28] His approach, however, was allusive rather than explicit, in line with his general aim of raising consciousness rather than directing audiences towards a specific response.

In 1963, after twelve heroic years, Vilar decided to give up the struggle and asked for his contract not to be renewed. His official explanation was the nature of his contract which provided an inadequate subsidy and demanded too much in return. In fact, he was also demoralised by constant criticism and the undermining of his position in the broader popular theatre movement.

There were so many conflicting hopes vested in the T.N.P. that it was impossible for Vilar to please everyone and difficult for him to satisfy anyone. The quarrels over the repertoire in the first three seasons showed how dangerously exposed his position was. The T.N.P. owed its existence to government subsidy and, while it was not expected to be the establishment's lackey, it was also not expected to bite the hand that fed it.

Throughout its early years Vilar was constantly being attacked by right-wing critics like Thierry Maulnier and François Mauriac who suspected him of using tax-payers' money for subversive anti-patriotic ends. The reaction to *Mother Courage* was one example. Kleist's *Prince of Homburg* was another: at least this could not be accused of being anti-capitalist but it was presented by the right as an offensive justification of German nationalism. When Vilar announced his intention of following these with a third German play, *Danton's death* by Büchner, there were even more angry outbursts from the right amid rumours of the government stepping in to ban the production.

For a while Vilar had the support of left-wing theorists and critics who rallied to the T.N.P.'s defense. The influential review *Théâtre Populaire* was founded in 1953 by a group of critics and intellectuals, principally in response to right-wing attacks on the T.N.P. Soon, however, with their adoption of a narrow Brechtian model and their espousal of a more dogmatic ideological approach to theatre, Vilar came to seem very unprogressive. As the Marxist bias of *Théâtre Populaire* became more pronounced, the T.N.P. was attacked for giving in to pressure from the establishment, for addressing a petit-bourgeois not proletarian public and for not introducing an authentic working class programme.

Vilar's contract, it should be remembered, specifically stated that one of the T.N.P.'s duties was to bring classics to the people, a condition which could only bring him into conflict with the more militant advocates of people's theatre who considered that fobbing the workers off with bourgeois classics was a betrayal of the cause. As early as 1955 Sartre criticised the T.N.P. for failing to live up to its name.[29] If people's theatre meant anything at all, he said, it meant plays written by working-class playwrights for working-class audiences, which was manifestly not the case at the T.N.P. Sartre, admittedly, was careful to lay the blame with the institution not its director – a courtesy roundly rejected by Vilar in his reply where he claimed full personal responsibility for the selection of plays. Sartre evidently felt that a genuine people's repertoire was impossible within the context of a state-subsidised theatre. No doubt he was right to draw attention to the conflict of interest, though it is hard to see how popular theatre could be spared from the commercial forces and concomitant high prices that affected other forms of theatre, other than by state subsidies.

Sartre also criticised the T.N.P. on another contentious issue, the social composition of its audiences. Its public, he declared, was not a popular public because it was not a working class public. Factually Sartre was certainly right in claiming that the majority of the T.N.P.'s new theatre-goers belonged to the lower middle class. Audience surveys suggest that blue-collar workers never accounted for more than about 7% of the T.N.P.'s public. Vilar agreed the proportion was disappointing, but it must be remembered that, while giving special attention to encouraging workers, he specifically dismissed the concept of proletarian theatre as divisive.

In 1968 and after, Vilar was treated even more harshly. The chaotic Avignon Festival of that year became a platform for the denunciation of its founder as a regressive and authoritarian traitor. Dissected with a Marxist scalpel, Vilar's ideal of cultural edification was easily exposed as hopeless liberal-humanist muddle. Recalling Vilar's stated aim of sharpening the workers' critical spirit, Emile Copfermann commented: "'Sharpening the workers' critical spirit': can theatre sharpen the workers' critical spirit? The alienation of the wage-earner from his work, which no-one now disputes, produces individual passivity. . . The energy expended on work, and the time spent travelling between home and work, result in workers opting for leisure activities where entertainment and relaxation predominate."[30] Or again: "'The workers' critical spirit': but critical of what? Of the cultural values embodied in the play? But the point is, the worker is not familiar with them." Copfermann also mocked the cosy "image of charming peace" promoted at Avignon, the unrealistic aura of human union and companionship, and Vilar's concept of the *fête* promoting the illusion of a perpetual holiday. All this, he implied, was pure escapism, sublimating reality instead of confronting it.

None of these criticisms can be seen as invalidating Vilar's achievements in the 1950s. If the popular theatre movement abandoned his generous humanist ideals in favour of a different, not necessarily better, ideology, that is not something that can be held against Vilar, nor is it even a matter of personalities. What has been called into question is the liberal tradition of *théâtre culturel* which Vilar embodied. Secondly, the rôle adopted by the T.N.P. cannot be separated from the historical moment that produced it. As Copfermann himself pointed out, unlike Piscator's proletarian theatre the T.N.P. corresponded to a period not of revolution but of national re-unification: "The mood at the Liberation of France in 1945 was one of class reconciliation in a spirit of national unity, the 'sacred union'. The French Communist Party shared power with the Popular Republican Movement and the Socialists. Class struggle was put in abeyance in the interest of 'national renewal'. There was thus no political basis in 1944-5 for a revolutionary popular theatre movement."[31]

It should also be recalled that Vilar was a realist who did what he could in the prevailing circumstances. Even if he shared Sartre's desire to see more working-class playwrights on the stage, he knew from experience how difficult this was to bring about. He also knew the material constraints imposed by his budget and the difficulties of operating in the Palais de Chaillot, difficulties which he complained were not recognised by his detractors. He described the Marxist criticism issuing from the *Théâtre Populaire* review as destructive and irresponsible, and said: "I would like to remind our friends of this. *Please consider the realities.* Why be content to judge us lazily in aesthetic terms? You are reputed to see yourselves as sociologists rather than dramatic critics, more intent on social realities than on humanist principles. Let me then quote Ulianov to you: 'When analysing a social question, theory demands that it be put in a specific historical context'. . . In writing of the T.N.P., you forget that it operates in a profit-based society. Vilar acts and produces, but he's also a shopkeeper. His playhouse will die if it fails to balance its budget."[32]

Finally, it should not be forgotten that while the ideological battle was being waged, Vilar made real advances where it counted, at grass roots level. Reviewing the first five years of its activities in 1957, he was able to claim with pride that its productions had been attended by over two million people. During the twelve years of his directorship a quarter of a million spectators saw *Le Cid*. His three productions of Shakespeare were seen by a third of a million and the most popular of his modern writers, Brecht, by nearly half a million. But it was not just attendance figures, impressive though they were, that made the T.N.P. unique: it was also the non-elitist sense of community, the spirit of adventure and the enthusiastic commitment of its followers. In its most illustrious period in the 1950s large numbers of ordinary people came to look upon it as their theatre. Many of them were discovering for the first time pleasures that were previously reserved for the educated middle class. For these people at least, Vilar had succeeded on his own terms in making theatre a passion.

Roger Planchon

Vilar's successor at the T.N.P. between 1963 and 1972 was Georges Wilson whose policy was to follow the general direction of his predecessor. On taking up the post he said: "On the ideological plane our theatre remains the same as before: not a weapon or a party platform but a way of helping our fellow citizens to think about present-day problems."[33] As the 'sixties wore on and this policy of "théâtre culturel" came to seem increasingly outworn, Wilson tried to inject new vigour into the repertoire by giving greater emphasis to adventurous contemporary writing, including plays by Dürrenmatt, Gatti, Arrabal, Kateb Yacine and Edward Bond, but the T.N.P. had lost its earlier sense of direction. It was already tottering when it received a double blow from the left and the right in 1968-9. The denunciation of its policies by the *contestataires* and the government's banning of Gatti's *La Passion du Général Franco* plunged the T.N.P. into a disarray from which it was unable to recover, and the last four years of Wilson's directorship were marked by quarrels over the repertoire, the collapse of attendance figures, and permanent budgetary crisis. In 1972 the government announced that the title of Théâtre National Populaire was to be transferred to Roger Planchon's Théâtre de la Cité in the communist municipality of Villeurbanne outside Lyon. It was a fresh start for an exhausted institution and a timely acknowledgement of the fact that Planchon had for fifteen years been France's most successful creator of committed popular theatre.

Despite his company's title, Planchon wisely makes no claim to being the embodiment of the popular theatre movement, hoping, perhaps, to avoid Vilar's fate when he became hostage to a movement that disowned him. He is wary of the word "populaire" because it corresponds to a utopian ideal not a present-day reality. The reality, he point outs, is that the only time workers are seen in theatres is when they are building them. As long as that continues to be the case *théâtre populaire* will remain an ideal to be striven for: "We shall do everything in our power to make sure that an audience which never normally goes to the theatre should come. But we shall do this without too many illusions. It's not the theatre that will get the working class into the theatre."[34] In other words, Planchon believes that only a major social upheaval can bring people's theatre into existence. Rather than pretending it can exist in the here and now, he aims "to go on making people aware that there is a violent cultural divide. Our job is to keep the wound open."[35]

Planchon's achievement in becoming director of the third national theatre was all the more remarkable in that his work has been carried out almost entirely in the provinces. From the outset of his career he took the attitude that theatre is not an isolated artistic phenomenon but belongs in a social context and must be rooted in a specific community. Instead of going to seek opportunies in Paris, as virtually every hopeful young director from the provinces before had done, he attempted an unprecedented enterprise of setting up a theatre in Lyon on the model of the Parisian studio theatres. The Théâtre de la Comédie which he formed at the age of twenty in 1951 was at that time the only permanently established theatre company operating on a regular basis outside the capital, other than the five national Centres Dramatiques. Planchon's theatre differed from the latter in that it aimed from the start to build up support in a single community. The Centres Dramatiques were set up to serve whole regions and would travel out from their centres to other towns where they would perform for two or three days at a time. In Planchon's view this horizontal spread resulted only in superficial contact with the population. His aim in Lyon was to recruit a public "in depth".[36]

For the first year the Théâtre de la Comédie had no fixed base and performed in various parish halls around Lyon. In 1952 the company converted the basement of an old printing works in the centre of the city into a small theatre which became their home for the next five years. It was a modest theatre with seating for 98 spectators and a tiny stage which somehow did not prevent Planchon from staging Elizabethan and Spanish Golden Age drama: Marlowe's *Edward II* (1954), Calderón's *Life is a dream* (1952) and *The Mayor of Zalamea* (1955). It was a strangely mixed repertoire, possibly in a calculated attempt to combine adventurousness with popular appeal but more probably simply reflecting the diversity of Planchon's interests. As well as the popular seventeenth-century drama which has always appealed to Planchon, there were signs of his early interest in poetry and surrealism in his choice of plays by Prévert, Vitrac and René Char. The company also wrote and produced several satirical burlesques which were tremendously popular with audiences: *Burlesque-digest* (1953), drawn from Tardieu's plays, *Cartouche* (1954), a thriller based on the life of a legendary bandit, and the most successful of all, an irreverent adaptation of Dumas' *Les Trois Mousquetaires* (1958). These anti-literary shows were mocking and self-mocking, making fun of their own conventions whilst also using the characters and situations to satirise personalities and events of the day.

A third group of plays, the most ambitious, consisted of contemporary avant-garde drama. Planchon directed plays by Ionesco (*Amédée* in 1955, *La Leçon* and *Victimes du devoir* in 1956), and two early absurdist plays by Adamov (*Le Sens de la marche* and *Le Professeur Taranne* in 1953) at a time when these writers were considered risky and experimental in Paris. The two productions of Adamov were particularly significant in that both were French premières, establishing the company's claim to be considered France's first provincial *théâtre de création*. Planchon also staged the first play of another young writer, *Les Coréens* by Michel Vinaver (1956). This was significant for a different reason: while the overwhelming tendency of new writing in the 1950s was towards timeless metaphysical themes, Vinaver's realistic play inspired by the Korean war signalled a return to contemporary social reality.

In the mid-1950s Planchon underwent a conversion to Brechtian theory which was to dictate his approach to theatre almost completely for several years. In 1954, the year of Brecht's first visit to France, Planchon staged the French pre-miere of *The Good Woman of Setzuan*. The production, by all accounts, was as unsuccessful as Vilar's experiment in 1951 with *Mother Courage* and for much the same reasons: Planchon had not acquired the distancing techniques that prevent spectators from becoming absorbed in the story and swayed by sympathy for the heroine. The following year, however, he saw Brecht's production of *The Caucasian chalk circle* when the Berliner Ensemble paid the second of its influential visits to Paris. He was also able to hold a long discussion with Brecht. "From this interview," he said, "and from the productions of the Berliner Ensemble, I was seized with the conviction that here was truth and that I should not hesitate to copy boldly."[37]

The discovery of Brecht was both an inspiration and a dispirit-ing experience. Planchon had never wanted to follow the aes-thetically-inspired work of the Cartel and had sensed that some-thing broader was needed. Brecht showed him the possiblity of a theatre intervening directly in society. But he also saw how far behind the French theatre lagged in its search for a new scenic language to express its incipient social awareness. He estimated it would take twenty years to catch up and concluded that the only possible response to Brecht's undisputed mastery was to serve a humble apprenticeship, learning from the master by making copies of his work.

Planchon meant this literally. He said "We should respect [Brecht's] productions to such a point that we not only draw our inspiration from them but try to make our own modest copies of them."[38] In 1958 he re-directed *The Good Woman of Setzuan*, this time in the style of the Berliner Ensemble. The production it was modelled on was not directed by Brecht him-self but by his assistant Benno Besson; and, unlike the Berliner Ensemble's production, Planchon's actors did not wear masks as he believed they did not have sufficient training or experience to master the art of masked performance. But in other respects he does seem to have implemented Brecht's theories assiduously and with some success. One complimentary review described the production as having "a power of provocation whose regular and tenacious pressure recalls that of the Berliner Ensemble".[39]

What Planchon learned from Brecht was, first, a view of theatre's ultimate purpose, with which he was already instinctively in agreement, and secondly, a way of staging plays. Apart from the most obvious and fundamental principle that art must inscribe itself in history and should try to explain life rather than merely express it, Brecht helped him to formulate the rôle of scenic language in relation to the overall meaning of a theatrical performance. In Planchon's words: "The lesson of Brecht the theoretician is to have declared that a performance is both dramatic writing and scenic writing; but – he was the first to say this and it seems to me very important – the scenic writing has an *equal responsibility* to that of the dramatic text. A movement on the stage, the choice of a colour, a costume etc., these things involve a total responsibility."[40]

To say that a text is incomplete until it is staged, that theatre consists of both text and performance, is to state the obvious. However, Brecht's lesson was more far-reaching. It encouraged Planchon to break away from the traditional view of *mise en scène* as an interpretative art geared to the text. "When I started working in the theatre," he said, "we all thought that directing a play involved making just a partial contribution. We were always asking ourselves 'Am I swamping the text? or am I underplaying it?'"[41] Brecht freed Planchon from this reticence by showing him the importance of *mise en scène* not merely as a way of representing a text but as a language in its own right, which Planchon calls *écriture scénique* or "scenic writing". As a result, he came to see that the much-vaunted ideal of a "neutral" or impersonal production of a text, subscribed to by Vilar amongst others, was a myth. *Ecriture scénique* being a visual grammar or system of signs, with each component of the production working with and in relation to the others, the choices that a director makes at every point in the staging process necessarily commit him to a statement which betrays a moral position. Brecht's concept of the *Gestus*, or visible external sign corresponding to a social reality, applied not only to the story of the play and the characters' gestures: it extended to every element of the production, from the actors' physique and the way they speak, to the setting, lighting, properties, costumes and music. Each of these things betrays assumptions and communicates an attitude to the spectators. For this reason none of them can be truly "innocent". This, I think, is what Planchon was referring to when he spoke of the "responsibility" of scenic writing. Consciously or otherwise, *mise en scène* is an act of criticism. And, if this is so, it is more honest for the director to recognise it and use his stage language in full awareness of the fact that it is a method of explanation both of the text and the world.

Brecht was also influential in forming Planchon's attitude towards characters and plot. In contrast to what he called the "dramatic form" which solicited an emotional response, Brecht's "epic form" was intended to force the spectator to make a rational judgement on the events portrayed. Brecht said this meant abandoning the traditional Aristotelian dramatic mode. In reality, Brecht's approach was less anti-Aristotelian than he supposed, and certainly far less so than Artaud's. Where Artaud, making a complete break with the logical-discursive approach to drama, opted for a full-bloodied Dionysian form, Brecht started with the conventional Aristotelian model of drama as the representation of an action, then proceeded to bend it to his own purposes. Without abandoning its two mainstays – the story and the characters – he assigned radically new functions to them. According to Brechtian theory, traditional drama presents the action as an unalterable linear sequence, which has the effect, first, of mesmerising spectators into a state of fascination where critical faculties are suspended; and secondly, by compelling the audience to accept the events as they are portrayed, of encouraging a fatalistic response. Brecht's epic formula, in contrast, demands that the spell be broken. By treating the story as a series of separate episodes and emphasising their discontinuity, it frees spectators to judge the events portrayed. Similarly, where the "dramatic form" offers insight into the characters' psychology and invites sympathetic understanding, the "epic form" presents the characters demonstratively and invites spectators to reflect critically on what their actions stand for.

Planchon set about applying these insights in a series of productions of modern and classical plays: Adamov's *Paolo Paoli* (1957), Shakespeare's *Henry IV* (1957), Molière's *George Dandin* (1958) and Marivaux's *La Seconde Surprise de l'amour* (1959). Adamov, whom Planchon described jokingly as his resident playwright, had also been profoundly influenced by the discovery of Brecht in 1954-5 and now repudiated his earlier absurdist plays for their nihilism and lack of historical perspective. In an article written for the bulletin of Planchon's theatre he stated that theatre must aim to show both the curable and incurable aspects of life. The incurable aspect was the fear of death which Adamov said had been the well-spring of his writing, as well as that of the absurdist theatre generally. The curable aspect was the social one ignored by the absurdists, and it was this that Adamov set out to explore in his plays after 1956. With *Paolo Paoli*, an exposé of the cruel laws of commerce and capitalism behind the elegant and frivolous façade of *belle époque* France, Planchon found a text written expressly in the Brechtian epic mode. In his production, the first by a French director to implement Brecht's theory of critical realism, he followed the play's semi-documentary composition, using the tableaux to break the narrative continuity and introducing factual interludes between the tableaux. For these, he projected photographs and newspaper clippings of the period on to large screens. For the main action, the tiny stage was crowded with a superabundance of real objects which had the estranging effect of making the actors seem dominated by the material world.

However, it was in his work with Shakespeare, Molière and Marivaux that Planchon's debt to Brecht was most obvious. In 1957 the company left Lyon to take over the municipal theatre at nearby Villeurbanne. Architecturally it was a badly conceived theatre with appalling acoustics and sight lines making three hundred of the 1300 seats virtually unusable. But it had the advantage of size, allowing Planchon to stage productions on a larger scale and to achieve greater distanciation than had been possible in the little Lyon theatre. His inaugural production here was Shakespeare's *Henry IV* which *Théâtre Populaire* hailed as the first Brechtian production of a classic in France. The play interested Planchon as a struggle for power depicting a world in flux and raising questions of order and disorder, legitimacy and usurpation. His production was a de-mystification of political power, exposing the shrewd calculation and self-interest behind the characters' idealistic rhetoric. It also sought to explain the action not by referring to some putative (and unverifiable) psychological continuity but with reference to the reality of the situations depicted. His approach to the characters and action, as he describes it, was obviously inspired by Brecht: "Truth, reality, emerges most clearly in the action. . . What counts is the development of the scenes, their relation one with another, the relation between a character and his language, the language he uses now, the language he uses later. It's not psychology that governs this. It's the situation that counts, its relation to the other situations of the same character."[42]

Planchon has claimed that what appeals to him in Shakespeare is the fusion of individual destiny with the historical venture. Whether this particular production succeeded in preserving the balance between the individual and the broader canvas is doubtful. It was to some extent a schematised production, incorporating a Marxist de-personalised view of history. But if some of Shakespeare's human insight was sacrificed to the history lesson, the ideas were carried through in the staging with great clarity. René Allio's set was a sloping wooden platform dominated by mediaeval maps which helped the spectators to follow the action and shifting political situation. Written signs, heraldic ensigns and portable pieces of scenery were added for specific scenes. The costumes were used emblematically to define groups of characters according to their social position and their political allegiances. Among the nobility, for example, aggressive strident costumes denoted the military leaders and sombre colours the politically-minded court intriguers. The materials used on stage, such as fustian, leather and rough-hewn furniture, had an earthy coarse-grained texture which gave the production a striking tactile quality. Along with the vast amount of down-to-earth business such as eating, polishing weaponry and so on, it created a vivid impression of realism in keeping with Planchon's anti-idealistic interpretation.

In Molière's *George Dandin*, a farce about a rich peasant who tries to marry out of his class, Planchon made a complete break with the traditional Italian style. Instead of exploiting stock character types and comic gags, the play was presented in a realistic setting with a wealth of concrete visual detail and sound effects evoking a picture of everyday provincial life in the seventeenth century. Rather than a satire of an individual it became the criticism of a class. As in *Henry IV*, everything seen on stage, from the setting itself, symbolically opposing a bourgeois house on one side with a farm on the other, down to the smallest props, was intended to carry meaning. Without altering a line of the text it made a conventional farce about a cuckold into a cruel realistic drama of social pretentions and exploitation. This was a refreshing new look at the play; a justifiable criticism was that it tended to overload a slight text with an excess of meaning.

One of Planchon's most interesting experiments at this time was his production of Marivaux's *La Seconde Surprise de l'amour* (1959). Traditionally Marivaux's plays are treated as refined comedies of subtle psychological analysis, but Planchon turned a critical eye on the eighteenth-century salon world they are set in. His production, the first to bring out the play's socio-historical significance in this way, brought to life the whole sub-world of domestic servants. Seen through the eyes of their masters, Marivaux's servants are either confidantes or clowns. Planchon made them characters in their own right, with lives and feelings of their own which their self-absorbed masters never suspect. When they were not involved in the action he made sure their presence was not forgotten. In one scene they would be seen shivering with cold in the background while their mistress sits comfortably by a fire; in another, they would go about their household business, apparently invisible to the aristocrats engrossed in their narcissistic banter. This may sound like a recipe for an un-subtle piece of class propaganda. In fact, however, Planchon was more concerned with understanding than denouncing. This came out most clearly in his treatment of the aristocratic characters. Without presenting them as crude caricatures, the production exposed the truth of their social situation, showing them to be the victims of an artificial code of behaviour which preferred wit, subtlety and *savoir-vivre* to honesty, and so precluded the direct expression of feelings. Planchon made this clear by showing explicitly the repressed sensuality concealed beneath the aristocratic veneer of amorous badinage. Nuptial beds and characters in their underwear had certainly never featured in previous productions of Marivaux, and their presence here was strongly contested by traditional-minded critics. André Boll likened it to introducing an elephant in a china shop.[43] Other critics such as Gabriel Marcel and Jean-Jacques Bernard objected that it was entirely contrary to the spirit of a playwright whose art is one of subtle suggestion. Bernard criticised Planchon for trying to make Marivaux accessible to people who, for want of culture, were incapable of appreciating the play's subtlety.[44] This was a complete misunderstanding of Planchon's aim which was not to vulgarise the play but to reveal the absurd artificiality of the social conventions it depicts.

These productions were highly influential in introducing new ways of looking at the classics. Apart from an early twentieth-century vogue for archaeological reconstructions in period production styles, most modern directors have been interested in finding contemporary relevance in the classics, but they have set about this in different ways. The Cartel directors, and Vilar, were at pains to square the search for relevance with a desire to keep their productions faithful to the "spirit of the play". They were able to do this by assuming that great works of art are not one-dimensional but are rich in possible interpretations. Their own interpretation could thus highlight this or that theme while still remaining within what a concensus would admit as the range of "permissible" readings. Marxist theory, however, regards as untenable the assumption that works of art somehow have an a-temporal universality that allows them to escape from the exact socio-historical context of their composition. Molière was not writing for some disembodied Humanity: he wrote plays to entertain the *honnête homme* in Louis XIV's France. Planchon's productions therefore try to restore the text's historicity, utilising the double awareness that although the performance is taking place in the here and now, what one is witnessing is a reflection, seen through contemporary eyes, of a given society at a given historical moment. They make no attempt to "modernise" the plays with twentieth-century dress and manners, as some directors have done. Instead, they extract contemporary relevance by introducing critical distance. By shifting the main attention from the characters to the action, and showing how both the characters and action are enmeshed in a particular social milieu at a precise moment in history, such productions are able to incorporate a general view of society without apparently making laboured explicit references to modern-day events.

Since 1957 when the company left Lyon to become the Théâtre de la Cité at Villeurbanne, Planchon's aim had been to make his theatre accessible to non-educated audiences. Villeurbanne, a working-class industrial town, had no existing theatrical tradition to build on; its municipal theatre had been used on and off for light operatic and occasional touring shows. In some ways this made things easier for Planchon because, although he had to build up a public from scratch, the opportunity existed to create a new theatre on the model he envisaged. Also, working with an unsophisticated public unschooled in dramatic conventions, he found a responsive audience for a theatre that abandoned artiness and spoke directly to the people about things that concerned them. Planchon's idea was for a "public service" theatre organised on similar lines to Vilar's T.N.P., working in and with a local community. As well as his research into scenic forms there was a programme of recruitment and education along the now classic lines: contacts with local factories, workers' organisations and schools, a subscription system, seminars and informal contacts between members of the company and the public. To publicise its activities, a journal, *Cité-Panorama*, was launched. Before that, the Théâtre de la Cité had announced its opening with a questionnaire designed to discover the public's attitude to theatre and asking what plays they would like to see performed. It was in response to their replies that *Henry IV* was chosen for the inaugural production.

Planchon's success in this field, coupled with his growing reputation as one of France's most progressive directors led to the Théâtre de la Cité being given the status of *troupe permanente*, a new category of government-subsidised provincial company introduced by Malraux in 1959. In 1963 it was upgraded to the rank of Centre Dramatique National.

By this time Planchon had moved beyond orthodox imitation of Brecht and was absorbing the experience into a more personal, less didactic approach. What has come to interest him most are not ideas but the relationship between individual experience and its social context. For this reason, he says, while Brecht's more ambiguous later plays such as *Mother Courage* and *Galileo* still appeal to him, he has no taste for the earlier didactic plays, the *Lehrstücke*, nor for a Sartrian-type theatre of ideas. "Compared with didactic theatre," he explains, "it's like the difference between giving street directions to reach the town hall across the road and giving directions to get to the railway station halfway across town. The targets aren't the same. If you want to make something on the stage that is very simple and unambiguously direct, you have to choose a target which is very close to hand. If you're talking about the railway station, you have to give directions which are much more complicated. It's not that the itinerary isn't clear, nor that it isn't rigorously accurate; it's just that the railway station is further away."[45]

Planchon has said that rather than working in political theatre he is working in theatre politically. This does not mean his work is less committed than previously, only that he is not interested in an over-simplified theatre of direct action which reduces complex human and social realities to ready-made political formulas. Planchon believes that the only honest way to involve the people in theatre is to represent the vast areas of human experience in the lives of ordinary people which most art totally ignores.

This thinking comes through clearly in his work as a playwright. Planchon turned to writing in the early 1960s when, having mastered Brecht, he became conscious of the danger of repeating himself in his productions. Writing plays was a way of re-discovering what he called the "bare bones" of drama after a prolonged period of working with the fleshy matter of *mise en scène*. Since *La Remise* (1961) he has written more than a dozen plays, some of them in collaboration with other members of the company.

Apart from two experimental comedies, neither of which was well received, his writing deals with imaginative reconstructions of history. The plays are inspired by real incidents or situations and are unusual in dealing with provincial and peasant life. Generally they centre on a violent criminal act: in *L'Infâme* (1969) the case of a priest who in 1956 murdered his pregnant mistress and cut out the foetus to baptise it; in *Le Cochon noir* (1972) the exorcism of a young woman who had been raped on the morning of her wedding; in *Gilles de Rais* (1976) the life and death of a fifteenth-century child murderer. These are not, however, documentary chronicles but complex plays working simultaneously on several levels: the individual's experience of everyday life set against the ideological context, and the local and topographical set against the wider historical canvas. David Bradby has said that Planchon's plays "emphasise the concrete, material realities of life while at the same time showing how these are mediated, interpreted, built into the imaginative responses of the individual's life".[46] Planchon's interest is not in the incidents which provide the *fable* but with the psychological and material circumstances that surround it and the reactions of the people involved. He said: "If I can't understand a character in real life, I try in the theatre to walk in their footsteps, to see how far I can follow them."[47]

Planchon's own plays have not been outstandingly successful with audiences, perhaps because of their multi-layered complexity, though they have attracted the admiration of critics. In *Theatre Quarterly* they were described as having the emotional incisiveness of Edward Bond, the epic range of Brecht and the imaginative fluency of Shakespeare: a large claim, but one which could be taken to indicate fairly the main directions of his writing. Planchon has sometimes been criticised for exploiting the T.N.P.'s national status and subsidy to promote his own writing. This is a curious objection to make when the Shakespearean and Molièresque examples of playwright and company working as one are constantly being invoked as the ideal model.

His plays are significant above all as examples of the sort of writing that the *théâtre populaire* movement conspicuously lacks.

Their approach is one of vivid but un-rhetorical descriptive realism, re-creating the material fabric of life in its detail while trying to preserve the human experience of which it is part. As such, they are unique. The abiding problem for people's theatre today, as at the time of Copeau, Vilar, Sartre etc., is still the absence of a modern repertoire engaging in the lives and history of the people. Planchon is one of the few Frenchmen to attempt to fill that gap by writing plays which avoid political rhetoric and try to represent proletarian experience, not only in moments of exceptional political or industrial struggle but through the unheroic substance of people's lives.

The relative scarcity of such writing is probably why there are so few contemporary plays in the T.N.P.'s repertoire. There have been occasional productions of Vinaver *(Par-dessus bord*, 1973), Adamov *(A.A. théâtres d'Adamov*, 1975) and Edward Bond *(Lear*, 1975). But in the absence of what might be described as a people's repertoire Planchon, like Vilar, has been forced to depend on the classics, especially Molière *(Tartuffe*, 1962, *Don Juan*, 1979) and Shakespeare *(Troilus and Cressida*, 1964, *Richard III*, 1966, *Pericles* and *Antony and Cleopatra*, 1978). However, unlike Vilar who aimed to help the people re-possess their cultural heritage, Planchon uses the classics as a way of showing the people their history.

It was in this sense that his famous production of *Tartuffe* was a revelation. Coming a mere twelve years after Jouvet's 1950 production, Planchon's marked a radical departure from the former's humanist orientation. Molière's genius is generally held to lie in the creation of living characters. Planchon, without denying Molière's human insight, believes that this on its own is pointless unless the characters can be seen against the material and ideological background of their time. In the case of *Tartuffe*, this means that one must take account not only of the authority of Catholic doctrine and the power of the Church but also of the citizen's position in relation to the monarchy, whose absolute power was firmly established by 1669, as well as the background of civil war some twenty years previously.

Planchon wanted his production to show how psychological, social and ideological forces inter-act to shape lives and events. Most approaches to *Tartuffe* start from the given fact that

Orgon is infatuated with Tartuffe. Planchon went behind this, to ask *why* a man should be so besotted that he entrusts his spiritual welfare, his worldly goods and his family, to such an obvious imposter. He produced a rather surprising answer: "For the past three hundred years these actions have not been understood. Critics have called Orgon stupid – but a man's actions cannot be explained away so easily. Orgon is not stupid but profoundly homosexual."[48] Less fancifully, he has also argued that Orgon's obsession reflects the position of the rich middle class in the 1660s, assured of its material welfare but powerless and unoccupied under a strong monarchy. In turning to religion, he suggested, Orgon is looking for a purpose in life to compensate for his lack of a clearly defined social rôle. According to Planchon: "the play shows in exemplary fashion the transference between ideology and feelings, how we live with ideas and how these ideas pass into our lives, how we think that we are expressing certain ideas when in fact what we say is entirely grounded in psychological impulse, or conversely, how what we think is a psychological state is really an unacknowledged social condition."[49]

The designer René Allio created an enormous and spectacular setting with a rich marquetry floor surrounded by huge fragments of devotional paintings of the period. At the end of each act the walls were flown to reveal another setting behind, in a scenic equivalent of the process whereby Orgon is stripped of his possessions, until at the end the family was seen surrounded by prison-like stone walls. In a later production (1973) designed by Hubert Monloup there was a more baroque set, dominated by scaffolding; the house was undergoing a transformation into something resembling Versailles, suggesting the enormous process of expansion undertaken by the wealthy middle classes. Planchon lifted the characters out of their usual homely bourgeois setting into a far grander milieu than the play suggests. The lavish settings, as well as making for an extremely spectacular production, helped to steer the emphasis away from bourgeois comedy to the play's meaning. The statues of Christ and of angels and the huge equestrian statue of Louis XIV were clearly not intended merely for decoration but to establish the ideological context. On the other hand, Planchon was able to preserve some sort of domestic framework within this opulence by introducing a wealth of naturalistic business. The play began with the family sitting down to a quarrelsome breakfast and ended with supper; Orgon entered in Act I dressed in formal court clothes and, as he enquired after Tartuffe's health, proceeded to change into dressing gown and slippers; and throughout the play the servants could be seen busying themselves with household duties.

The production reserved its biggest surprise for the end. Molière's use of an eleventh-hour *deus ex machina* to rescue Orgon from his own folly has been seen as a theatrical device to contrive a satisfying end to the comedy, or as a means for Molière to flatter a monarch whose support and protection he had good reason to be thankful for. In Planchon's production it became a scene of terrifying brutality. In place of the King's urbane Officer one saw a squad of armed militia who burst through the walls and drove the terrorised family into a dungeon before turning to arrest and gag Tartuffe. Planchon implied that Tartuffe was to be executed: not for his treatment of Orgon or his alleged criminal past, but because absolutism required the elimination of a disruptive anarchist. Orgon, as the royal emissary says, had been saved because he was a loyal supporter of the King in the civil war. But the Officer's manner as he said this – deliberate and menacing – made this seem less an act of magnanimity than a warning against future disobedience. Where Orgon's pardon had previously been seen as the far-sighted wisdom of a divine monarch, Planchon presented it as a calculated political act by the head of an efficient police state.

Planchon's mature style, of which *Tartuffe* is the best-known example, is a highly personal synthesis of various influences: his passion for history, which Brecht helped him to formulate in a stage language; but also his fascination with people and psychology and a love for the detailed texture of everday life. He said: "I have a passion for what is concrete. Everything that is really palpable, concrete, pleases me. I like life in its most elementary state, without heightening. . . I love garbage, potato peel, bits of broken wood, all the things left over from life – not the things themselves, perhaps, but the life they point to."[50]

As his approach has become less didactic and more descriptive, so his work has allowed more room for the expression of what might be called a poetry of the everyday. Although some critics have likened this tendency, especially in the plays he writes, to a form of neo-naturalism, Planchon's realism never limits itself to describing the surface of things, nor does it show any of the traditional Naturalist tendency to dwell on the sordid. His response to reality is never one of disgust, but is closer to wonderment.

One feature of Planchon's best productions, therefore, is their ability to communicate the slightly miraculous quality of being, both on the surface and in depth. Needless to say, this descriptive treatment of reality is always subsumed in a dialectic world view. The element of experiential awareness, the sense of "what it is like to be", is always related to a second level of response, namely understanding. Describing and deciphering are bound up in a single theatrical process. Probably Planchon's most distinctive contribution to theatre is the way his productions combine the richness of immediate experience with an understanding of social, historical and psychological causality.

Ariane Mnouchkine and the Théâtre du Soleil

We're trying to make the Théâtre du Soleil as democratic as possible, to try as far as possible to give the actors control over their art, so that they will be as prepared and ready as possible to use it in the service of what people need – not by asking them what they want but by representing their experience of life. That's what *théâtre populaire* means. So, obviously, it doesn't exist. But that doesn't mean it can never exist.[51]

To this end Ariane Mnouchkine created the Théâtre du Soleil which for twenty years has been one of the most inventive companies in France, presenting spectacles that are theatrically exciting as well as relevant and intelligent. But rarely demagogic: like Planchon, the Théâtre du Soleil is not so much creating political theatre as creating theatre politically. Its members too approach their work from a leftist political stance and with the premise that theatrical activity must be rooted in an awareness of historical and contemporary social realities, and must aim to reach into the lives of as many people as possible. However, while Planchon has worked on politicising the classics, Mnouchkine and her company have pursued a more radical experimental approach to the language of the stage, an approach which has led them to break with conventional forms of theatrical institution and creation and to experiment with improvisation, collective creation, audience participation, and performance styles inspired by *commedia dell'arte*, Noh, Bunraku and Kathakali. Like Artaud, Mnouchkine encountered the impact of stylised oriental theatre during a visit to the Far East and this has inspired much of her later work with acting styles.

As a company it is unusual in the non-hierarchical way it operates. It harnasses the multiple talents and resources of its members in a way that is often found in amateur theatre, where actors will turn their hands to carpentry, sewing and selling tickets, but very rarely in professional theatre. It can do this because it has worked consistently to abolish specialised functions in the theatre, beginning with that of the director. If the Théâtre du Soleil owes its existence to the inspiration of Mnouchkine, it owes its success to the contribution of every one of its forty-odd members, who constitute a "Société Coopérative Ouvrière de Production" (workers' co-operative). In the case of the Théâtre du Soleil this is not a nominal distinction: the group is a self-determining community, with decisions taken by majority vote, and the work is distributed equally; its members can turn their hands to a variety of skills, from acting and making costumes and props, to keeping the company archives, and each of them takes turns at mundane chores like sweeping, cleaning and washing up. In return, each member receives the same salary. Most crucially for the spectacles they produce, many of their shows are researched, rehearsed, and in a sense "written" and "directed" by the entire production team working together on an equal footing.

Going to a performance by the Théâtre du Soleil is refreshingly different from the usual ritual of theatre-going. It requires some act of commitment, since it involves an inconvenient journey by metro and bus into the wooded park of Vincennes where the Cartoucherie (a former munitions factory) is located. For an evening performance spectators start to arrive in the late afternoon, and find members of the company manning the reception area, building props, repairing costumes or preparing meals in the large kitchen. There is a sense of a community at work, where visitors are made welcome and are free to wander about unchallenged. Inside the theatre itself, which occupies three adjoining sheds, the stage, seating, wardrobes and dressing areas occupy one large open space. All this is no gimmick but a natural expression of the company's collective organisation and their efforts to demystify theatre for the people. The Théâtre du Soleil remove the veil from the artifices of theatre and expose the secret machinery to public view, just as Peter Brook has urged. "Once," he wrote, "the theatre could begin as magic: magic at the sacred festival, or magic as the footlights came up. Today, it is the other way round. The theatre is hardly wanted and its workers are hardly trusted. So we cannot assume that the audience will assemble devoutly and attentively. It is up to us to capture its attention and compel its belief. To do so we must prove that there will be no trickery, nothing hidden. We must empty our hands and show that there is nothing up our sleeves."[52]

The Théâtre du Soleil was catapulted to international fame with *1789*, its phenomenally successful spectacle about the French Revolution, (Milan 1970, Paris 1971, London 1971). This was the first of their shows to be produced entirely by the method involving documentation, improvisation and *création collective*, but in fact it was the culmination of experiments with creative methods stretching over the previous six years. Their earlier productions, mostly based on existing texts, had helped them to discover their identity as an ensemble and had also shown them the limitations of conventional patterns of theatrical work – a realisation which was particularly sharpened by the radicalising influence of the events of May '68.

The Théâtre du Soleil was created in 1964 as an offshoot of the Association Théâtrale des Etudiants de Paris, a university group which Mnouchkine had formed when she was a student of psychology. At this stage the company was more like

Copeau's than the theatre collectives such as the Living Theatre and Open Theatre which it later came to resemble. Although it was organised as a co-operative from the start, the principle of equal salaries was not introduced until four years later and its working methods to begin with were still relatively conventional. As well as a team of actors, the company had a stage designer, a costume designer and a teacher specialising in movement and mime. Mnouchkine herself was its director, though her methods were already less prescriptive and authoritarian than most directors'. (Two non-members involved in the first production resigned from the cast because they did not regard her as a "real" director). They prepared their first play, *Les Petits Bourgeois* (Adamov's adaptation of Gorky's *The smug citizens*), in a country retreat in the Ardèche where the troupe lived together and worked on improvisations, trying to discover their characters using well-tried Stanislavskian methods. Neither *Les Petits Bourgeois*, which was performed in Paris in 1964, nor their next production, the company's own adaptation of Théophile Gautier's *Le Capitaine Fracasse* (1966), attracted much attention and the company had to continue working in daytime jobs in order to survive.

But with their third production, Arnold Wesker's *The kitchen* (1967), they scored a major critical and public success: 62,000 spectators, compared with 3,000 for their previous shows. This was the first production of a play by Wesker in France, and it was performed not in a regular theatre – which the company could not afford – but in the disused Cirque Médrano, which gave the show an extra novelty value. The play's reception was also, no doubt, helped by the critical acclaim in the press: *Le Monde*, for example, described it as the most original and important discovery of the season.[53]

One thing which made the production stand out from the dozens of others running at the time was the relevance of its subject matter. Wesker's play, based on his experiences as a pastry cook and exposing the working conditions of ordinary people, captured the underlying social discontent which broke to the surface the following year in 1968. But the production was also significant as an expression of the group's artistic as well as political convictions. The parts were not cast to begin with, and each actor worked on a number of rôles for most of the rehearsal period before fixing on his or her character. And rather than rehearsing the play, they spent several months observing working conditions in the kitchens of large Paris restaurants, trying to understand the various functions and relationships in operation. They also invited kitchen staff to watch their rehearsals and criticise. In case this sounds like a sociological enquiry conducted by actors whose background, it might be added, is overwhelmingly middle-class, it should be understood that their purpose was the thoroughly practical one of formulating theatrical techniques and a style to express the play's milieu authentically. Authenticity, in this case, did not mean giving a naturalistic copy but finding the essential rhythms and gestures which could be transposed into images of inhuman working conditions. In one scene the cast mimed their frantic attempts to keep pace with the demands made on them, as dishes were despatched to the dining room, empty plates appeared, and orders were bellowed out by waiters at a progressively more intolerable tempo. Thanks to the stylised techniques they had developed, they were able to present the play not as a realistic "kitchen sink" drama but as a metaphor for alienating working conditions generally. This was well understood by factory workers in 1968 – admittedly in a rather special period of heightened political consciousness – when the company was invited by strike leaders to perform the play in several occupied factories in the Paris region. These performances were extremely well received and were followed by lively discussions about the play and the problems it dealt with, showing how even a politically "negative" play (negative in that its characters were seen as passive and a-political) could act as a positive stimulus to political awareness

Mnouchkine's other experiment at this time was a highly controversial production of *A midsummer night's dream* (Cirque Médrano, 1968), a play rarely performed successfully in France and a surprising choice, one might think, in view of the company's political leanings. It may be that both *The kitchen* and *A midsummer night's dream* shared a common concern with liberating the individual. Mnouchkine said in connection with the former: "A person's life, in the final analysis, consists of two essential activities: work and love. Failure in the world of work is just as serious as inability to succeed in love."[54] If *The kitchen* was a play of protest against a system which prevents people from realising themselves in work, *A midsummer night's dream* was concerned with the possibility of people realising themselves in love. Mnouchkine's production broke completely with fay Romantic traditions and aimed at something less dreamlike, more elemental. It presented a savage, cruel Dionysian spectacle of real eroticism and frustrated sensuality, with the frenzied lovers set against a perverse and manic Puck. Mnouchkine felt that Puck should really be naked, but stopped short of full nudity because she estimated that it would be interpreted as a calculated act of provocation. It was nevertheless an intensely physical, sensuous production performed on slopes with the entire arena covered in goatskin, and with much emphasis on tactile qualities, movement (Mnouchkine brought in dancers from Béjart's ballet company to play Oberon and Titania) and seductive lighting effects. Critics saw it as being in the Artaudian tradition – and indeed Artaud may be the thread linking it with Peter Brook's later Stratford production (1970) with which it has also been compared.

The company's distinctive identity emerged more clearly in its first attempt at a non-scripted spectacle, *Les Clowns* (1969). In part this was a logical progression from the work on improvisation that had gone into their previous productions, but its immediate stimulus was their response to the events of May. One fruitful consequence of the social upheavals of 1968 was a quantum leap in thinking about theatre: first, in the sense that they led to the more general adoption of ideas previously held by a minority about theatre's political rôle; and secondly, in stimulating real thought about the difficulties involved in radicalising theatre. In particular they led to a sharper realisation that if theatre is to achieve a political rôle without being demagogic or propagandist, it must constantly question its own aesthetic and institutional conditions. It was in this sense that the events of May were significant where the Théâtre du Soleil was concerned. Its members had always believed that theatre's rôle is to awaken people to the conditions of their existence and where possible suggest how these might be changed, but the events of May stimulated them to reassess how this might be achieved. In 1968 the group resolved to organise itself on even more democratic lines, to abandon written texts and to re-examine more critically the relationship between the artist and society.

Les Clowns, a series of improvised sketches, was the first fruit of these resolutions. The image of the clown was chosen to express the artist's rôle in society, perhaps because of the licence which society gives to clowns to mimic the fundamental folly of the world in their antics. But the spectacle's real subject was not clowns as such, rather the creative process through which the performers expressed their vision of the world. With no pre-existing text, the actors and their creative resources furnished both the raw materials for the spectacle and its subject. Each actor worked separately to compose his or her own clown – the persona which corresponded most to his own personality – by improvising autobiographically inspired sketches and choosing his own costume and make-up. In a second stage the actors worked in twos and threes to develop scenarios and skits, with the work constantly being modified by self-criticism from within the group. Mnouchkine's rôle as director involved giving objective criticism to the actors and, later, "editing" the spectacle by selecting from the mass of material that had been generated the parts to be retained in performance.

Les Clowns was performed in the Paris suburb of Aubervilliers and at the Avignon Festival in 1969. Although it drew large audiences it was not an entirely successful experiment. Traditional-minded critics rejected the whole concept of *création collective* – "After all," wrote one, "what do people want when they go to the theatre? To see *a play*, surely"[55] – but that was to be expected. The company themselves questioned the spectacle's effectiveness and wondered if its success wasn't partly due to the public's appetite for novelty.[56] Apart from its inward-looking subject matter, where *théâtre populaire* surely requires something closer to the public's own concerns, there was the major failing, as Mnouchkine herself described it, that there had been no real *création collective*. Instead there had been been a series of parallel *créations individuelles*, with the various products being stitched together to make a spectacle.

But Mnouchkine also identified *Les Clowns* as a capital stage in the company's development because it led to the troupe finding a theatrical language to express itself. Five months of research had gone into its preparation, involving intensive exploration of gesture, of techniques to expand the actors' vocal range, and perfecting their physical and gymnastic skills. It is such work on performance techniques that has made the Théâtre du Soleil one of the most articulate and expressive companies since Copeau's.

No less important was the fact that the actors were now using these techniques to express directly their own individuality, rather than, as previously, speaking through characters in a written play. In this connection Mnouchkine's unusual conception of her rôle as director in a company committed to *création collective* was crucial. Instead of directing the actors in the conventional way she defined her rôle as that of "first spectator", able to offer criticism and guidance while leaving the creative initiative with the performers. To this should also be added the company's co-operative structure (modified to make it more open after 1968) which allows the actors to feel they are involved as whole people in the life of the troupe, as opposed to selling their talents in a capitalist market place. These factors combine to produce a unique sense of involvement; in the words of Louis Samier who joined the company in 1970:

> Previously I would be hired by a theatre, I was paid for rehearsals and paid for performances, but I remained an outsider, an employee. Whereas here... I feel I'm not just an actor, I'm completely in accord with what I'm doing, and the work I do is a part of me... Here an actor is also a creator *of the spectacle*. What we allow into a spectacle is the result of work which isn't seen in the spectacle, and intimately linked to the group's life and work.[57]

This level of personal involvement is an invisible ingredient in the company's distinctive stage language, but it is an element which audiences undoubtedly sense and respond to.

By 1970 the Théâtre du Soleil was an experienced, articulate ensemble company which Mnouchkine believed was now ready to tackle an important popular subject, using the "clear, direct and luminous" language she felt they had mastered in *Les Clowns*.[58] Several projects were sketched out then abandoned. A spectacle based on folk tales was rejected when it was realised that their acquired cultural status had severed them irrevocably from their popular origins. A production of Brecht's *Baal* was dropped because of its possibly limited public appeal. And a documentary play to celebrate the centenary of the 1871 Commune was abandoned because the company believed it did not have the necessary historical and political understanding to tackle such an advanced subject without making it into a simplistic platform for their ideological beliefs. They decided that instead of putting the cart before the horse they should go back to first principles and study the French Revolution, which would serve both as a political apprenticeship and provide the major subject familiar to every spectator.

At this time, in 1970, the company still had no permanent base. Mnouchkine applied to use one of the disused but not yet demolished market buildings in Les Halles in the centre of Paris. These halls were already being used very successfully on an *ad hoc* basis by theatre groups experimenting with open performance spaces. Mnouchkine's application, however, was rejected and instead she rented one of the warehouses at the old Cartoucherie in the suburb of Vincennes. Originally it was intended to use this simply for storage and rehearsals, but when it was pressed into service its value as a performance space was immediately obvious. Now a thriving base for a cluster of companies, the Cartoucherie has been one of the success stories of the last twenty years.

1789 had a short initial run in Milan before moving to the Cartoucherie where it was an instant hit. It was a complex spectacle played for two and a half hours without a break, and involving an enormous variety of popular styles and techniques: *commedia dell'arte*, puppets and acrobats, song and chant, readings from historical documents and *tableaux vivants* as well as more conventional dramatisations for certain scenes.

Overall it aimed to present a view of the Revolution as experienced by the common people. As a people's theatre group they naturally wanted to avoid treating the Revolution in the manner of history manuals, as a heroic story of major events and famous individuals, played out on the stage of national life. But they also felt that the obvious alternative, a play depicting the lives of the common people at the time of the Revolution, ran the risk of being equally hackneyed and misleading. Instead, they looked for a solution in the para-theatrical device of transposing the subject on to a second level of theatricality and imagined the spectacle being performed by eighteenth-century fairground actors who enacted and interpreted a series of events, real and imaginary, public and private, for their contemporaries.

This allowed a de-mystified view of historical events. It meant that one was seeing the well-known events and figures through the eyes of people who were not leading actors on the political stage but who gave meaning to the images that formed in their mind. It provided a logical pretext for the introduction of techniques drawn from traditional popular types of entertainment. Also, by using the device of theatre-within-theatre the company was able to exploit the audience's double awareness, involving them directly in the spectacle while also maintaining a critical distance, giving the spectators space to reflect on the meaning of the events portrayed. In fact this double awareness was built into the spectacle and reinforced because the theatre was arranged in such a way that there were really two audiences. The performance space, which was about the size and shape of a basketball hall, occupied part of the interior of one of the Cartoucherie warehouses. There were five small platform stages, connected by walkways and steps, arranged around a central space, with a single bank of seating benches down one side of the rectangle. The performance took place in the entire area. Some scenes were played on the platforms against rapidly erected backdrops, while at other times the action came down to the stage floor. The audience, as they arrived before the show, could choose to stand in the central space, in which case they were absorbed into the spectacle, or else opt for a more conventional passive rôle by sitting on the benches, watching a promenade-type performance which included other spectators. In either case each group of spectators' experience of the performance was conditioned by the presence of the other.

The spectators' ambivalent status was also mirrored in the way the action was presented which stressed that an event's meaning varies according to whether one is a participant, an observer, or if one is viewing it from a historical distance. In fact the question of historical truth had become one of the spectacle's dominant leitmotifs. In the course of its preparation the actors had become aware of the inaccuracies in what they had assumed they knew about the Revolution. Drawing on their recollections of what they (like every French child) had learnt at school, they began with the common notion of the Revolution as a popular democratic uprising. In the course of their extensive research and documentation they came to see that this supposed historical truth was just one way of representing the Revolution, the one favoured by bourgeois history books. The interpretation given in *1789* presented the Revolution as the event which carried the bourgeoisie to power. It covered the period 1789-91 and showed a popular uprising against the nobility and clergy being taken over by the bourgeoisie, leaving the common people enslaved in the capitalist order of the new dominant class. To alert the spectators to what was being proposed and to stimulate critical reflection, the spectacle constantly sought to contrast it with the traditional history-book version of events. In the opening scene, for instance, the flight of the King and Queen to Varennes was enacted in a sentimental Romantic style, close to melodrama. The beleagured couple were seen fleeing from the ugly mob, strains of a Mahler sympathy added to the pathos, and a strolling player narrated the sad tale in a manner designed to enlist the audience's sympathy. As the couple disappeared from sight the music stopped and the Narrator announced in a robust voice that what one had just seen was one way of telling history: now, he said, the Théâtre du Soleil was about to show another. . .

Throughout the spectacle there was a continual juxtaposition of famous historical events and imagined scenes using a great variety of theatrical devices, from readings of historical documents, straight dramatisations of political meetings, and morality type vignettes showing the suffering of the people, to caricatural sketches involving the aristocracy and satirical guignol shows. Some events were depicted several times from different angles. The flight to Varennes which was presented in the prologue as a tear-jerking vignette was depicted again later with no attempt to arouse the audience's sympathy. Some scenes used irony and other distancing effects to make their point. Others, on the contrary, called for the audience's complete identification. A striking example of the latter was the way news of the fall of the Bastille was spread through Paris by word of mouth. The theatre had suddenly gone dark and quiet, but one became aware of whispering around the hall. The actors had spread out among the audience and were telling what they had seen to little knots of spectators who gathered round to hear a vivid first-hand account of the event. Gradually the speakers became more excited and voluble as they relived the event. There were drum rolls as they built to a climax proclaiming the taking of the Bastille. Then the celebrations erupted with lights and music, acrobats and jugglers poured into the theatre and a fairground trundled in with booths and side-shows which the audience could take part in.

In general no actor was identified with a consistent character and the historical figures were played by different actors whenever they appeared. (The one exception was the people's friend Marat who, by denouncing the betrayal of the popular cause and calling for the Revolution to continue, embodied the Théâtre du Soleil's viewpoint). Thus Louis XVI who had appeared briefly as a tragic victim in the prologue, was next seen as a confident self-assured monarch reading out his proclamation to the people to submit their grievances (a gesture shown as futile in the scenes which followed). Later he was represented as a derisory marionnette manipulated by an actor in a scene showing a meeting of the Estates General, and later still, when the women of Paris were bringing the King and Queen back from the remote safety of Versailles to the Tuileries in Paris, by a ten-foot high carnival puppet jostled along above the crowds' heads. In this way one saw how images of the mighty and influential were fashioned in the popular mind.

In scenes towards the end of the play the bourgeois deputies of the National Assembly (dressed anachronistically in high Romantic period costumes to emphasise the consolidation of middle-class power in the nineteenth century) played an increasingly prominent rôle, declaring the Revolution to be finished and calling for a return to order. The play ended predictably with the words of Marat and another revolutionary, Gracchus Babeuf, urging the citizens to recognise what had happened and continue the struggle by civil war. There was, however, a more ambiguous message in the ironic penultimate scene where one group of actors enacted a little history of the Revolution for the entertainment of an audience of satisfied bourgeois spectators. The Théâtre du Soleil probably hoped here that the audience would see a link with the events of May '68. But it must also have been conscious of the paradox of its own revolutionary spectacle being rapturously acclaimed by audiences where the middle class presence, as usual, predominated.

It is impossible to gauge the political impact of a show like *1789*. The audience, it seemed to me, who applauded so enthusiastically were primarily manifesting their delight at a festive spectacle, so brilliantly executed, and performed with such gusto, that it was impossible to resist. (This must have been even more the case in London where the subject did not hold the special meaning it had for French audiences). If this were so, it would not necessarily mean the group had failed in its general aims, because these are not concerned so much with propaganda as with raising political awareness by means of a pleasurable theatrical experience. Certainly as far as the theatrical side is concerned, *1798* is rightly regarded as marking an epoch in popular theatre in France: its mastery of innovative techniques and its rich and varied theatrical vocabulary made it the most convincing demonstration yet of the validity of collective creation as a process.

After the huge success of *1789* the company was resolved to continue experimenting with progressive theatrical techniques at the same time as striving towards a more rigorous and focused political analysis. The follow-up to *1789*, dealing with a later phase of the Revolution and entitled *1793*, and its successor *L'Age d'or*, set in the present time, built on the lessons learned in *1789* and followed on logically from the latter but without reproducing its format or style.

1793 followed the activities of the *sans culottes* in one of the Paris *sections* or district assemblies which were a major forum for political activity in the period 1791 to their suppression in September 1793. By choosing to recreate this successful but short-lived experiment in direct democracy the company was expressing its own ideal and, indirectly, its opposition to representational democracy. The play also provided a logical sequel to the political analysis of *1789* which had shown how the betrayal of the people in the transition from the *ancien régime* to the new order was made possible by their lack of political awareness. *1793* showed the people's growing political self-awareness and their acquisition of a political language to formulate their situation and needs as they grappled with the problems of democracy.

Mnouchkine realised that if they were to bring this less familiar episode of the Revolution to life and make it generally accessible they would have to learn a new style of presentation and new approaches to characterisation. *1793* was created using the same process of documentation, improvisation and collective creation as *1789*, but in place of the traditional popular forms and fairground style it adopted a more dramatic tone. And instead of the broad canvas of *1789*, where the historical process was seen in the interaction of social classes represented by mostly allegorical figures, it focused more on individual characters. Each actor played one *sectionnaire* whose character, occupation and ideas were imagined from historical readings and developed in depth through improvisations. This permitted a more personalised view of history and also led to a much closer analysis of defined political positions.

The theatre was set out like a section hall with a timber floor. The spectators were integrated into the set, some of them perched on wooden galleries along two walls, others sitting directly on the floor at the actors' feet. This time there was no direct audience participation in the action but, instead, a stronger sense, as the play progressed, of experiencing history on the level of ordinary people living it in their everyday lives. It was also, perhaps, a more meticulously prepared spectacle with great care given to fulness of characterisation expressed in a wealth of significant detail, and to plastic effects, especially in the costumes and lighting. For all that, audiences did not respond with quite the degree of enthusiasm as they had for *1789*, possibly because of the expectations created by the previous spectacle. The decision not to repeat the successful formula of *1789* was certainly a correct one for the company's artistic development, but it disappointed many spectators who came to *1793* hoping for the animated, boistrous fairground atmosphere of *1789* and instead found a more discursive, demanding piece, more dramatic than spectacular.

The third spectacle in the triptych was different again. *L'Age d'or, première ébauche (The golden age, first draft*, 1975) dealt with present-day social problems and again involved the company in a quest for a new theatrical style. Like Joseph Chaikin who described his Open Theatre as a laboratory performing unfinished work, they called the play a first draft to emphasise the fact that with unscripted spectacles there can never be a definitive product: what the audience sees is "work in progress" captured at a particular moment in its development. This can be true of all theatre to some extent, but the Théâtre du Soleil wanted to stress the fact that its spectacles are not finished products offered for consumption: they are an invitation to spectators to join with the company in an exploration, conducted in a present moment, of both social reality and theatrical form.

The group's general aims when they approached *L'Age d'or* were identical to their previous ones. They wanted "a theatre in direct contact with social reality: not just a representation of reality but an incitement to change the conditions we live in".[59] The working methods, too, were well established: background investigation (for *L'Age d'or* this involved field work in factories, mines, schools and hospitals, together with newspaper articles); initial work on characterisation; improvised sketches which expressed the characters' essential situation; and group sessions in which findings were pooled and the spectacle's general shape was decided upon. The idea was to take a small, everyday news item – in this case "Death of worker in building site accident" – and around this imagine the background, in terms of people and concrete social situations, that could lead to an immigrant worker falling to his death from scaffolding. This provided a narrative thread serving as a framework for a series of sketches introducing issues such as economic exploitation, bad working conditions, problems of housing, health, communication and so on. The spectacle was imagined as a chronicle of the 1970s performed by actors in the year 2000, a theatrical transposion designed to introduce a critical distance between the spectators and the contemporary subject matter.

What distinguished this show from many politically motivated spectacles was not the sophistication of its analysis – the need to put a limited number of points across unambiguously resulted in a play which politically was far from subtle – but its inventive and very precise use of theatrical language. The designer Guy-Claude François completely redesigned the theatre, dissecting the hangar into four valleys made from beaten earth and covered in hessian, with two ridges crossing in the centre. All the action was performed in the hollows with no scenery and very few props. The audience sat either on the ridges, where they commanded a view of several playing areas, or camped on the slopes and followed the actors from one playing area to another. It was an uncomfortable arrangement for a spectacle lasting over three hours, and the constant displacement was felt by some members of the audience to be gimmicky, but others responded positively to the closeness of the actors mingling with spectators.

The real departure for the company was in borrowing theatrical conventions of the past, adopting masks and performance styles inspired by traditional Chinese theatre and *commedia dell'arte*. For most of the twenty months the spectacle was being prepared the actors spent half of each day perfecting new acting styles. They saw this work as being in the spirit of Copeau who had argued that the best hope for a popular theatre lay in a new improvised form similar to the *commedia dell'arte* but with modern types and themes.[60] Their masked commedia-like characters were immediately recognisable as contemporary social types: the capitalist boss (based on Pantaloon), the ingenuous immigrant worker (a character inspired by Harlequin) and so on.

L'Age d'or was the last in the Soleil's cycle of historical chronicles and perhaps the least successful. Although audience figures

were good it was sensed that on this occasion the company's
theatrical brilliance was not matched by their material. Its weakness was noted by critics who were generally supportive of the
company. Alfred Simon found its politics superficial and naive.[61]
Raymonde Temkine criticised the weakness of the text which
on the level of expression was prosaic and overall gave the
impression of an arbitrary collocation of scenes.[62] On the technical side, however, with its rigorous exploration of acting styles
and use of environmental staging techniques, *L'Age d'or* confirmed the Théâtre du Soleil as having a distinctive theatrical
language as innovative and accomplished as any to be seen. It
is precisely this stunning theatrical brilliance that has been the
company's most consistent hallmark, both in the experiments
with collective creation which culminated in *L'Age d'or* and in
the most recent phase of its existence.

Like all innovators Mnouchkine puts great stress on the need
to take risks, to keep changing and break new ground, in order
to avoid the artistically deadening effects of habit. This has
disappointed those who continue to regard *1789* as the
touchstone and high point of the company's work, but it has
also meant that the Théâtre du Soleil has continued to come
up with surprising and challenging productions. Mnouchkine's
work with the Soleil during the last ten years has taken her into
film, with her highly successful celebration of Molière's theatre
in *Molière, une vie* (1979), and away from collective creation
back to scripted plays.

Mephisto (1979) was an adaptation by Mnouchkine herself of
the novel by Klaus Mann. Tracing the progression of a famous
actor Hendrik Höfgen (a barely disguised double for Mann's
brother-in-law Gustav Gründgens) from radical agit-prop
worker in the 1920s to Nazi collaborationist, it depicts the life
of a theatre company in Germany in the 1920s and '30s. In
addition to its political interest, this subject allowed the company to pursue its earlier reflections on the actor and his social
rôle. The published text is interesting also in showing how
Mnouchkine approached the question of supplying a scripted
play for a company with such a special formation as the Théâtre
du Soleil's. The "presentational" way in which the characters
are built up, relying on characteristic gestures and actions rather

than explanatory speech, owes a lot to the economical stage language which the troupe has developed, and there are unscripted areas in the text which were filled in the production by improvisations developed by the actors themselves.

In the 1980s the company embarked on an ambitious Shakespearean cycle beginning with *Richard II* and intended eventually to include three further history plays *(Henry IV* parts one and two, *Henry V)* and two comedies *(Twelfth night* and *Love's labours lost)*. So far only three have been produced, *Richard II* (Cartoucherie, 1981, and Avignon, 1982), *Twelfth night* (Avignon, 1982, then Cartoucherie), and *Henry IV part one* (Cartoucherie, 1984), and the cycle appears to be abandoned. These prodigious and much disputed productions have been remarkable not so much for their interpretations of the texts as for their aesthetic and stylistic innovations. An impression of the strange effect of Mnouchkine's experiment can be gleaned from the following report on the first production: *"Richard II,"* wrote Robin Smyth, "is a compulsive ritual in which the actors leap and swoop across the stage, lifting their knees in front of them like pedigree trotters. Richard and his court of white-faced or masked samurai hack their lines into rough shouts, their every movement underlined by drums and gongs. The characters are either flailing warrior-marionnettes or broken rag-dolls."[63] In effect what Mnouchkine has attempted is an oriental Shakespeare played in a ritualistic style inspired by Noh, Kabuki and Kathakali, with a dash of *commedia dell'arte*.

It might be wondered why anything so outlandish should be attempted, but the project fits well with the history of the Théâtre du Soleil which is essentially one of a search for a form and a language in which to interpret and comment upon reality. The company's concern with political and social reality and their quest for new ways of interpreting the past and relating it to the present made Shakespeare's histories an obvious subject for their experiments. By grafting an original stage language on to the Shakespearean texts Mnouchkine hoped, as in all her productions, to introduce new ways of seeing the world. At the same time, the company believed that by studying Shakespeare's stagecraft they would advance their understanding of the medium. At the start of the cycle, in the programme for

Richard II, Mnouchkine wrote that they were embarking on it in the spirit of apprentices "entering the master's workshop with the hope of learning how to depict the world on a stage". Like Copeau, who turned to Molière not only for inspiration but for a source of pure theatrical technique, she said they were consulting Shakespeare the expert in order to learn the proper instruments with which to present some future spectacle depicting the contemporary world.

There was never any intention of creating authentic reconstructions of foreign theatrical traditions. In *Richard II* the dominant influence was Kabuki, while *Twelfth night* was more Indian in its inspiration and *Henry IV* seemed to combine the Far East and the Middle East, with a decidedly Arabian Prince Hal. In all the productions it was a pervasive orientalism that emerged rather than precise references. Mnouchkine's aim, in other words, was not archaeological or anthropological but to fabricate a new theatrical language for contemporary audiences by drawing on what seemed most universal from a range of sources.

The result was an eccentric and eclectic peformance style which nevertheless achieved its own coherence. At the Cartoucherie the entrance to the theatre was decked in black and white vertical stripes, suggesting an Elizabethan atmosphere, but passing into the main hall where the stage, seating and dressing areas were situated, the environment became more oriental. The acting area for all three plays was a large square platform sumptuously carpeted and backed by huge symbolically coloured drapes which could be rolled up or dropped to give a stage which was predominantly gold, green or blue according to the action. At each corner there were curtained entrances giving on to raised ramps, as in Kabuki theatre, along which the actors would glide, run or tumble their way on to the stage. To one side, and in full view of the audience, stood a vast array of exotic instruments where musicians could be seen engaging in prayer-like ritual before the play began. None of this, however, prepared the audience for the initial impact when, to the accompaniment of a resounding clash of cymbals and drums, the performers hove into sight. Resplendent in oriental dress, some with Elizabethan ruffs, and sporting a mixture of masks, half-masks and white make-up, they glided at breakneck speed on to the stage and circled round to line up facing the audience with their flattened hands resting on their hips. All the court scenes were in fact played in this extreme anti-naturalist, ritualistic manner, with the actors not addressing each other directly but declaiming their lines to the audience, their speeches underlined by cymbals and gongs. As in Kabuki theatre, music was an important and ever-present feature of the performance – mainly percussion for the histories, but with more melodic instruments such as Peruvian and Bolivian flutes and other wind instruments or Indian string instruments, for the comedy – and the actors employed a precise system of gesture to express emotion. Like the design of the productions as a whole, this visual language was not copied from a source but loosely inspired by the universal language of gesture codified in Eastern theatrical traditions. One did not need to be versed in Kabuki conventions in order to understand the significance of flared nostrils, an inclination of the head or a sudden flick of the wrists.

While there was not much that was recognisably Shakespearean in this, the overwhelming impression was of a prodigiously skilled and well drilled troupe performing spectacles of great energy, beauty and polish. They played to packed houses in Paris and were given rapturous acclaim at Avignon where each performance attracted over three thousand spectators. Though the acclaim was certainly justified, these impressive aesthetic experiments did also raise legitimate doubts about the company's identity. The Soleil seemed to have abandoned its radical left-wing position in favour of spectacles where production values and technical achievements dominated all else. Moreoever, for a company previously noted for its ability to personalise rôles and exploit the performers' personal resources, the adoption of a style where actors were manipulated like impersonal instruments seemed a dubious step forward. It did rather look as though conviction had given way to technical virtuosity.

Such doubts should be dispelled by the company's latest production, *L'Histoire terrible mais inachevée du Norodom Sihanouk, roi du Cambodge (The terrible but unfinished history of Prince*

Sihanouk of Cambodia: Cartoucherie, 1985). Written by Hélène Cixous in collaboration with the company, this eight-hour epic, presented over two evenings, chronicled the events in Cambodia from Sihanouk's accession in 1955 to the invasion by Vietnam and the overthrow of Pol Pot in 1979. The intrinsically dramatic nature of its subject – the clash of ideologies, the super-power politics of America, Russia and China – and the human fascination of its central character, combined to make it a compelling spectacle. Sihanouk, played with outstanding vitality and sympathy by Georges Bigot as an engaging, hyper-theatrical figure, energetically wheeler-dealing to preserve his country's neutrality and independence, and constantly betrayed by allies and friends, completely dominated the play and welded the vast, sprawling subject together.

The company drew on its previous experiments to create a performance style which, although visibly oriental in its precision, economy and use of rhythm, was tamed and westernised. It was an altogether more human production which, instead of using the actors like hieroglyphs, placed greater emphasis on characterisation. The orientalism naturally sat more comfortably with the subject here compared with the Shakespeare productions where it was deliberately applied against the grain of the text. Once again, the company's technical achievement, the spectacle's precision and finish, were breathtaking. But, beyond that, the production demonstrated that when the company's unrivalled performance skills are combined with an important new text the result can be both theatrically exciting and relevant to the modern world. In this respect – and notwithstanding any nostalgic hankerings one might have for the roughness of *1789* – *Sihanouk* marks an important stage in the Théâtre du Soleil's development.

In many ways the Soleil's progress mirrors the wider pattern of development in French theatre during the past twenty years. After the wave of militancy released by the May '68 rebellion, the 'seventies saw a waning of political theatre generally and a return to more formalist aesthetic experiments. And meanwhile, after the heyday of *création collective*, as text-based productions, especially in the shape of radical re-interpretations of the classics, have become the main focus of innovation, so too the Théâtre du Soleil has become a much more director-orientated company. Its spectacles are still an expression of corporate ideas and involve actors, director, designer, musician and (most recently) author working together. But it is no longer possible, as it once seemed, to imagine a hypothetical Théâtre du Soleil surviving more or less unchanged the departure of Mnouchkine. Clearly, the experiment with *création collective* has not made the director redundant. What has changed irreversibly, however, at least for the Théâtre du Soleil, is the nature and extent of the director's rôle. What makes Mnouchkine's achievement as a director so unusual is the degree of overall command and artistic discipline she attains – her spectacles are outstanding for their consistence, with no word or gesture out of place – within a democratic structure which leaves a high degree of creative initiative with the actor. The popularity and success of the Théâtre du Soleil's spectacles suggest that this is a much-needed formula in the theatre today.

Conclusion

It is the fate of all all theatrical experiments to be ephemeral. A great performance is like a firework display, momentarily brilliant but incapable of repeating itself. As Pirandello wistfully put it in *Tonight we improvise*, "the art of the stage, the only one capable of rescuing the dramatic work from its irremediable fixity, is the most beautiful and tragic of all. It lives like life and it dies like life". But if nothing tangible subsists of the experiments I have described, this is not to say that the world has not been changed by them. An art form which is static is a dying art form. In their experiments to implement their vision of the kind of theatre they wanted the world to have, each of these directors has made a special contribution to the process of transformation and renewal without which the art of theatre cannot live.

But not unaided. The artists discussed in this book remind us that theatre is also a collective art where an individual's experiments cannot succeed without the collaboration and consent of everyone who combines, on stage, backstage and in front of the stage, to realise the theatrical event. It is not by coincidence that the greatest directors almost without exception have been actors themselves or have understood, as Appia did, that for theatre to be a living art it must harnass the creative instincts of the performer. It took the unrivalled pictorial skills of a Baty, the "magician of *mise en scène*", to infuse life and soul into the inanimate matter of the stage. Such exceptions apart, there seems to be something fundamentally unsound in an idea of theatre which does not take account of the fact that actors supply the original and most valuable of its resources. The abiding danger, which Craig seemed to court, is that if it stifles the actor's living presence, theatre will be beautiful but sterile, incapable of producing lasting responses in the watcher.

As for the other element in the theatrical equation, the public, we have seen that it has been the concern of progressive theatre practitioners to discover new forms of theatre in accord with the preoccupations and needs of the public. "Art for art's sake" is a well accredited doctrine, but its application to such a public art as the theatre is fraught with danger. One of the fatal weaknesses of late nineteenth-century Symbolism where theatre was concerned was its tendency to lose contact with reality, a weakness of which Lugné-Poe became conscious and which later practitioners have strived to avoid. It is true that the great unified public dreamed of by men of the theatre, from Gémier and Copeau to the present day, remains an elusive ideal. *Théâtre populaire*, as Planchon and Mnouchkine readily acknowledge, remains a goal, possibly even a utopian idea, rather than a present-day reality. But the need to stay in contact with the public is one which theatre ignores at its peril.

It is this double preoccupation – with exploiting the resources of the actor in new creative ways, and with theatre's social responsibility – that has characterised the most significant theatrical experiments. It is the same two preoccupations that provide the clearest link between the innovators of the past and those of today. What is true of the directors I have discussed is also true at present of such directors as Patrice Chéreau, Bernard Sobel, Jean-Pierre Vincent, Georges Lavaudant, Daniel Mesguich and Antoine Vitez, to name but a few.

As possibly the most representative example of present trends, and certainly the most respected, Vitez demands a few more words here. A charismatic teacher of acting at the national Conservatoire and an ambitious and committed Marxist director, he established his reputation as one of France's star directors in the 1970s at the Théâtre des Quartiers d'Ivry in one of the communist suburbs of the "red belt". Since 1981 he has been the artistic director of the Théâtre National de Chaillot. His productions, most notably his radical re-workings of the classics like Racine's *Phèdre* (1975) and *Britannicus* (1981) and his Molière cycle *(L'Ecole des femmes, Tartuffe, Don Juan and Le Misanthrope)*, combine strong political beliefs with the aim of freeing the actor from the conventions of naturalism and character portrayal. Free to explore and invent, Vitez's actors deconstruct their characters and comment on them, using their voices, and especially their bodies, to create original and challenging effects through abrupt, radical juxtapositions of naturalistic and non-naturalistic playing styles. Their lines and even their emotions are "quoted", while, in a similar way, scenes are extracted from the general narrative flow and presented as isolated moments charged with a significance which will be modified by the surrounding scenes. The use of such techniques makes a performance not a straightforward reading of the play but, properly decoded, a complex network of signs and gestures to illuminate its message. Vitez, who rejects the Stanislavskian idea of the actor's identification with his rôle, has been strongly influenced by Brecht's ideas about the social "responsibility" of *mise en scène* and Meyerhold's constructivist methods. But the main inspiration behind his approach to the language of performance is the non-theatrical language of structural linguistics and semiology.

Such uncompromising intellectualism, which appears in a more extreme form in Lavaudant and Mesguich, marks a new trend in French directing and poses a new set of questions which may well dominate the debate about theatre for some time to come. Semiology (the "science of signs and signifiers"), although primarily a critical tool for analysing performance, is clearly of enormous relevance in the quest for new, richer and significant languages of performance. How its lessons can be absorbed while producing spectacles which are not intimidatingly intellectual is not yet clear. For the present, theatre seems to have abandoned the attempt to be both experimental and popular, as activist theatre is replaced by sociologically-inspired research of a more intellectual and philosophical nature. Vitez would like there to be no contradiction between popular and elitist, between experimental and accessible. Dismissing such oppositions as small-minded, he said: "We do not fit our work into these categories. We think that theatre is, in fact, an elitist art, but an elitist art for everyone."[1] In practice this is wishful thinking, at least for a current crop of intellectualising directors who have drawn encouragement from Vitez's prestige. It is surely not philistinism to object when a theatrical performance invites the reflection that its ideal audience would be composed entirely of Ph.D.s in performance theory. Even Vitez, for all his unquestionable brilliance, does not seem to me to escape this charge. He has succeeded in moulding an extremely talented and cohesive company, and on a certain level there is pleasure to be had from the extreme theatricality of its performances. But it is a specialised taste. Audience defections during the course of performances suggest that Vitez's encouragement to his actors to revel in "ludic pleasure" is not being successfully communicated to the audience.[2]

While director's theatre continues to dominate the French stage, one feature which has become less common is directors' *theatres*. With the exception of Vitez's, there are few permanent repertory companies operating as did those of Jouvet, Pitoëff, Dullin and Barrault in the Marigny period. Of other companies which bear the imprint of a creative director many, like the Théâtre du Soleil or Peter Brook's at the Bouffes du Nord, now devote several months, sometimes even years, to research and preparation, only emerging at long intervals with a public performance. It can be questioned whether the gain in terms of quality and finish sufficiently offsets the loss in terms of sustained contact with a regular public.

To some extent this gap is being filled by theatrical centres. The Cartoucherie at Vincennes, where a number of experimental groups operate in the group of sheds, is one example. Another outstanding example is the Le Lucernaire, a National Centre for Art and Creation located in the Latin Quarter in the heart of Paris. Created by Christian Le Guillochet,[3] a writer, administrator and occasional director, with the director Luce Berthommé, the Lucernaire is a thriving, bustling artistic complex which houses two theatres, a concert hall and a cinema, with a restaurant in its cobbled covered courtyard. In a typical week in 1985, spectators could choose from six spectacles: two premières, one a tribute to Simone Weil, the other an evocation of Parisian cabaret in the 1930s, Audiberti's *La Fête noire* directed by Georges Vitaly, and plays by Dario Fo, Kateb Yacine and Yukio Mishima. This is achieved by means of intensive scheduling, with three performances starting in the early evening, mid-evening and late-evening in each of the theatres.

Le Guillochet belongs to no ideological or aesthetic camp. In contrast to what is currently the most prestigious form of theatrical research, that involving new approaches to the classics, he has resurrected an older notion of the avant-garde, aiming to provide a forum for risky, non-commercial new ventures in writing and *mise en scène*. The Lucernaire operates a "mixed economy", using profits from the restaurant and film and television work, supplemented by a small state subsidy, to underwrite the cost of non-commercial productions. It is not, at present, a theatrical company with a strong ensemble identity, but with Le Guillochet's intention to concentrate more on its acting school in the future it could become a worthy and welcome successor to the Vieux-Colombier and the Atelier.

While the search for new languages and structures continues, the central problem for theatre today remains the same as it always has been: what is theatre's rôle? All other questions of form and technique, of material resources and profitability, and the immediate practical matters which dominate the theatre worker's day to day activities, are subsumed in this central question. Whether, in today's fragmented society, an art form which lives by constant self-questioning and by going against orthodoxy can once again capture the assent of the vast public, is an unresolved dilemma. But it is only by offering a vision of life that is relevant to a given public at a given moment that theatre can hope to survive. This is why Vilar's question, "why am I making theatre, and for whom?" remains the most pertinent one of all.

Notes

Publication details of works listed in the Bibliography are not given here.

Introduction: *The advent of the director*

1 La Grange, *Préface des Oeuvres de Molière* (Edition de 1682), ed. Georges Monval, (Paris: Librairie des Bibliophiles, 1882), p. 28.
2 Jouvet, "Point de vue du metteur en scène", *Revue d'Histoire du Théâtre*, III, 1951, pp. 378-87 (p. 380).
3 Mercier, *Du théâtre* (Amsterdam: Van Harrevelt, 1773), p. 106.
4 Diderot, "De la poésie dramatique" in *Oeuvres complètes*, VII (Paris: Garnier, 1875), p. 374.
5 Ibid.
6 Ibid., pp. 374-5.
7 Charles Collé, *Journal et mémoires*, II (Paris: Firmin Didot, 1868), p. 172.
8 Lekain, *Mémoires, précédées de Réflexions sur l'art de cet acteur et sur l'art théâtral, par F. Talma*, (Paris: Ponthieu, 1825), pp. XLVII-XLIX.
9 W. C. Macready, *Reminiscences* (London: Macmillan, 1876), p. 180.
10 Copeau, "Un essai de rénovation dramatique" in *Registres*, I, pp. 19-32 (p. 27).
11 Quoted by Vilar in *De la tradition théâtrale*, pp. 71-2.
12 *The Athenaeum*, 2797, 4 June 1881, p. 762.
13 Antoine, *Mes souvenirs sur le Théâtre Libre*, p. 109.
14 Zola, "Le Naturalisme au théâtre" in *Oeuvres complètes*, XXXVIII (Paris: Bernouard, 1887), pp. 26-7.

1 *New theatres for new playwrights*

(Antoine)

1 Becque, "Souvenirs d'un auteur dramatique" in *Oeuvres complètes*, VI (Crés, 1924-6), p. 119.
2 Becque, "Deuxième préface (1887)" in *Oeuvres complètes*, VI, p. 128.
3 *Mes souvenirs sur le Théâtre Libre*, pp. 94 & 208.
4 Performed in October 1888. The sheep's carcasses have come to be seen as examples of extreme Naturalism. In fact, Icres's *Les Bouchers* was not a

naturalist play but a Romantic melodrama and Antoine's production was probably intended in the spirit of "local colour" rather than as a piece of naturalist staging. See Pruner, *Les Luttes d'Antoine*, pp. 249-52.

5 Francisque Sarcey, *Quarante ans de théâtre*, VIII (Paris: Bibliothèque des Annales, 1902), p. 255.

[Médan: Reference to Alexis, Céard and Hennique, members of the Médan group which spearheaded efforts to impose Naturalism in the theatre in the 1880s.]

6 Letter to Sarcey, 1892, transl. Samuel Waxman. Cited in Waxman, *Antoine and the Théâtre Libre*, p. 174.

7 Antoine, "Causerie sur la mise en scène". The translations used here are from Cole & Chinoy (eds.), *Directors on directing*, pp. 89-102 (p. 94). The italics are mine.

8 Ibid., pp. 98-9.

9 Zola, "Le Naturalisme au théâtre", p. 77.

10 "Causerie sur la mise en scène", p. 102.

11 Baty, *Rideau baissé*, p. 212.

(Fort)

12 Claudel, *Oeuvres complètes*, XVI (Paris: Gallimard, 1959), p. 190.

13 J. Rivière – P. Claudel, *Correspondance* (Paris: Plon, 1926), p. 104.

14 Ibid.

15 *Echo de Paris*, 24 Feb. 1891.

16 Anon., "La mise en scène symboliste", *Le Gaulois*, 14 December 1891, p. 2.

17 "Crayonné au théâtre", in *Oeuvres de Mallarmé* (Paris: Garnier, 1985), p. 245.

18 *La Jeune Belgique*, 9, 1890, p. 331.

19 Quillard, "Argument de la mise en scène", *Théâtre d'Art*, 3 (undated review). [1891]

20 Henri Fouquier, "L'art mystique", *Le Figaro*, 15 December 1891.

21 Camille Mauclair, *Servitude et grandeur littéraires* (Paris: Ollendorff, 1922), p. 99.

22 Ibid., p. 97.

(Lugné-Poe)

23 Anon., "Causerie dramatique", *Le Moniteur Universel*, 5 March 1894, p. 1.

24 For a recent study of Jarry's play and a detailed account of the first performance see Claude Schumacher's *Alfred Jarry and Guillaume Apollinaire* (London: Macmillan, 1984).

25 Lugné-Poe, *Acrobaties*, p. 160.

26 Ibid., p. 174.

27 Gémier, interview in *Excelsior*, 5 November 1921.

Yeats, *Autobiographies* (London: Macmillan, 1955), pp. 347-8.

Symons, *Studies in seven arts* (New York: Dutton, 1906), pp. 371-80.

28 *Acrobaties*, p. 183.

29 *Le Figaro*, 2 April 1894.

30 Copeau, "Ibsen au Vieux-Colombier", *Nouvelles Littéraires*, 12 May 1934, p. 10.

31 Robichez, "L'Introduction de l'oeuvre d'Ibsen en France", *Revue d'Histoire*

du Théâtre, IX, 1957, pp. 23-35 (p. 27).

32 *Acrobaties*, p. 183.

33 In *Bulletin du Théâtre de l'Oeuvre* (1897), quoted by Lugné-Poe in *Acrobaties*, pp. 203-4.

34 E. Sée, "Souvenirs de Lugné-Poe", *Revue Théâtrale*, 1, 1946, p. 17.

35 Some new plays, however, continued to slip through the net, including Rostand's highly original *Cyrano de Bergerac* (1899) which was rejected by every manager he showed it to. Like Becque a quarter of a century earlier – and in the same theatre, the Porte St Martin – Rostand was forced to stage at his own expense what turned out to be the runaway success of the century.

36 Lugné-Poe, "A propos de l'inutilité du théâtre au théâtre", *Mercure de France*, October 1896, p. 96.

37 Lugné-Poe, "A propos de 'La mise en scène théâtrale d'aujourd'hui'", *Revue de l'Oeuvre*, November 1927, pp. 22-3.

2 *The scenic revolution*

(Theorists)

1 Antoine, "Causerie sur la mise en scène", p. 91.

2 Appia, *L'Oeuvre d'art vivant*, p. 22.

3 Ibid., p. 92.

4 *The art of the theatre*, pp. 17-18.

5 *Towards a new theatre*, p. 1.

6 *The art of the theatre*, p. 52.

(Copeau)

7 "Un essai de rénovation dramatique" in *Registres*, I, p. 27.

8 Ibid., p. 20.

9 *Notes sur le métier de comédien*, p. 38.

10 Ibid., p. 39.

11 "Un essai de rénovation dramatique", p. 25.

12 Copeau, "Le poète au théâtre", *Revue des vivants*, May-June 1930, pp. 678-87 & 769-77 (p. 686).

13 "Un essai de rénovation dramatique", p. 28.

14 *Continental stagecraft*, p. 182.

15 *The producer and the play*, p. 60.

16 "Un essai de rénovation dramatique", pp. 29-30.

17 Ibid., pp. 30-1.

18 Ibid., p. 32.

19 Léautaud, *Le Théâtre de Maurice Boissard*, II (Paris: Gallimard, 1958), p. 126.

20 Quoted in Marshall, pp. 59-60.

21 "Un essai de rénovation dramatique", p. 27.

22 Gide, *Journal, 1939-49* (Paris: Gallimard, 1954), p. 466.

23 Salacrou, "Note sur le théâtre" in *Théâtre*, II (Paris: Gallimard, 1944), p. 209.

24 Copeau decided to give the first performance of *Le Cid* on 11 November,

the anniversary of the 1918 Armistice – a patriotic gesture which cost him his dismissal.

25 Jouvet, "Hommage à Jacques Copeau", *Arts*, 28 October 1949, pp. 1 & 7.
26 Copeau, "Dialogue avec le metteur en scène", *Correspondance*, 19, 1930, pp. 13-20.
27 Dullin, "Le Théâtre, ses conditions actuelles, ses tendances", *Correspondance*, 4, 1929, p. 13.

(Dullin)
28 Dullin, *Ce sont les dieux qu'il nous faut*, p. 76.
29 Ibid., p. 117.
30 Marshall, pp. 80-1.
31 *Ce sont les dieux qu'il nous faut*, p. 242.
32 Ibid., pp. 149-50.
33 "Le déploiement ad libitum de la décoration est un obstacle certain à la mise en valeur d'un texte" – ibid., p. 78.
34 Ibid.
35 Dullin, "Les Ames des vieux théâtres" in *Souvenirs et notes de travail d'un acteur*, p. 71.

(Jouvet)
36 Jouvet, *Témoignages sur le théâtre*, p. 85.
37 Letter to Copeau dated 9 February 1916, in *Cahiers de la Compagnie Renaud-Barrault*, 7, 1954, p. 115.
38 *Témoignages sur le théâtre*, pp. 99-100.
39 *L'Information*, 4 May 1932.
40 *Revue d'Histoire du Théâtre*, IV, 1952, p. 51.
41 Crémieux, "Le Théâtre", *Nouvelle Revue Française*, 1 June 1928, pp. 867-9.
42 Jouvet, Introduction to Sabbattini, *Pratiques pour fabriquer scènes et machines au théâtre* (Neuchâtel: Ides et Calendes, 1942).
43 Brasillach, *Animateurs de théâtre* (Paris: Corréa, 1936), p. 40.
44 Jouvet, "Molière", *Theatre Arts*, XXI, 1937, pp. 694-5.
45 Quoted in Marshall, p. 323.
46 *Témoignages sure le théâtre*, p. 103.
47 Jouvet, *Prestiges et perspectives du théâtre française*, pp. 51-2.
48 Ibid., p. 53.
49 *Studies in the contemporary theatre*, pp. 178-9.
50 Strehler, *Un théâtre pour la vie* (Paris: Fayard, 1980), p. 121.

(Pitoëff)
51 *L'Information*, 31 August 1925.
52 *Le Journal*, 1 September 1927.
53 Letter dated 9 August 1921, reproduced in Jomaron, *Georges Pitoëff, metteur en scène*, p. 343.
54 Pitoëff, *Notre théâtre*, p. 11.
55 Ibid., p. 7.
56 Ibid., p. 12.
57 Ibid., p. 12-13.
58 Ibid., p. 13.

59 Ibid., p. 23.
60 Ibid., p. 9.
61 *L'Information*, 2 March 1925.
62 *Notre théâtre*, pp. 21 & 25.
63 *L'Information*, 4 May 1925.
64 Marshall, p. 75.
65 Palmer, pp. 182-3.
66 *Comoedia*, Spring 1924.
67 *L'Information*, 30 April 1933.
68 *Notre théâtre* pp. 44-5.
69 Lenormand, *Les Pitoëff: souvenirs*, p. 93.
70 *Le Peuple*, 22 April 1921.
71 *Notre théâtre*, p. 14.
72 Ibid., p. 48.
73 Ibid., p. 21.
74 Barrault, *Souvenirs pour demain*, p. 70.

(Baty)
75 Baty, "Vérités premières et paradoxales sur l'art du théâtre", *Marges*, 13 December 1920, pp. 275-80 (p. 280).
76 "Tous les auteurs qui ont travaillé avec lui vous diront qu'il avait le plus grand respect des textes qui lui étaient confiés, même quand il cherchait, par-delà ces textes, à découvrir l'esprit de la pièce." (Jean-Jacques Bernard in *Les Droits et les devoirs du metteur en scène: Entretiens de Vienne, présentés par P.-L. Mignon*, p. 20).
77 Baty, *Rideau baissé*, p. 81.
78 Ibid., p. 83.
79 Ibid., p. 84.
80 Ibid., pp. 103-4.
81 F. Porché, "Gaston Baty", *Revue de Paris*, 15 August 1935, p. 922.
82 *Rideau baissé*, p. 217.
83 Ibid.
84 Bernard, "Le Silence au théâtre", *Bulletin de la Chimère*, 2, May 1922, p. 67.
85 Bernard, *Mon ami le théâtre*, (Paris: Albin Michel, 1958), p. 48.
86 *Revue d'Histoire du Théâtre*, V, 1953, p. 19.
87 Henri Bidou, "L'Année dramatique", *Journal des débats*, 3 July 1922, p. 3.
88 "Présentation du *Malade imaginaire*", *Cahiers Gaston Baty*, 1, 1963, p. 45.
89 Ibid., p. 46.
90 *Rideau baissé*, p. 177.
91 Ibid., pp. 7-8.
92 Ibid., p. 224.

3 Total theatre – ritual theatre – festive theatre

(Artaud)
1 Letter to Max Jacob, 1921. In *Oeuvres complètes*, III (Paris: Gallimard, 1961), pp. 117-8. (Artaud's italics).

2 Barrault, *Réflexions sur le théâtre*, p. 61.

3 Tzara, *Oeuvres complètes*, I (Paris: Flammarion, 1975). This much under-valued play was performed at the Théâtre de la Cigale, 17 May 1924, directed by Marcel Herrand.

4 "Je m'étonne que M. Benjamin Crémieux dressant un tableau du mouvement théâtral dans ces années bénies du théâtre de 1926-7 s'attache encore à ces pourritures branlantes, à ces fantômes anti-représentatifs que sont Jouvet, Pitoëff, Dullin, voire Gémier etc. Quand aura-t-on fini de remuer de l'ordure?" – Letter to Jean Paulan (1927), in *Oeuvres complètes*, III, p. 130.

5 "Théâtre Alfred Jarry (Saison 1926-7)" in *Oeuvres complètes*, II, p. 16.

6 *Jet de sang (Spurt of blood)* was eventually performed as part of Peter Brook's Theatre of Cruelty programme at the LAMDA Theatre in London, 1964.

7 A. Melzer, "Homage to Robert Aron", *Theatre Research International*, II, 1977, pp. 131-9.

8 *Oeuvres complètes*, V, p. 262.

9 *Oeuvres complètes*, IV, p. 95.

10 "Théâtre Alfred Jarry (Saison 1928)" in *Oeuvres complètes*, II, p. 31.

11 *Oeuvres complètes*, IV, pp. 12-13.

12 Ibid., p. 50.

13 Ibid., p. 96.

14 Ibid., p. 38.

15 Ibid., p. 39.

16 Ibid., p. 38.

17 Ibid., p. 102.

18 Ibid., p. 123.

19 Esslin, *Artaud*, p. 70.

20 *Oeuvres complètes*, IV, p. 118.

21 Ibid., p. 111.

22 *Cahiers de la Compagnie Renaud-Barrault*, 22/3, 1958, p. 149.

23 *Réflexions sur le théâtre*, p. 60. (Barrault names *Le Théâtre et son double* as the most recent of five profoundly seminal works. The others he mentions are Aristotle's *Poetics*, Corneille's *Trois discours*, Hugo's *Préface de Cromwell* and Craig's *The art of the theatre*).

24 Brook, *The empty space*, p. 49.

(Barrault)

25 *Réflexions sur le théâtre*, p. 93.

26 Barrault, "On Stanislavsky and Brecht", *Theatre Quarterly*, III, no.10, 1973, p. 3.

27 *Réflexions sur le théâtre*, p. 32.

28 Ibid., p. 49.

29 Quoted by Barrault in *Réflexions sur le théâtre*, p. 50.

30 Ibid., p. 59.

31 Barrault, *Souvenirs pour demain*, p. 83.

32 Artaud, *Oeuvres complètes*, IV, pp. 58ff.

33 *Réflexions sur le théâtre*, p. 71.

34 *Souvenirs pour demain*, p. 203.

35 Ibid., p. 204.

36 In *Phèdre, mise en scène et commentaire* Barrault gives an illuminating dis-

cussion of Racinian versification considered in thoroughly practical and non-academic terms.

37 *Réflexions sur le théâtre*, p. 145.

38 This unusual device is often assumed to foreshadow the Brechtian alienation effect. I think it is more likely that it harks back to the mediaeval Mystery, and, as in the Mysteries, its function is not to distance the spectators but to draw them more intimately into the spectacle.

39 J.-J. Gautier, "*Rabelais* à l'Elysée-Montmartre", *Le Figaro*, 19 December 1968.

40 *Cahiers de la Compagnie Renaud-Barrault*, 33, 1961, p. 125.

41 *Souvenirs pour demain*, p. 157.

42 Ibid., pp. 205-6.

43 "Conviction et malaise dans le théâtre", *Cahiers de la Compagnie Renaud-Barrault*, 71, 1970, p. 69.

44 Ibid., p. 82.

(Garcia)

45 Ossia Trilling, "The defiant ones", *The Guardian*, 2 February 1971, p. 8.

46 Garcia, "Déshumaniser" in *Le Théâtre 1968-1*, p. 72.

47 This is how Jean-Marie Serreau and Gisèle Tavet had presented, respectively, *Pique-nique en campagne* (1959) and *Fando et Lis* (1965).

48 Théâtre des Mathurins (1966), director Georges Vitaly.

49 "I always tell my directors: 'You must create something fabulous, even if it means betraying me.' Sometimes I'm shocked by the result but I always give the director a completely free hand." – Arrabal, in Alain Schifres, *Entretiens avec Arrabal* (Paris: Belfond, 1969), p. 85.

50 Anon., *Gazette de Lausanne*, 27 January 1968. Reproduced on back cover of Arrabal, *Théâtre*, II (Paris: Bourgois, 1968).

51 "Déshumaniser", p. 76.

52 Ibid.

53 Ibid., p. 77.

54 Garcia's only recorded acting rôle was an appearance in Arrabal's film *Viva la muerte!* (1971).

55 "Déshumaniser", pp. 79.

56 Ibid., pp. 71-2.

57 Ronald Bryden, "Desert island fantasies", *The Observer*, 7 February 1971, p. 23.

58 "Déshumaniser", p. 72.

59 *Les Voies de la création théâtrale*, IV, pp. 251-3. Hopkins later told Garcia: "It's the first time I've experienced that and I won't forget it. I'm human, I'm lazy, but I'll try not to lose what you've given me." (Ibid.)

60 So great was the success of the first production of *Les Bonnes* that when a French version was announced, the Centre National de la Recherche Scientifique created a team of ten specialists to follow the production through to performance. Their findings, published in *Les Voies de la création théâtrale*, IV, provide a uniquely detailed anatomy of the production.

61 *Les Voies de la création théâtrale*, IV, p. 274.

62 Genet, "Lettre à J.-J. Pauvert" in *Les Bonnes* (Décines: L'Arbalète, 1958), p. 145.

63 M. Galey, *"Les Bonnes de Genet"*, *Combat*, 9 April 1970.

64 *Sunday Times*, 23 May 1971.

65 *Les Voies de la création théâtrale*, IV, p. 309.

66 Espert, "Adios Victor", *Plays and Players*, 351, 1982, p. 47.

67 For detailed studies of *Gilgamesh* and Garcia's earliest productions (1963-5), see *Les Voies de la création théâtrale*, XII.

(Savary)

68 B. Rogers, "Chaos in 43 scenes", *The Daily Telegraph Magazine*, 424, 15 December 1972, pp. 9-12 (p. 10).

69 Savary, "Nos fêtes" in *Le Théâtre 1968-1* (Paris: Bourgois, 1968), pp. 81-6 (p. 82).

70 "I don't believe in sets. I have no faith in the designer's function in the theatre; nor do I believe that the musician has a special function there. All these divisions are out of date and no longer valid" – Savary, in Knapp, *Off-stage voices*, p. 64.

71 Arrabal, *Le Panique* (Paris: Union Générale d'Editions, 1973), p. 52.

72 Savary, "Comment est né le Grand Magic Circus", *L'Avant-scène*, 496, 1972, p. 5.

73 Knowles, "Fernando Arrabal and the Latin-Americans", *Modern Language Review*, LXX, 1975, pp. 526-38 (p. 528).

74 "Nos fêtes", pp. 84-5.

75 Ibid., p. 85.

76 Knapp, p. 66.

77 Ibid., p. 68.

78 Rogers, "Chaos in 43 scenes", p. 10.

79 Savary, "Le public et nous", *L'Avant-scène*, 496, p. 44.

80 Ibid.

81 C. Alexander, "Le Grand Magic Circus à Suresnes", *L'Express*, 30 April-6 May 1973, p. 19.

82 David Bradby, *Modern French drama, 1940-1980*, p. 220.

83 L'Express, 11-17 December 1981, p. 17.

(Lavelli)

84 Knapp, *Off-stage voices*, pp. 58-9.

85 Quoted in Nores, *Jorge Lavelli*, p. 26.

86 Gilles Sandier, *Arts*, 15 January 1964.

87 Gabriel Marcel, quoted in Nores, p. 34.

88 "The spectacle must be governed by a rigorous theatrical concept or, in the case of a text, its composition must be perfect while still reflecting the chaos and confusion of life. Beneath the apparent disorder it is imperative for the *mise en scène* to be a model of precision." – Arrabal, *Théâtre*, V (Paris: Bourgois, 1967), p. 8.

89 Nores, p. 169.

90 Ionesco, *Notes et contre-notes* (Paris: Gallimard, 1962), p. 74.

91 Interview with C. Alexander, *L'Express*, 998, 24-30 August 1970, p. 48.

92 Quoted in Nores, p. 64.

93 Lavelli, "Ethique" in Nores, pp. 187-90, (p. 187).

94 Ibid., pp. 188-9.

95 Ibid., p. 189.

96 Quoted in Nores, p. 223.

97 A. Chesneau & A. Berenguer, *Entretiens avec Arrabal* (Presses Universitaires de Grenoble, 1978), p. 76.

98 Ibid., pp. 77-8.

99 Quoted in Nores, p. 220.

100 *La Traviata* (Aix-en-Provence, Paris, Bordeaux etc.); *Pelléas et Mélisande* (Paris Opera); *Fidelio* (Toulouse, Angers); *Madame Butterfly* (La Scala); Handel's *Alcina* (Aix-en-Provence); *Carmen* (Rhine Opera).

101 Quoted in Satgé, *Lavelli, opéra et mise à mort*, p. 18.

102 Ibid., p. 157.

103 J. Lonchampt, *"Idoménée* aux Champs-Elysées", *Le Monde*, 28 May 1976, pp. 1 & 5.

104 A. Lanceron, "Entretien avec Lavelli", *L'Avant-scène Opéra*, 2, 1976, pp. 75-81 (p. 75).

105 Lonchampt, "Heureux ceux qui verront *Faust*", *Le Monde*, 5 June 1975, p. 17.

4 Théâtre populaire

(People's theatre)

1 Copeau, "Le Théâtre populaire" in *Registres*, I, p. 285.

2 Ibid.

3 "Le Théâtre Populaire est avant tout une question de répertoire. Il faut mettre à la disposition du peuple une production dramatique émanant de notre époque". From an article dated 1920, reproduced in *Registres*, I, p. 315.

4 *Bref*, 15 October 1955.

5 See Dorothy Knowles, *French drama in the inter-war years*, pp. 299-301.

6 See *People's theatre* by David Bradby and John McCormick, Chapter 5: "France between the wars".

(Gémier)

7 *L'Etudiant*, 17 February 1848. The translation used here is from *Theatre Quarterly*, VI, no.23, 1976.

8 In *Theatre Quarterly*, VI, no.23, p. 22.

9 Cited in Blanchart, *Firmin Gémier*, p. 125.

10 Gémier, *Le Théâtre*, p. 273.

11 "Le Théâtre populaire", p. 291.

(Vilar)

12 Vilar, *Le Théâtre, service public*, p. 81.

13 *Action Française*, November 1943. Jacques Lemarchand made a similar remark: "Coming out after one of those performances at the Théâtre de Poche we asked ourselves if we weren't witnessing the birth of the Vieux-Colombier of our time". (*Figaro Littéraire*, 2 March 1963).

14 Vilar, *De la tradition théâtrale*, p. 85.

15 Vilar, *Memento*, p. 9.
16 *De la tradition théâtrale*, pp. 64-5.
17 Ibid., p. 175.
18 Ibid., p. 176.
19 Ibid., p. 40.
20 Ibid., p. 105.
21 Gontard, *La Décentralisation théâtrale en France*, p. 319.
22 *Le Théâtre, service public*, p. 173.
23 Ibid., p. 147.
24 Ibid., p. 146-7.
25 Vilar, "Memorandum" in *Le Théâtre, service public*, pp. 233-62, (p. 251). (Originally published in *Théâtre Populaire*, 40, 1960, pp. 1-18).
26 Ibid., p. 235.
27 *Le Théâtre, service public*, p. 371.
28 *Bref*, 49, 1961, p. 1.
29 Sartre's criticisms were made in an interview with Bernard Dort in *Théâtre Populaire*, 15, 1955, pp. 1-9.
30 Copfermann, *Le Théâtre populaire, pourquoi?*, p. 183.
31 Ibid., p. 127.
32 "Memorandum", loc.cit. The translation used here is from *Theatre Quarterly*, VI, no.23, 1976, p. 55.

(Planchon)
33 Wilson, "Servir ce théâtre", *Théâtre Populaire*, 51, 1963, p. 6.
34 Planchon, "Taking on the T.N.P.", *Theatre Quarterly*, VII, no.25, 1977, p. 32.
35 Ibid., p.33.
36 Broadcast interview, 20 January 1969, quoted in Gontard, pp. 327-8.
37 Quoted in English in Bradby, *Modern French drama, 1940-1980*, p. 107.
38 "Note sur le théâtre épique", *Le Travail au Théâtre de la Cité*, 1, 1959, pp. 2-3.
39 Quoted in Daoust, *Roger Planchon*, p. 33.
40 "Où en sommes-nous avec Brecht?" (interview with Roger Planchon and René Allio), in Adamov, *Ici et maintenant* (Paris: Gallimard, 1964), p. 214.
41 Ibid.
42 Interview in *Théâtre Populaire*, 28, 1958, p. 15.
43 Boll, *Théâtre total*, p. 32.
44 In *Les Droits et les devoirs du metteur en scène: Entretiens de Vienne, présentés par P.-L. Mignon*, p. 22.
45 "Creating a theatre of real life" (interview by Michael Kustow), *Theatre Quarterly*, II, no.5, 1972, p. 49.
46 Bradby, *Modern French drama, 1940-1980*, p. 119.
47 John Burgess, "Roger Planchon's *Gilles de Rais* at Villeurbanne", *Theatre Quarterly*, VI, no.21, 1976, p. 23.
48 Knapp, *Off-stage voices*, pp. 50-51.
49 Letter to a spectator, reproduced by Emile Copfermann in *Théâtres de Roger Planchon*, pp. 380-7 (p. 384).
50 "Creating a theatre of real life", p. 54.

(Mnouchkine)

51 D. Bablet, "Rencontres avec le Théâtre du Soleil", *Travail Théâtral*, 18/19, 1975, p. 20.

52 *The empty space*, p. 97.

53 B. Poirot-Delpech, *"La Cuisine* d'Arnold Wesker", *Le Monde*, 9-10 April 1967, p. 22.

54 Quoted by D. & M.-L. Bablet in *Le Théâtre du Soleil*, p. 20.

55 J.-J. Gauthier, *Le Figaro*, 5 May 1969.

56 One actor admitted that after visiting a factory (for the first time in his life!) and talking to workers on the shop floor he suddenly saw how remote the artistic preoccupations of *Les Clowns* were from the factory workers' reality. He added that it was not the workers who attended the performances and participated in the discussions afterwards but the managers. (Gérard Hardy, quoted by Bablet & Bablet in *Le Théâtre du Soleil*, pp. 39-40).

57 *Travail Théâtral*, 2, 1971, p. 13.

58 Ibid., p. 4.

59 *L'Age d'or*, p. 14.

60 Copeau, "Appels" in *Registres*, I, pp. 308-10.

61 A. Simon, "Un rêve vécu de théâtre populaire", *Esprit*, 447, June 1975.

62 Temkine, *Mettre en scène au présent*, I, pp. 132-4.

63 "Murdering sleep", *The Observer*, 8 August 1982, p. 29.

Conclusion

1 "Vitez on Molière: freeing the actor", *Performing Arts Journal*, V, 1980, p. 86.

2 For a discussion of Vitez's work and ideas, see Campos, C. & Sadler, M., "The complex theatre of Antoine Vitez", *Theatre Quarterly*, X, no. 40, 1981, pp. 79-96.

3 See "La folle et merveilleuse aventure du Lucernaire", interview with Le Guillochet in Schumacher (ed.), *Forty years of Mise en scène*, pp. 45-57.

Bibliography

The following list includes works which I found useful in preparing this study and is intended as a guide to further reading.

A Theatre & mise en scène

Anders, France, *Jacques Copeau et le Cartel des quatre* (Paris: Nizet, 1959).
Appia, Adolphe, *Die Musik und die Inscenierung* (Munich: Bruckmann, 1899). In translation: *Music and the art of the theatre* (Miami University Press, 1962).
— — *L'Oeuvre d'art vivant* (Geneva: Atar, 1921). In translation: *The work of living art* (Miami University Press, 1960).
Bablet, Denis, *Les Révolutions scéniques du XXe siècle* (Paris: Société Internationale d'Art, 1975). In translation: *The revolutions of stage design in the 20th century* (Paris/New York: Amiel, 1977).
Blanchart, Paul, *Histoire de la mise en scène* (Paris: Presses Universitaires de France, 1948).
Boll, André, *La Mise en scène contemporaine, son évolution* (Paris: Nouvelle Revue Critique, 1944).
— — *Le Théâtre total* (Paris: Perrin, 1971).
Borgal, Clément, *Metteurs en scène* (Paris: Lanore, 1963).
Bradby, David, *Modern French drama, 1940-1980* (Cambridge University Press, 1984).
— — & McCormick, John, *People's theatre* (London: Croom Helm, 1978).
Braun, Edward, *The director and the stage* (London: Methuen, 1982).
Carlson, Marvin, *The French stage in the nineteenth century* (New Jersey: Scarecrow Press, 1972).
Champagne, Lenora, *French theatre experiment since 1968* (Ann Arbor: UMI Research Press, 1984).
Cole, Toby & Chinoy, Helen (eds.), *Directors on directing*; revised edition (Indianapolis: Bobbs-Merrill, 1963).
Copfermann, Emile, *Le Théâtre populaire, pourquoi?* (Paris: Maspero, 1969).
Craig, Edward Gordon, *The art of the theatre* (Edinburgh: Foulis, 1905).
— — *On the art of the theatre* (London: Heinemann, 1968. First published 1911).
— — *Towards a new theatre* (London: Dent, 1913).

Dhomme, Sylvain, *La Mise en scène contemporaine d'Antoine à Brecht* (Paris: Nathan, 1959).

Dort, Bernard, *Théâtre public, 1953-1966* (Paris: Seuil, 1967).

— — *Théâtre réel, 1967-1970* (Paris: Seuil, 1971).

— — *Théâtre en jeu, 1970-1978* (Paris: Seuil, 1979).

Féral, Josette (ed.), *Théâtralité, écriture et mise en scène* (Quebec: Hurtubise, 1985).

Godard, Colette, *Le Théâtre depuis 1968* (Paris: Lattès, 1980).

Gontard, Denis, *La Décentralisation théâtrale en France* (Paris: SEDES, 1973).

Henderson, John, *The first avant-garde, 1887-1894* (London: Harrap, 1971).

Hort, Jean, *Les Théâtres du Cartel et leurs animateurs* (Genève: Skira, 1944).

Innes, Christopher, *Holy theatre: ritual and the avant-garde* (Cambridge University Press, 1981).

Kirby, Ernest (ed.), *Total theatre, a critical anthology* (New York: Dutton, 1969).

Knapp, Bettina, *Off-stage voices: interviews with modern French dramatists* (New York: Whitston, 1975).

Knowles, Dorothy, *French drama of the inter-war years* (London: Harrap, 1967).

— — "Principles of staging" in *Forces in modern French drama*, ed. John Fletcher (London University Press, 1972), pp. 11-32.

— — *La Réaction Idéaliste au théâtre depuis 1890* (Geneva: Droz, 1934; reprinted Geneva: Slatkine, 1972).

Macgowan, Kenneth & Jones, Robert, *Continental stagecraft* (New York: Benn, 1922; reissued New York: Blom, 1964).

Marshall, Norman, *The producer and the play*; third edition (London: Davis-Poynter, 1975).

Mignon, Paul-Louis (ed.), *Entretiens de Vienne: Les Droits et les devoirs du metteur en scène* (Paris: Brient, 1963).

Miller, Anna, *The independent theatres in Europe* (New York: Long & Smith, 1931; reissued New York: Blom, 1966).

Miller, Judith, *Theatre and revolution in France since 1968* (Lexington: French Forum Monographs, 1977).

Palmer, John, *Studies in the contemporary theatre* (London: Secker, 1927).

Robichez, Jacques, *Le Symbolisme au théâtre: Lugné-Poe et les débuts de l'Oeuvre* (Paris: L'Arche, 1957).

Roose-Evans, James, *Experimental theatre from Stanislavsky to Brook*; revised edition (London: Routledge & Kegan Paul, 1984).

Roubine, Jean-Jacques, *Théâtre et mise en scène* (Paris: Presses Universitaires de France, 1980).

Sanders, James (ed.), *Aux sources de la vérité du théâtre moderne* (Paris: Minard, 1974).

Schumacher, Claude (ed.), *40 years of Mise en scène* (Dundee: Lochee Publications, 1986).

Temkine, Raymonde, *L'entreprise-théâtre* (Paris: Cujas, 1967).

— — *Mettre en scène à présent*; 2 vols (Lausanne: L'Age d'Homme, 1977-79).

Theatre Quarterly, VI, no.23, 1976. Issue devoted to people's theatre in France since 1870.

Veinstein, André, *Du Théâtre Libre au Théâtre Louis Jouvet: les théâtres d'art à travers leurs périodiques (1887-1934)* (Paris: Librairie Théâtrale, 1955).

— — *La Mise en scène théâtrale et sa condition esthétique* (Paris: Flammarion, 1955).

B Individual directors

Antoine

Le Théâtre Libre (Paris: Imprimerie Eugène Verneau, 1890).
"Causerie sur la mise en scène", *Revue de Paris*, X, 1 April 1903, pp. 596-612. In selected translation: "Behind the fourth wall" in Cole & Chinoy (eds.), *Directors on directing*, pp. 89-102.
Mes souvenirs sur le Théâtre Libre (Paris: Fayard, 1921). In translation: *Memories of the Théâtre Libre* (University of Miami Press, 1964).

on Antoine

Pruner, Francis, *Les Luttes d'Antoine* (Paris: Minard, 1964).
Sanders, James, *André Antoine, directeur à l'Odéon* (Paris: Lettres Modernes, 1978).
Thalasso, Adolphe, *Le Théâtre Libre* (Paris: Mercure de France, 1909).
Waxman, Samuel, *Antoine and the Théâtre Libre* (Harvard University Press, 1926).
also discussed in Braun, Carlson, Henderson, Miller (A.), Sanders.

Artaud

Lettres d'Antonin Artaud à Jean-Louis Barrault (Paris: Bordas, 1952).
Oeuvres complètes, I-XX (Paris, Gallimard, 1956-84). In translation: *Collected works*, I-V (London: Calder & Boyars, 1968-76).
Le Théâtre et son double (Paris: Gallimard, 1964). In translation: *The theatre and its double* (New York: Grove Press, 1958).

on Artaud

Esslin, Martin, *Artaud* (London: Fontana, 1976).
Hayman, Ronald, *Artaud and after* (Oxford University Press, 1977).
Sellin, Eric, *The dramatic concepts of Antonin Artaud* (University of Chicago Press, 1968).
Virmaux, Alain, *Antonin Artaud et le théâtre* (Paris: Union Générale d'Editions, 1977).
– – & Virmaux, Odette, *Artaud: un bilan critique* (Paris: Belfond, 1979).
– – *Artaud vivant* (Paris: Nouvelles Editions Oswald, 1980).
also discussed in Bradby, Braun, Roose-Evans.

Barrault

Phèdre, mise en scène et commentaire (Paris: Seuil, 1946).
Réflexions sur le théâtre (Paris: Vautrain, 1949). In translation: *Reflections on the theatre* (London: Rockliff, 1951).
Nouvelles réflexions sur le théâtre (Paris: Flammarion, 1959). In translation: *The theatre of Jean-Louis Barrault* (London: Barrie & Rockliff, 1961).
Journal de bord (Paris: Julliard, 1961).
"Conviction et malaise dans le théâtre contemporain", *Cahiers de la Compagnie Renaud-Barrault*, 71, 1970, pp. 52-91.
Rabelais (Paris: Gallimard, 1970).
Jarry sur la butte (Paris: Gallimard, 1970).
Souvenirs pour demain (Paris: Seuil, 1972). In translation: *Memories for tomorrow* (London: Thames & Hudson, 1974).

Comme je le pense (Paris: Gallimard, 1975).
Saisir le présent (Paris: Laffont, 1984).
(with) Madeleine Renaud, *Paris notre siècle* (Paris: Messine, 1983).
on Barrault
Chancerel, Léon, *Jean-Louis Barrault* (Paris: Presses Littéraires de France, 1953).
Frank, André, *Jean-Louis Barrault* (Paris: Seghers, 1971).
Wallis, Roger, "Jean-Louis Barrault's *Rabelais*", *Theatre Quarterly*, I, no.3, 1971, pp. 83-97.
also discussed in Bradby, Knapp.

Baty
Le Masque et l'encensoir (Paris: Blond et Gay, 1926).
Masques (Cahiers d'art dramatique dirigés par Gaston Baty), nos. 1-34 (1926-42). Contents listed in *Revue d'Histoire du Théâtre*, V, 1953, pp. 94-6.
Vie de l'art théâtral des origines à nos jours (Paris: Plon, 1932).
Rideau baissé (Paris: Bordas, 1949).
on Baty
Blanchart, Paul, *Gaston Baty* (Paris: Nouvelle Revue Critique, 1939).
Cahiers Gaston Baty, nos. 1-8 (1963-71).
Cogniat, Raymond, *Gaston Baty* (Paris: Presses Littéraires de France, 1953).
Pastorello, Félie, "*L'Opéra de quat'sous* de Brecht, mises en scène d'Erich Engel et Gaston Baty" in *Les Voies de la création théâtrale*, VII (Paris: CNRS, 1979), pp. 475-543.
Porché, François, "Gaston Baty", *Revue de Paris*, 15 August 1935.
Revue d'Histoire du Théâtre, V, nos. 1/2, 1953. Double issue devoted to Baty.
Simon, Arthur, *Gaston Baty, théoricien du théâtre* (Paris: Klincksieck, 1972).
also discussed in Anders, Blanchart, Boll, Borgal, Dhomme, Hort.

Copeau
"Un essai de rénovation dramatique", *Nouvelle Revue Française*, 57, 1 September 1913, pp. 337-53. Reprinted in *Registres* I. In selected translation: "The manifesto of the Vieux-Colombier" in Cole & Chinoy (eds.), *Actors on acting* (New York: Crown, 1970), pp. 217-8.
Souvenirs du Vieux-Colombier (Paris: Nouvelles Éditions Latines, 1931).
"La Mise en scène", *Encyclopédie Française*, XVII, 1935. In translation: "Dramatic economy" in Cole & Chinoy (eds.), *Directors on directing*, pp. 214-25.
Le Théâtre populaire (Paris: Presses Universitaires, 1941).
Notes sur le métier de comédien (Paris: Brient, 1955).
Correspondance Copeau-Martin du Gard (Paris: Gallimard, 1972).
Registres, I-IV, in progress (Paris: Gallimard, 1974-). I: *Appels*; II: *Molière*; III: *Les Registres du Vieux-Colombier 1*; IV: *Les Registres du Vieux-Colombier 2, America*.
on Copeau
Bablet, Denis, "Copeau et le théâtre théâtral", *Maske und Kothurn*, XV, 1969, pp. 74-81.
Borgal, Clément, *Jacques Copeau* (Paris: L'Arche, 1960).
Frank, Waldo, *The art of the Vieux-Colombier: a contribution of France to the*

contemporary stage (New York: Gallimard, 1918).

Gontard, Denis, *Le Journal de bord des Copiaus, 1924-9* (Paris: Seghers, 1974).

Katz, Albert, "The genesis of the Vieux-Colombier: the aesthetic background of Jacques Copeau", *Educational Theatre Journal*, XIX, 1967, pp. 433-46.

Kurtz, Maurice, *Jacques Copeau, biographie d'un théâtre* (Paris: Nagel, 1950).

Revue d'Histoire du Théâtre, II, no.1, 1950; XV, no. 4, 1963; XXXV, no. 1, 1983. Issues devoted principally or exclusively to Copeau.

Rudlin, John, *Jacques Copeau* (Cambridge University Press, 1986).

also discussed in Anders, Borgal, Dhomme, Hort, Macgowan & Jones, Marshall, Sanders, *Theatre Quarterly* VI, no.23.

Dullin

Souvenirs et notes de travail (Paris: Lieutier, 1946).

L'Avare (Paris: Seuil, 1946).

Cinna (Paris: Seuil, 1948).

Ce sont les dieux qu'il nous faut (Paris: Gallimard, 1969).

on Dullin

Arnaud, Lucien, *Charles Dullin* (Paris: L'Arche, 1952).

– – "Charles Dullin et la mise en scène", *Théâtre Populaire*, 2, 1953, pp. 27-33.

Arnoux, Alexandre, *Charles Dullin, portrait brisé* (Paris: Emile-Paul, 1951).

Sarment, Jean, *Charles Dullin* (Paris: Calmann-Lévy, 1950).

also discussed in Anders, Borgal, Hort.

Fort

Mes mémoires (Paris: Flammarion, 1944).

also discussed in Henderson, Robichez.

Garcia

"Déshumaniser" in *Le Théâtre 1968-1* (Paris: Bourgois, 1968), pp. 71-9.

on Garcia

Arnott, Brian, "A scenography of light", *Drama Review*, XVII, no. 2, 1973, pp. 73-9. [*The Architect and the Emperor of Assyria*]

Compte, Carmen, "*Yerma*: une nouvelle lecture de Lorca", *Travail Théâtral*, 11, 1973, pp. 127-34.

Knowles, Dorothy, "Fernando Arrabal and the Latin-Americans", *Modern Language Review*, LXX, 1975, pp. 526-38.

– – "Michel Parent and experiments in simultaneity", *Theatre Research*, XI, 1971, pp. 23-41.

Les Voies de la création théâtrale, I (Paris: CNRS, 1970), pp. 309-40. [*Le Cimetière des voitures*]

Les Voies de la création théâtrale, IV (Paris: CNRS, 1975), pp. 103-315. [*Les Bonnes*]

Les Voies de la création théâtrale, XII (Paris: CNRS, 1984),pp. 14-131. [*Gilgamesh*]

Zanotto, Ilka, "An audience-structure for *The Balcony* (Victor Garcia, Brazil)", *Drama Review*, XVII, no. 2, 1973, pp. 58-73.

also discussed in Féral, Knowles (1975), Temkine (1977).

Gémier
Le Théâtre (Paris: Grasset, 1925).
"Creating a travelling theatre for the provinces", Theatre Quarterly, IV, no. 23, 1976, pp. 28-9.
on Gémier
Blanchart, Paul, Firmin Gémier (Paris: L'Arche, 1954).
Gontard, Denis, "An example of 'popular' itinerant theatre: Gémier's National Travelling Theatre (1911-12)" in Western Popular Theatre, edited by David Mayer & Kenneth Richards (London: Methuen, 1977), pp. 123-32.

Jouvet
"The profession of the producer, I", Theatre Arts, XX, 1936, pp. 943-9.
"The profession of the producer, II", Theatre Arts, XXI, 1937, pp. 57-64.
"Molière", Theatre Arts, XXI, 1937, pp. 686-98.
Prestiges et perspectives du théâtre français (Paris: Gallimard, 1945).
Réflexions du comédien (Paris: Librairie Théâtrale, 1951).
Témoignages sur le théâtre (Paris: Flammarion, 1952).
Le Comédien désincarné (Paris: Flammarion, 1954).
on Jouvet
Kérien, Wanda, Louis Jouvet, notre patron (Paris: Editeurs Français Réunis, 1963).
Knapp, Bettina, Louis Jouvet: man of the theatre (Columbia University Press, 1957).
Revue d'Histoire du Théâtre, IV, nos. 1/2, 1952. Double issue devoted to Jouvet.
also discussed in Anders, Borgal, Hort.

Lavelli
"Le Concile d'amour" in Le Théâtre 1968-1 (Paris: Bourgois, 1968), pp. 61-70.
on Lavelli
Campos, Christopher, "Experiments for the people of Paris", Theatre Quarterly, II, no. 8, 1972, pp. 57-67.
Knowles, Dorothy, "Fernando Arrabal and the Latin-Americans", Modern Language Review, LXX, 1975, pp. 526-38.
Nores, Dominique & Godard, Colette, Jorge Lavelli (Paris: Bourgois, 1971).
Satgé, Alain, Lavelli, opéra et mise à mort (Paris: Fayard, 1979).
also discussed in Knapp.

Lugné-Poe
La Parade, I-III (Paris: Gallimard, 1930-33).
Dernière pirouette (Paris: Sagittaire, 1946).
Rolland et Lugné-Poe: correspondance, 1894-1901, ed. Jacques Robichez (Paris: L'Arche, 1957).
on Lugné-Poe
Lié, P. (pseud.), "Comment Jarry et Lugné-Poe glorifièrent Ubu à l'Oeuvre", Cahiers du Collège de 'Pataphysique, nos. 3/4, 1952, pp. 37-51.
Robichez, Jacques, Lugné-Poe (Paris: L'Arche, 1955).
also discussed in Braun, Knowles (1934), Robichez, Sanders.

Mnouchkine & the Théâtre du Soleil
Mnouchkine, Ariane, "Une prise de conscience" in *Le Théâtre 1968-1* (Paris: Bourgois, 1968), pp. 119-26.
— — "Entretien avec Ariane Mnouchkine", *Travail Théâtral*, 2, 1971, pp. 3-14.
— — "*L'Age d'or*: the long journey from 1793-1975", *Theatre Quarterly*, V, no. 18, 1975, pp. 5-13.
Théâtre du Soleil, *1789* (Paris: Stock, 1971).
— — *1793* (Paris: Stock, 1972).
— — *L'Age d'or* (Paris: Stock, 1975).
— — *Mephisto* (Paris: Solin, 1979).
on Mnouchkine & the Théâtre du Soleil
Bablet, Denis & Bablet, Marie-Louise, *Le Théâtre du Soleil* (Paris: CNRS, 1979).
Campos, Christopher, "Experiments for the people of Paris", *Theatre Quarterly*, II, no. 8, 1972, pp. 57-67.
Kirkland, Christopher, "Théâtre du Soleil: *The golden age, first draft*", *Drama Review*, XIX, no. 2, 1975, pp. 53-60.
Nes Kirby, Victoria, "*1789*", *Drama Review*, XV, no. 4, 1971, pp. 73-91.
Travail Théâtral nos. 2 (1971), 3 (1972), 8 (1972), 9 (1972), 18/19 (1975), 20 (1975).
Travail Théâtral: Le Théâtre du Soleil (Lausanne: La Cité, 1976).
Les Voies de la création théâtrale, V (Paris: CNRS, 1977), pp. 121-278. *[1793; L'Age d'or]*
also discussed in Bradby, Dort (1979), Kirby, Champagne, Godard, Miller (J.), Temkine (1977).

Pitoëff
Notre théâtre (Paris: Messages, 1949).
on Pitoëff
Frank, André, *Georges Pitoëff* (Paris: L'Arche, 1958).
Hort, Jean, *La Vie héroïque des Pitoëff* (Genève: Caillier, 1966).
Jomaron, Jacqueline, "Lenormand mis en scène par Georges Pitoëff" in *Les Voies de la création théâtrale*, VII (Paris: CNRS, 1979), pp. 307-38.
— — *Georges Pitoëff metteur en scène* (Lausanne: L'Age d'Homme, 1979).
Lenormand, Henri-René, *Les Pitoëff: souvenirs* (Paris: Lieutier, 1948).
also discussed in Anders, Borgal, Hort, Knowles (1967), Knowles (1972), Marshall, Palmer.

Planchon
"Orthodoxies", *Théââre Populaire*, 46, 1962, pp. 117-34.
"A frenzy of images", *Drama Review*, XI, no. 1, 1966, p. 133.
"Creating a theatre of real life", *Theatre Quarterly*, II, no. 5, 1972, pp. 46-55.
Le Cochon noir & La Remise (Paris: Gallimard, 1973).
"Blues, whites and reds: the humours of a history play", *Theatre Quarterly*, IV, no. 15, 1974, pp. 27-31.
Gilles de Rais & L'Infame (Paris: Gallimard, 1976).
"Taking on the T.N.P.", *Theatre Quarterly*, VII, no. 25, 1977, pp. 29-33.
"I'm a museum guard", *Performing Arts Journal*, 16, 1981, pp. 97-109.

on Planchon
Bradby, David, *The theatre of Roger Planchon* (Cambridge: Chadwyck-Healey, "Theatre in Focus", 1984).
Burgess, John, "Roger Planchon's *The black pig* at Villeurbanne", *Theatre Quarterly*, IV, no. 14, 1974, pp. 56-87.
— — "Roger Planchon's *Gilles de Rais* at Villeurbanne", *Theatre Quarterly*, VI, no. 21, 1976, pp. 3-24.
Copfermann, Emile, *Théâtres de Roger Planchon* (Paris: Union Générale d'Editions, 1977).
Daoust, Yvette, *Roger Planchon* (Cambridge University Press, 1981).
Duvignaud, Jean, *Itinéraire de Roger Planchon, 1953-64* (Paris: L'Arche, 1970).
Kustow, Michael, "Life and work of an illuminated man", *Theatre Quarterly*, II, no. 5, 1972, pp. 42-5.
Travail Théâtral, 1, 1970, pp. 55-91; 17, 1974, pp. 11-51.
also discussed in Bradby, Copfermann, Dort (1971), Knapp.

Savary
"Nos fêtes" in *Le Théâtre 1968-1* (Paris: Bourgois, 1968), pp. 81-6.
"*Zartan*, a scenario", *Drama Review*, XV, no. 1, 1970, pp. 88-91.
"*Zartan ou le frère malaimé de Tarzan* and *Les derniers jours de solitude de Robinson Crusoé*", *L'Avant-scène*, 496, 1 June 1972. Issue devoted to the Grand Magic Circus.
"Une grande fête pour adultes tristes", *Preuves*, XI, 1972, pp. 137-45.
"*De Moïse à Mao*", *L'Avant-scène*, 539, 15 April 1974, pp. 3-42. Text of play and illustrations.
Album du Grand Magic Circus (Paris: Belfond, 1974).
on Savary
Knowles, Dorothy, "Fernando Arrabal and the Latin-Americans", *Modern Language Review*, LXX, 1975, pp. 526-38.
also discussed in Knapp.

Vilar
De la tradition théâtrale (Paris, L'Arche, 1955).
Chronique romanesque (Paris: Grasset, 1971).
Mot par mot (Paris: Stock, 1972).
Le Théâtre, service public (Paris: Gallimard, 1975).
Mémento (Paris: Gallimard, 1981).
on Vilar
Bermel, Albert, "Jean Vilar: unadorned theatre for the greatest numbers", *Tulane Drama Review*, V, no. 2, 1960, pp. 24-44.
Leclerc, Guy, *Le T.N.P. de Jean Vilar* (Paris: Union Générale d'Editions, 1971).
Roy, Claude, *Jean Vilar* (Paris: Seghers, 1968).
Serrière, Marie-Thérèse, *Le T.N.P. et nous* (Paris: Corti, 1959).
Travail Théâtral, 5, 1971, pp. 89-118; 8, 1972, pp. 19-56.
Wehle, Philippa, *Le Théâtre populaire selon Jean Vilar* (Avignon: Barthélemy, 1981).
also discussed in Bradby, Bradby & McCormick, Copfermann, Dort (1979), *Theatre Quarterly* VI, no. 23.

Index